The Sutras
Healing and Enlightenment

by Matthew Brownstein, CIHt

Anahat Education Group
SILENT LIGHT PUBLISHERS
www.silentlightpublishers.com

Published by Silent Light Publishers. Tampa, Florida

The Sutras on Healing and Enlightenment
Copyright © 2015 by Anahat Education Group, Inc.

First Edition, 2004
Second Edition, 2015

All rights reserved. No part of this book may be reproduced or transmitted in any form or by any means, electronic or mechanical, including photocopying, recording or by any information storage and retrieval system without permission in writing from the Publisher.

Information in this book is provided for informational purposes and is not meant to substitute for the advice provided by your own physician or other medical professional. You should not use the information contained herein for diagnosing or treating a health problem or disease, or prescribing any medication. If you have or suspect that you have a medical problem, promptly contact your health care provider. Information and statements given here are not intended to diagnose, treat, cure or prevent any disease.

LCCN 2005901550

ISBN 978-1518743559

Printed in the United States of America.

Preface

During the spring of 2003, while living in the Kullu Valley of the Himalayas in India, I was inspired to begin sharing what I know about the processes of healing and enlightenment. When I sat down to write, I was surprised to see so much information coming out in such a clear format. It felt very natural to write in the style of the Sanskrit texts of old because I was studying the Yogic sutras so intensely. All in all, 366 sutras unfolded in a matter of days. However, it took many months to write a commentary for each sutra to explain what was being presented in these writings. The sutras and their commentaries really need no introduction; however, I would like to share a few points with you first.

I recommend that you read this book in the order that it was written. The sutras are presented first and then their commentaries. Many books place sutras after their commentaries as if the commentator feels that his interpretations of someone else's sutras are apparently more important than the sutras themselves, for the reader obviously needs his interpretation to understand them. It is my belief, however, that we all understand Truth when we hear it, even if we cannot grasp it all intellectually. I, therefore, would like to give credit to my reader and ask that you first read all of the sutras, which stand by themselves. Then, if you connect with the sutras and care at all about what I have to say, you can read the commentary with the sutras.

The word *Sutra* literally means "string" or "thread," in the sense that sutras are beads strung together on a common theme or thread. As the underlying theme occurs over and over, one sutra blends into the other, and

Preface

the next sutra often loops back on previous sutras. A beautiful string of sutras acts more like waves on a river, than a linear presentation of text. The major themes come up again and again until the mind of the reader is completely saturated. This is a deliberate effect that is not meant for redundancy but in the spirit of teaching through repetition.

Repetition is the mother of all learning, and the mother of all learning is repetition. No matter how many ways you say it, repetition remains the mother of all learning. The great saints and sages of our world spoke One Certain Truth and spoke of it repeatedly through many different words, metaphors, styles and philosophies. However, in the end, they were simply saying the same one thing over and over. This process acts as a sort of mantra that draws the attention of the reader back time and time again to the object of meditation. In this case, the object of the meditation is the One Self that underlies all manifest existence and is the core theme of the sutras as a whole.

The sutras repeatedly cover the essence of healing and enlightenment while strung together by the thread of eternal existence. The sutras are not only designed to inform the reader about the nature of health, healing and spiritual growth but also to act as a meditation and a healing session in and of themselves.

The sutras are meant to heal and not simply to teach, to enlighten and not simply to inform and to lead the consciousness of the reader continuously into the Source of his own being where true peace and healing can be found. They define healing and the process of enlightenment; but more importantly, their purpose is to promote these.

Preface

These teachings are deep and not meant for everyone. They are actually written for the advanced healer more than for the one being healed, which is to say that they are directed more to the "physician" than to the "patient." However, in the sutras there is no doctor-patient relationship. Honoring the inherent Oneness of all beings, the sutras refer to the "healer" and the "client" but only in the sense that both are always playing both roles. The "healer" is always healed in true healing just as his client is. Therefore, this book is for both the healer and the client, even though it serves the healer more as a text for his work.

This book is an attempt to assist more people to do what I do in my healing practice with others. One person can only do so much, but many duplicates of a system that works can influence the world in incredible ways. I, therefore, offer this work not only as a meditation and teaching tool, but also as a textbook for those who wish to dive deeply into the mysteries of health, healing and enlightenment.

This book should be given to the clients of healers who follow its methods and philosophies, because it is my belief that the more a person knows about his healing the better. The philosophies in this book are very deep and quite controversial; not many people will accept them at face value. The common-sense view of health and healing is very unevolved, and modern medicine and psychiatry are seriously lacking in their views concerning who a man really is. This book therefore will be very difficult for many to grasp and accept. It is for those who are willing to really look deep and experiment for themselves that the truths of the sutras will come out.

Preface

This book is therefore not meant to be theoretical but to be practiced. Its major premise is that a human being can be free from suffering and be healed. This could simply be dismissed as idealistic or fanciful, but that would undermine the many people I have seen healed, enlightened and relieved of suffering in my years of practicing this work. First-hand knowledge of these truths from direct experience is what really will count in the end.

I do wish to apologize now to my readers for the use of masculine and not masculine/feminine terms when referring to the healer and the client. Writing "he or she" in every sutra would have been quite excessive, so please know that when I say "he," I really mean "we." I believe that each and every one of us is absolutely Divine in our essence and that our true immortal Self is not gendered. When I say "he," I am really in the deepest Truth referring to the "I," which is the non-dual Oneness that is the Source of All That Is.

I would also like to share that the sutras come from no one particular tradition. My background in the spiritual and healing arts is extensive, and I claim no one specific tradition as my own. Rather I believe in the Divine Nature of all existence and that healing is a natural process that will unfold for anyone who is willing to put any form of effort into it at all. Once that intention for healing is clear, then the specific modalities of the healer will simply fall into place. I personally claim no hold on any specific healing modality but have come to trust in the Divine Truth as the Ultimate Healer.

You will also notice in Section II that certain sutras have no commentaries. Two or more sutras may be explained in the commentary below or a sutra may need no further explanation.

Preface

I leave you with the sutras to speak for themselves. I offer these introductory words to encourage readers to embrace the pages with an open mind and an open heart and to trust in the wisdom of their presentation style. When a point seems very clear to you, but you are hearing it again, consider that to be your mantra, which constantly brings you back to that One Truth. Use this book as a meditation and as a practical text for relieving your own suffering and the suffering of those around you. In the end, the wisdom of the sutras should be infused into your being in a way that is deeply lived in compassion, service and love. This is meant to be a living sutra that the practitioner becomes in every aspect of Life.

Contents

Preface   iii

Section One - The Sutras   1

Chapters
One—Truth and Healing   3
Two—The Order of Manifestation   5
Three—Mind and Matter   10
Four—The Manifestation of Illness and its Reversal   13
Five—The Healer and the One Healed   16
Six—Understanding Illness   20
Seven—Misconceptions about Healing   26
Eight—The Process of Healing   29
Nine—The Breath   34
Ten—Long-Distance Healing and Taking on Karma   35
Eleven—Creating and Manifesting   37
Twelve—Empowering the Client   40
Thirteen—The Knower 42
Fourteen—The True Spiritual Path   43

Section Two—The Sutras with Commentary   45

Chapters

One—Truth and Healing   47
Two—The Order of Manifestation   73
Three—Mind and Matter   101
Four—The Manifestation of Illness and its Reversal   125
Five—The Healer and the One Healed   155
Six—Understanding Illness   187
Seven—Misconceptions about Healing   227
Eight—The Process of Healing   253
Nine—The Breath   295
Ten—Long-Distance Healing and Taking on Karma   303
Eleven—Creating and Manifesting   323
Twelve—Empowering the Client   343
Thirteen—The Knower   359
Fourteen—The True Spiritual Path   365

Section One
The Sutras on Healing and Enlightenment

Chapter One—Truth and Healing

1:1   Now an exposition on healing and enlightenment is to be made.

1:2   Healing and enlightenment, which are synonymous terms, both arise with the knowledge and awareness of Truth.

1:3   Healing is the process of transforming illusions into Truth.

1:4   Enlightenment is the process of transforming illusions into Truth.

1:5   Illusions are false beliefs, which deny Truth and have no basis in Reality.

1:6   Truth can be experienced as Pure Existence, Pure Consciousness and Pure Bliss.

1:7   Truth can also be experienced as God the Unchanging Source, which is One Substance, One Power and One Love.

1:8   Truth is Absolute and is Immortal, Eternal and Infinite—One without a second.

1:9   Truth also can be experienced as Pure Goodness, Pure Harmony and the Only Reality.

1:10 Truth can be experienced as Soul, Spirit and Pure Light and even beyond Light.

1:11 Truth is Divine Intelligence, Mind and Life and is absolutely non-dual.

1:12 Truth is the Whole, the All-in-All, the Great I Am

1:13 All true healing is mental healing, for God is All and All is Mind.

1:14 Symptomatic relief is not true healing.

1:15 True healing comes from God and God alone.

1:16 True healing is not of the body, but of the mind.

1:17 True healing is of the mind, yet the body may become healthy again in the process of true healing.

1:18 All illness is psychosomatic because the body itself is psychosomatic.

1:19 Illness is illusion and can only be resolved through Truth, which is God.

1:20 A healer who is well evolved on the path of enlightenment can facilitate this process.

The Sutras on Healing and Enlightenment

1:21 True healing removes the cause of disharmony, allowing for its manifestation to drop away.

1:22 Illness, which is disharmony, can only occur in the realm of manifestation, because Consciousness remains forever the same and is eternally pure, free and forever.

1:23 Consciousness is unchanging and can never be disharmonious, yet it has an ability to manifest itself to appear as form while still retaining its True Nature.

1:24 Consciousness is like a mirror in which the whole universe is reflected. The mirror remains forever the same even though the forms reflected in it are changing.

1:25 Understanding, experiencing and knowing one's Self as this Absolute Bliss Consciousness is the primary qualification of a true healer.

Chapter Two—The Order of Manifestation

2:1 The order of manifestation from Pure Consciousness happens both macrocosmically and microcosmically.

2:2 Macrocosmic manifestation refers to the various levels that make up the entire Universe, and its levels are called planes or worlds.

The Sutras on Healing and Enlightenment

2:3 Microcosmic manifestation refers to the various levels that make up a human being, and its levels are called bodies or vehicles.

2:4 These levels are here based on the system of the seven chakras and relate to both microcosmic and macrocosmic creation.

2:5 The seven chakras are known in Sanskrit as sahasrar, ajn, vishuddh, anahat, manipur, svadisthan and muladhar.

2:6 Sahasrar chakra is associated with the Absolute Reality of Godhead, which is Absolute Bliss Consciousness.

2:7 This is the seventh chakra and here there are no planes and no bodies as there is no movement or vibration.

2:8 Its color is often seen as white, golden or violet light and it is associated with the crown of the head; yet in essence it is beyond all name, form, time, space and color.

2:9 Ajn chakra is associated with the level of manifestation in its first movements as Light, creativity, the Vision of Oneness, Pure Ideas and the arising and movement of the subtle particles of creation.

The Sutras on Healing and Enlightenment

2:10 This is the sixth chakra, which is associated with the causal plane and the causal body.

2:11 The sixth chakra, which is often seen as indigo, is associated with the third eye in the forehead region.

2:12 Vishuddh chakra is associated with the level of manifestation where the Divine expresses itself as mind, intelligence, ego-sense and mind-sense.

2:13 This is the fifth chakra associated with the mental plane and the mental body.

2:14 Its color is often seen as blue, and it is associated with the throat.

2:15 Anahat chakra is associated with the level of creation which vibrates at the density of emotions, the purest being love and compassion.

2:16 This is the fourth chakra, which is associated with the astral plane and the astral body.

2:17 The fourth chakra, often seen as green, is associated with the region of the heart.

2:18 Manipur chakra is associated with personal power.

The Sutras on Healing and Enlightenment

2:19 It is the third chakra associated with the lower mental plane and lower mental body.

2:20 The third chakra, often seen as yellow, is associated with the solar plexus.

2:21 Svadisthan chakra is associated with Consciousness, taking pleasure in its creations and in itself.

2:22 This is the second chakra, which is associated with the etheric plane and the etheric body.

2:23 The second chakra, often seen as orange, is associated with the region just below the navel.

2:24 Muladhar chakra is associated with Consciousness in its appearance in physical form.

2:25 This is the first chakra, which is associated with the physical plane and the physical body.

2:26 The first chakra, often seen as red, is associated with the region of the tailbone.

2:27 The order of manifestation, governed by Divine Intelligence, is perfect and harmonious in every way.

The Sutras on Healing and Enlightenment

2:28   A human being—the Divine made manifest on every level of creation—is perfect in every way.

2:29   A human being is a self-conscious entity who is often unaware of his Divine origins and who can choose to become conscious of his True Nature, which is pure, free and forever.

2:30   Disharmony, disease, pain and suffering in the human experience are not based on the Divine Intelligence of God, but are an apparent manifestation of illusion, delusion and error.

2:31   Through Truth, all disharmony, disease, pain and suffering are transformed back into harmony, health, comfort and peace.

2:32   Enlightenment is the process by which a human being transfoms illusions into Truth and realizes his True Nature.

2:33   The enlightenment process culminates in Absolute Self-Realization, which is a state of being totally independent of the health of the body, where Consciousness experiences that Self is All That Is.

The Sutras on Healing and Enlightenment

Chapter Three—Mind and Matter

3:1   Pure Consciousness is the Only Reality, which is eternal, formless and forever unchanging.

3:2   The manifestations of Consciousness, which are temporary forms, are always changing.

3:3   Truth is that which is real, and its manifestations are said to be unreal.

3:4   Physical form is a manifestation of Consciousness and has no absolute existence.

3:5   Physical form, which is a mirage, is said to be unreal, having only an apparent and relative reality.

3:6   All physical form is dependent in nature and is empty of any sense of being a separate self.

3:7   Nothing exists in physical form that does not exist on the more subtle levels of creation.

3:8   The physical world is a belief system, and belief systems are thoughts.

The Sutras on Healing and Enlightenment

3:9   Thoughts can manifest whether harmonious or disharmonious.

3:10 Divine Mind only creates perfect and harmonious realities and has created the mind of a human being as perfect in its image and likeness.

3:11 A human mind has the free will to choose between the real and the unreal, between Truth and illusions.

3:12 Choices based on that which is true and real create harmony; choices based on that which is untrue and false create disharmony.

3:13 One can choose to nurture false illusory beliefs, or at any moment one can choose Truth, which transcends beliefs.

3:14 Illness is disharmony and is not of God.

3:15 The physical world of matter has no inherent intelligence, sensation or power in and of itself.

3:16 Sensation is in mind and not in matter.

3:17 Matter is not a cause.

3:18 The world of form is the result of mind and not matter.

The Sutras on Healing and Enlightenment

3:19 Things are thoughts, only apparent realities perceived through the limitations of the five senses.

3:20 The Consciousness of a human being identifies itself with the human form and the human mind and becomes misidentified with matter.

3:21 In the misidentified state, the mind concludes that it is the body and not Pure Consciousness.

3:22 Its beliefs about who it is come from its self-created ignorance and illusion.

3:23 It concludes that it has the attributes of the body and the body's experiences rather than the attributes of Source.

3:24 These conclusions are false beliefs, which are thoughts; and these false thoughts do affect the order of manifestation.

3:25 The order of manifestation is perfect, and false thoughts will perfectly manifest as disharmonious realities.

3:26 False thoughts are beliefs, which can appear as negative emotions, suppression, destructive behaviors, illness and disharmonious life situations.

3:27 The remedy for all disharmony on any level of manifestation is Truth.

Chapter Four—The Manifestation of Illness and its Reversal

4:1 The essence of a human being is Pure Consciousness, which is often called I Am.

4:2 Any thought placed after "I Am" that is held long enough will manifest into form.

4:3 All thoughts have creative power.

4:4 In the order of manifestation in a human being, Consciousness associates with its mind, emotions and physical body and forgets who it really is.

4:5 Its thoughts then become based on the limitations of the object of Consciousness, which are body, mind and emotions.

4:6 As a creative force, Consciousness will manifest realities based on the thoughts of the mind with which it is associated.

4:7 Thoughts of Truth and right knowledge are harmonious and manifest only harmonious realities.

The Sutras on Healing and Enlightenment

4:8 Thoughts that are not true and not of right knowledge are disharmonious and manifest only disharmonious realities.

4:9 Thoughts that are not true are beliefs, and all beliefs are false.

4:10 False beliefs manifest as negative emotions, which are often expressed through speech and action.

4:11 Expression only reinforces negative beliefs and emotions.

4:12 In an ignorant state the human being often suppresses beliefs and emotions to avoid having to experience them.

4:13 These suppressed beliefs and emotions cause blockages in the energy flow of the subtle bodies.

4:14 These blockages, which are mental impressions that cause disharmony in the physical system, must be removed for healing to occur.

4:15 Healing does not occur from the dense levels of manifestation inward, but from the more subtle levels outward.

The Sutras on Healing and Enlightenment

4:16 Suppressed beliefs and emotions manifesting as physical symptoms or negative behaviors must be resolved through Truth.

4:17 Truth shatters false beliefs and their associated emotions and symptoms.

4:18 To treat physical symptoms and emotions alone is not true healing.

4:19 The mechanism of suppression must be reversed.

4:20 Emotions and beliefs must be brought to the Light of Consciousness.

4:21 Truth must end up replacing negative beliefs.

4:22 The heart must remain open.

4:23 Forgiveness must occur.

4:24 Consciousness must be re-established in its True Nature.

4:25 The mind must learn to see itself as a manifestation of Divinity on all levels.

4:26 Consciousness must learn to know itself as Itself and to avoid identifying with the new positive self-image established in the mind.

The Sutras on Healing and Enlightenment

4:27 Enlightenment, which is the process of establishing the Self within Itself, has nothing to do with physical or emotional well-being.

4:28 Healing can assist in the enlightenment process, but perfect harmony on any level is not required for full realization.

4:29 Harmony on the lower levels assists in the enlightenment process.

4:30 A strong and flexible body, an open heart, a clear mind, a good memory, high energy and a well-evolved intellect all assist in the enlightenment process.

4:31 There are many modalities, exercises and techniques that can assist in creating harmony on the lower levels of reality.

4:32 However, true healing and enlightenment occur only through Divine Mind, which is Truth.

4:33 Once a being is fully established in Truth, then he is free from all misfortune and pain regardless of the condition of the physical body.

Chapter Five—The Healer and the One Healed

5:1 Truth is the only healer there is.

The Sutras on Healing and Enlightenment

5:2 A human being fully established in Truth becomes an exceptionally powerful healing force, because his True Nature is known as being one with Truth.

5:3 A true healer can see only Truth and knows that all disharmony is a manifestation of a deluded mind.

5:4 A true healer knows that illness does not exist in God's Order of Manifestation and that God did not create illness.

5:5 A true healer does not believe in illness because he knows that only the creations of God are real and all else is unreal.

5:6 A true healer does not see his client as sick or support the client in his beliefs about illness, disharmony, pain and suffering.

5:7 A true healer must be healed himself.

5:8 In true healing both the healer and the client are healed simultaneously.

5:9 The one being healed is referred to as a client because they must offer some form of compensation for the healing that is being done.

5:10 Compensation need not be monetary, but there must be some form of giving and receiving, no matter how small.

The Sutras on Healing and Enlightenment

5:11   In true healing the healer must see the client as already healed.

5:12   In true healing the healer must know that the client is not and can never be sick.

5:13   The true healer must see illness only as a fleeting mirage.

5:14   The healer should know that he is absolutely one with his client, even if the client does not.

5:15   The client must come to the healer asking for help; the healer should never try to convince a client to begin therapy.

5:16   The healer must evaluate whether or not his client meets certain criteria or healing cannot occur.

5:17   However, if the majority of the criteria are met, then the healer can help to nourish the criteria lacking in his client.

5:18   Not only must the client meet the criteria, but the healer as well.

5:19   The client and the healer must both have a willingness to heal.

5:20   They have to be ready to let go of their suffering.

The Sutras on Healing and Enlightenment

5:21   They must believe they can heal.

5:22   They must believe that the healer can heal them.

5:23   It is very helpful for them to believe in God and to have a strong spiritual viewpoint; otherwise, a desire for discovering the Truth is imperative.

5:24   They must want to heal and to be healed.

5:25   They must be willing to accept being healed and the responsibility of being Whole.

5:26   They should be made to expect that healing will occur and that it already exists in Truth.

5:27   They both must be committed to the healing process.

5:28   They must both surrender the outcome of the healing work to God and be non-attached.

5:29   The healer should work within the client's model of reality, while always holding the Space of Truth.

5:30   To a great extent, the healer must be freed from false beliefs or he will not be able to free his client from such beliefs.

The Sutras on Healing and Enlightenment

5:31 A healer's modalities and credentials are entirely secondary to his degree of enlightenment.

5:32 A healer is to be used by Truth to free a client from illusions, and therefore the healer must be a clear channel for Truth to come through.

5:33 A healer must know that healing does not take time because false beliefs can be transformed in an instant.

5:34 Physical symptoms may take time to change because they are in the realm of time.

5:35 Once the cause of a symptom is removed, the symptom has no more power and cannot last long.

5:36 True healing can occur regardless of a change in physical symptoms.

5:37 True healing is only true if both the healer and the healed know themselves as Self in the end.

Chapter Six—Understanding Illness

6:1 The body communicates to the mind the mind's denials of the Self.

The Sutras on Healing and Enlightenment

6:2 The body is a metaphor for the beliefs and emotional patterns of the mind.

6:3 The body is a three-dimensional reflection of one's thinking.

6:4 The body does not cause false beliefs and emotions, rather false beliefs and emotions cause the illusion of the body.

6:5 Many believe that sickness causes negative feelings, but the reverse is true: negative feelings cause sickness.

6:6 Pure Consciousness identifies with body, mind, emotions and life experiences and defines itself as such.

6:7 Instead of knowing itself to be Perfect Divinity, Pure Consciousness takes on belief systems based on life experience.

6:8 The range of false beliefs is proportional to the infinite experiences that a Soul can have.

6:9 The Universe will always support a person in what he believes.

6:10 These false beliefs create negative emotions.

6:11   The range of negative emotion is proportional to the number of false beliefs held in the mind.

6:12   Experiences of love, joy, peace, bliss, ecstasy and true happiness are not emotions, but are direct experiences of Truth when not clouded by beliefs and emotions.

6:13   Depression is not an emotion but the result of suppressed emotion.

6:14   False beliefs and negative emotions in and of themselves are not the cause of illness; when these are suppressed and unresolved, they truly create disharmony.

6:15   Suppressed beliefs and emotions combined with the memory of the events that created them are stored in the mind and are called mental impressions.

6:16   Mental impressions that remain suppressed form the subconscious mind and are blockages in the energy flow of a human being, which can eventually manifest as disease.

6:17   In Truth there is no subconscious mind.

6:18   The heart is the root of the mind because whatever the heart is feeling, the mind will talk about.

6:19   When the heart is pure, then heart and mind are seen as one.

6:20   Where and how disease manifests in the body is very relevant because the body is telling the story of the mental impressions stored in the heart.

6:21   How a person feels about his symptoms is an exceptionally good indicator of the mental impressions causing these symptoms.

6:22   Through skillful means the healer can determine which false beliefs and emotions are causing the illness and through which chakra the illness is manifesting.

6:23   Where an illness manifests in the body is related to a specific chakra and its energetics.

6:24   A chakra's energetics are complex, and only the most general and practical explanation is given here.

6:25   Problems in the hands, feet or tailbone region deal with muladhar chakra and are associated with issues of one's security.

6:26   Problems in the wrists, ankles and sacral region deal with svadisthan chakra and are associated with pleasure and sexuality.

The Sutras on Healing and Enlightenment

6:27 Problems in the forearms, lower legs and solar plexus region deal with manipur chakra and are associated with personal power.

6:28 Problems in the elbows, knees and heart region deal with anahat chakra and are associated with love.

6:29 Problems in the upper arms, upper legs and throat region deal with vishuddh chakra and are associated with expression.

6:30 Ajn and sahasrar chakras do not manifest in the body directly, but problems in these chakras will manifest as poor creativity, lack of purpose and a lack of spirituality.

6:31 Problems that arise in the region of the head are often the result of the suppression of emotions through the closing of the heart and throat chakras, causing a lack of energy flow to the higher chakras.

6:32 Each chakra functions through each and every other chakra; problems can manifest in multiple chakras simultaneously because much larger patterns are all interconnected in the system as a whole.

The Sutras on Healing and Enlightenment

6:33　The mental level of a chakra must be healed, because chakras are not a cause of disharmony but are only the channels through which disharmony can manifest.

6:34　By knowing the underlying beliefs and emotions of a symptom and its corresponding chakra, a healer can begin a true process of healing for his client.

6:35　If the underlying cause of a symptom is not brought to the surface, then it will manifest again in an even more powerful way.

6:36　There is nothing wrong with treating symptoms to relieve another's pain and suffering, but a true healer should never call this healing.

6:37　Symptomatic relief is not true healing because the negative beliefs and emotions that manifested the problem still remain intact.

6:38　Once negative beliefs and emotions are transformed, Truth will take their place, healing will occur, and harmony will be restored.

The Sutras on Healing and Enlightenment

Chapter Seven—Misconceptions about Healing

7:1 Negative beliefs and emotions combined with the act of suppression block chakras and energy channels and cause illness; chakras and energy channels do not get blocked by themselves.

7:2 Chakras, energy channels, energy and matter are not the cause of illness.

7:3 Modalities that simply manipulate these lower levels of reality never provide true healing.

7:4 Any form of healing that does not put its full faith in God is a disservice to the client in his spiritual growth.

7:5 Any modality that does not lead one back into a true knowledge of Self only supports ignorance and illusion and does not honor God as the Ultimate Healer.

7:6 Chakras, beliefs, emotions, energy channels, energy and matter have no power in and of themselves except for the power given to them.

7:7 God is the Only Power and the only true healer.

The Sutras on Healing and Enlightenment

7:8 These Truths should never exclude practical forms of hygiene, medical care, proper nutrition, rest and exercise.

7:9 Most people are not aware of Truth and should be helped on the level that is appropriate for them.

7:10 Healing is not of the body.

7:11 Healing is not done through a rebalancing of energy.

7:12 Healing is not done through chakra balancing.

7:13 Healing is not done through medications, herbs, drugs, needles or homeopathies.

7:14 Healing is not done through massage or bodily manipulations.

7:15 Healing is not done through crystals or stones.

7:16 Without true forgiveness, healing does not occur.

7:17 Without Self-Realization, healing does not occur.

7:18 A human being is never the healer; his skillful means only make room for Truth to enter.

The Sutras on Healing and Enlightenment

7:19 The belief that healing takes time is a false belief.

7:20 The belief that it is difficult to heal is a false belief.

7:21 The belief that symptoms must get worse before they get better is a false belief.

7:22 The use of the hands, magnets or energetic transfer is not necessary for true healing.

7:23 True healing can and often does heal the physical body, but not always.

7:24 A saint's curing touch is not true healing even if it does partially or fully relieve symptoms, although it certainly can spark true healing.

7:25 Any modality can spark true healing, even though it is not the direct cause of true healing.

7:26 True healing does not stop the body from dying, although it could.

7:27 A person is not healed simply because the body has ceased to function in what is commonly called death.

Chapter Eight—The Process of Healing

8:1 There is no one way to assist a person in healing, yet there are principles a healer should know to make him a more effective healer regardless of his methods.

8:2 The most important principle is that the healer knows who he truly is and only sees his client as that One Self—which is pure, free and forever.

8:3 The healer must not accept the client's illusions as real, including physical symptoms, destructive behaviors, emotional responses or false beliefs.

8:4 The healer must assess his client's ability to heal based on the criteria given earlier.

8:5 If the client is ready to heal, then the healer should gather a thorough understanding of the client.

8:6 All healing must be rooted in Spirit; both the healer and the client must have a rapport on many levels, especially on the level of Spirit.

8:7 With rapport established and a good understanding of the client's complaints, the healer should become clear about what the client wants the results of the healing to be.

The Sutras on Healing and Enlightenment

8:8   Then the client's underlying beliefs and emotions that cause the physical problem should be brought to Consciousness, along with the negative self-image that goes with this.

8:9   Then the corresponding chakras that relate to the problems should be noted along with their corresponding energetics.

8:10 Once the physical symptoms or behaviors are addressed, along with the underlying beliefs, emotions and chakras, then Truth should be discussed.

8:11 The healer must explain to the client the unreality of illusions and assess the client's model of Truth.

8:12 While discussing the Absolute Truth, the client should be made to see the falseness of suffering and be willing to let it go.

8:13 The list of negative beliefs and emotions should be checked against the Light of Truth, and a client should make new lists with words that speak to the Truth of who he is on all levels—physically, emotionally, mentally and spiritually.

8:14 Then a new positive image of the person should be established in the mind with this image representing his Divinity made manifest in human form.

8:15 The client's new image should present himself as he wants to be—free from his suffering and illusions.

8:16 This image is then used to dismantle all false images with their corresponding negative beliefs and emotions.

8:17 The new image should access a client's visual, auditory and kinesthetic senses.

8:18 The new image should address his intelligence, ego-sense and mind as a whole.

8:19 The new image should address his emotional state and feelings.

8:20 The new image should address the condition of his physical body and his behaviors.

8:21 Suggestions and affirmations should be made that remind the client of who he truly is.

8:22 These suggestions and affirmations, along with the new visual images and powerful emotions, should be repeated often in the client's mind.

The Sutras on Healing and Enlightenment

8:23 It is important to understand that this new positive self-image is not the True Self, but is a healthier construct for the person to live out of.

8:24 The new self-image will help to allow for the Light of Truth to come more easily and for illusions to drop away more quickly.

8:25 After a new self-image based on the highest Truth is established, then the underlying events, beliefs and emotions must be dealt with.

8:26 Negative emotions must be released so that physical and energetic shifts can occur if necessary.

8:27 The belief that there is a valid reason to be angry must be eliminated.

8:28 Anger is love without understanding.

8:29 Understanding, acceptance, commonality, forgiveness and compassion must arise.

8:30 Past memories must be reframed from the perspective of Truth and present-day spiritual awareness.

8:31 False beliefs must be transformed to Truth.

The Sutras on Healing and Enlightenment

8:32 The new self-image should replace the old self-image; the healer must be sure that the client knows who he truly is aside from this more beneficent new model.

8:33 Visualizations and suggestions for symptomatic relief should be given if necessary.

8:34 Chakras that were out of balance can be visualized with their corresponding locations and colors.

8:35 A chakra's emotional energetics can be placed into suggestions and affirmations to balance a specific chakra or chakras.

8:36 Through these steps, if negative beliefs are transformed, emotions are released, forgiveness occurs and suggestions and visualizations for symptomatic relief are given, then success will be easy.

8:37 True healing only occurs when a person is enlightened to the Absolute Truth of his being.

8:38 False beliefs and self-images must be replaced with healthier ones, but in the end only Self-Realization can be considered true healing.

Chapter Nine—The Breath

9:1 Here we begin an explanation of the breath-within-the-breath.

9:2 The word *breath* here is synonymous with the body's life force energy.

9:3 This life force energy is the breath-within-the-breath.

9:4 Unless this energy flows freely and in balance, illness will manifest.

9:5 The biggest cause of the blockage of breath energy is emotional suppression and denial.

9:6 To stop emotion or thought, one can stop the breath, yet this blocks life force energy.

9:7 Blocked energy must be made to flow freely again.

9:8 Within blocked breath energy are mental impressions that house memories, beliefs and emotions.

9:9 These must be released and brought to Consciousness.

9:10 This is done exceptionally well by the healer assisting the client through Breath Work.

9:11 The breath will reverse the order of the manifestation of disease.

The Sutras on Healing and Enlightenment

9:12   The breath will expose suppressed mental impressions, which the healer can transform with his client.

9:13   When this is accomplished and true healing occurs, the client must be taught never to block this energy again.

Chapter Ten—Long Distance Healing and Taking on Karma

10:1   Healing can occur regardless of whether the client is physically present or not.

10:2   The healer and the client are not two separate realities and are not limited by time and space.

10:3   True healing, which is the transformation of illusions into Truth, happens only on the mental level.

10:4   The healer is again reminded not to acknowledge illness or error as real.

10:5   The healer is to visualize his client and to see him only as perfect, whole and complete.

10:6   He should deny the client's false beliefs and affirm only the Truth.

10:7   The healer must believe that it is possible to heal a client in this way.

10:8   The healer must want to do this.

The Sutras on Healing and Enlightenment

10:9 The healer must be willing to accept this power and any responsibility that goes with it.

10:10 The healer must expect that his efforts will yield the results he imagines.

10:11 The healer must surrender the outcome with non-attachment.

10:12 It is possible for the healer to read the mind of the client during a long-distance healing session and to become aware of the negative beliefs that are causing the problem.

10:13 The healer can then work out those beliefs within his own mind.

10:14 Karma is belief in action.

10:15 If the beliefs are very strong, then the healer may experience the client's symptoms within his own body.

10:16 If the healer is well evolved and does not believe in the client's false thoughts, emotions and symptoms, then the healing can be quite rapid.

10:17 If the healer does hold similar beliefs, then the healing will take longer only because now the healer must heal himself as well.

10:18 A healer should never attempt to take on another person's karma without the total confidence that he can resolve it quickly and easily.

10:19   It is an unparalled act of selflessness and compassion to even consider this.

10:20   A healer must find his own limit as to how much he is willing to work this way with his clients.

10:21   Because of this ability for an evolved Soul to take on another being's karma, a healer who does not believe in illness may have sickness within his own body.

10:22   Healing and enlightenment are synonymous terms, yet a fully liberated being can appear to have a sick body. He knows that he is not the body and can work out another's karma in his body.

10:23   As long as any Soul still believes in sickness, then it will still exist.

10:24   The more evolved the healer, the more influence he shall have over creation, whether he is present or working long-distance.

Chapter Eleven—Creating and Manifesting

11:1   Anything that exists physically was created on more subtle levels and then manifested in form.

11:2   An evolved being who is in touch with his Source can easily use a simple formula to create and manifest on any level of creation.

The Sutras on Healing and Enlightenment

11:3   This process can be applied to healing or anything else that one would wish to manifest.

11:4   This process should only be used for the greatest good.

11:5   It should only be used to heal someone who is willing to heal and who has asked for help.

11:6   In the case of those who cannot ask for help, it is up to the healer to listen to his inner guidance and to act only from the highest intentions and intuitions.

11:7   This process works for healing whether the client is physically present or located at a distance from the healer.

11:8   If both the healer and the client do this process together, it is even more powerful.

11:9   Although the more people involved the better, the healer must be aware of unevolved or disharmonious minds that could sabotage the process.

11:10   First, one must become clear on what is to be created and manifested.

11:11   Then he should only act with intentions set for the highest good for all involved.

11:12   Next, he should be aware of and work in accordance with universal laws.

The Sutras on Healing and Enlightenment

11:13   He is then to go into deep meditation and access his Source, the place of Pure Potentiality, Pure Consciousness and creativity.

11:14   Here the image of the desired result is to be held in the mind.

11:15   The visual image should be seen as if it already exists with all those involved.

11:16   Intense positive emotion should be added.

11:17   Thoughts affirming the outcome should be added.

11:18   The healer then affirms his belief that this will work.

11:19   He then affirms that he wants this to happen.

11:20   He then affirms that he is willing to accept the outcome.

11:21   He then affirms that he expects this to manifest.

11:22   He affirms his commitment to the process of doing what must be done to achieve the result.

11:23   He then surrenders the outcome to God through non-attachment.

11:24   The process is repeated until the desired result manifests.

The Sutras on Healing and Enlightenment

> 11:25 The healer understands that present knowledge supercedes prior commitment.
>
> 11:26 The client is also to use this process in conjunction with his other methods of transformation.
>
> 11:27 The highest use of this process involves the healer totally in harmony with the Will of God and not acting selfishly or with ulterior motives.

Chapter Twelve—Empowering the Client

> 12:1 Clients must be empowered to discover the True Self on their own outside of therapy.
>
> 12:2 They should be taught to meditate very early on in the therapeutic process.
>
> 12:3 They must learn to keep the heart open.
>
> 12:4 They should understand not to suppress or act out on their emotions.
>
> 12:5 They must learn what to do with their emotions—not to block, suppress, deny or act out.
>
> 12:6 They should be taught how to breathe properly and to relax.
>
> 12:7 They should be taught when the voice of ego is communicating to them and when it is the voice of Truth and how to tell the difference.

The Sutras on Healing and Enlightenment

12:8 They should be taught how to witness their body, mind and emotions from the seat of Witness Consciousness.

12:9 They should be taught how to meditate on the Knower.

12:10 A client should understand that illness is a call for Love and that Consciousness is Love.

12:11 A client should be encouraged not to withdraw from or deny pain, but to bring the presence of the Knower directly into the core of the pain.

12:12 The Knower is Love, and Love is the most healing force there is.

12:13 When Consciousness finds the core of a problem, then the problem is seen to be nonexistent.

12:14 Many times illness arises because the person has withdrawn his Consciousness from a certain region of his body due to fear, shame or judgment.

12:15 The remedy is a state of maturity that is willing to be fully intimate with What Is and to embrace What Is totally and completely.

12:16 In the core of any manifested phenomena resides the Self.

12:17 The client must learn how to take his Consciousness and place it on the Consciousness within a problem.

The Sutras on Healing and Enlightenment

14:4   Only the Self is an end in Itself.

14:5   Enlightenment is not dependent on the condition of the body, the emotions, the belief systems or the chakras.

14:6   The knowledge of one's True Nature transcends all manifest reality.

14:7   The health and harmony of the lower levels can help one to attain the goal of Self-Realization; therefore, healing is beneficial for this reason.

14:8   The lower levels do not ever change the Self and the Knower of the Self, which is the Self.

14:9   The true spiritual path is about one's ability to discern that which is changing from that which is not.

14:10   It is the ability to discern the real from the unreal and to know who one truly is in Truth.

14:11   When the Knower of the Self is fully established in his True Nature, then healing and enlightenment are completed, and there is no more healing and enlightenment left.

Section Two
The Sutras on Healing and Enlightenment with Commentary

The Sutras on Healing and Enlightenment

Chapter One—Truth and Healing

-1:1-
Now an exposition on healing and enlightenment is to be made.

The Sutras on Healing and Enlightenment begin by acknowledging the content of the information that is to follow this first sutra. Beginning in this way is very similar to the style of the Ancient Sages of India, such as Patanjali, who began his Yoga Sutras with the words *Atha Yoganusasanam*, which are often translated as "Now, an exposition of Yoga (is to be made)." In honor of the great saint Patanjali, who offered one of the most profound scriptures for all mankind, The Sutras on Healing and Enlightenment begin in a similar fashion.

The word *Sutra* can be translated from the Sanskrit to mean "thread," in the sense that many aphorisms are linked together like the beads of a rosary to form one whole. The thread is a basic theme that links a set of aphorisms together, and it is here that the themes of healing and enlightenment shall be discussed. The style of writing in sutras allows the author to convey his or her point most succinctly. In ancient times before books, adepts memorized sutras, which were often created as songs that could be sung and easily recalled. Such a system also allowed a teacher to impart only the most basic meanings of a theme while encouraging a serious student to dive much deeper into the teachings to discover the real meaning of the sutras.

Commentaries by many authors often would follow a set of sutras, which were written sometimes hundreds of years after the original aphorisms had been given.

The Sutras on Healing and Enlightenment

This led to many different interpretations derived from different commentators from different places and times. Once the Sutras on Healing and Enlightenment were written, commentaries immediately followed, allowing the author's full meaning and intentions to be made clear. Each sutra and its commentary are meant to be studied thoroughly, meditated on and then mastered in one's daily life and service to others.

-1:2-
Healing and enlightenment, which are synonymous terms, both arise with the knowledge and awareness of Truth.

The Sutras on Healing and Enlightenment begin with an exceptionally important statement that declares that there is no difference between the use of the terms *healing* and *enlightenment* in the given context. The context of the work is that a healer or a teacher can assist another in being free of suffering. The ancient spiritual traditions from all over the world basically have this aim. Any spiritual, mystical or religious system that does not lead a human being to his freedom from suffering cannot be called much of a system at all. Whether it is the promise of a future heaven or a state of being that transcends all pain and suffering, it can be clear that in the end a human being simply wants to be free.

Healing then can be considered as a process that liberates a human being from his suffering. The word *healing* implies that a human being can be healed, but it is an often-misunderstood term that usually implies the mere treatment of symptoms. Removing the symptoms of suffering or trying to cure disease is not true healing. For a human being to be healed, the root cause of his suffering must be extinguished. This is why the words *healing* and *enlightenment* are used synonymously, because in all of the world's great traditions, the word *enlightenment* implies freedom from suffering for the one who has been enlightened. Yet if we look deeply into the world's great systems of enlightenment, we find a few exceptional beings active in assisting humanity to become enlightened—the world's great teachers, healers, saints, sages and gurus.

The word *Guru* can be translated as "one who leads from darkness to Light." It is a sacred word implying a very sacred relationship. A Guru is a healer in the truest sense as he works to lead others from the darkness of ignorance to the Light of their own True Nature where suffering is transcended. However, there are very few True Gurus, because there are very few human beings who have truly reached such a state. Therefore, the use of the term *healer* refers to one who assists himself and others in the process of enlightenment and healing. The world needs more Gurus, and it needs more healers. Few can claim to be True Gurus, but anyone with an open and willing heart can work toward being a healer.

A healer works to enlighten his client about the cause of his suffering and heals through loving service in removing its cause. What a healer is will be described throughout the course of these sutras; however, the definition of the term is mentioned here because true enlightenment and true healing do not happen in an isolated case. Healing is a process where two or more beings come together to assist each other in reaching a state where suffering is eliminated.

Suffering happens on many levels and in many ways, but through the process of healing and enlightenment

The Sutras on Healing and Enlightenment

it can be significantly reduced. If we believe the great sages of our mystical traditions, then we can safely say that suffering can be entirely eliminated. The premise underneath such a bold statement is that in Truth there is no disharmony in any way. When a person is led from illusions to Truth, then suffering ceases and healing and enlightenment are said to have arisen. This is a most sacred work and should be considered of the utmost importance.

-1:3-
Healing is the process of transforming illusions into Truth.

To understand healing, we must understand how the illusions of the human mind are the root cause of suffering and how the unfolding of Truth is the only real solution. Healing is often misunderstood as the relieving of symptoms through various means and modalities, yet it is stressed throughout the sutras that this is not true healing. True healing addresses the root cause of suffering, which is ignorance; and the only place this ignorance is found is within a human mind. The human mind is ignorant of its True Nature and therefore lives in an illusion, plagued with false beliefs and terrible negative emotions. It will be seen throughout the course of this work that these false beliefs and emotions are causing all human suffering, and nothing else. It is the ignorance of one's True Nature that creates disharmony on any level of reality.

Disease is disharmony, and the premise here is that all disharmony comes from the ignorance within the human mind. Truth—being God—does not create disharmony. Only in the illusion of the human psyche

The Sutras on Healing and Enlightenment

does suffering actually arise. When one assists oneself or another back into the awareness of Truth, then all illusions drop away and so too does all disharmony. This sutra says that this is a transformation process, yet we must understand what is being transformed. It is only the mind that is transformed in true healing. As we shall see later, everything is mind, and it is only the mind that needs transformation. Simply stated, ignorance causes illusion, which causes suffering. Only through a strong dose of Truth can true healing occur.

The reader should not be expected to be convinced of these statements but should experiment with this premise himself to experience directly its exceptionally pragmatic and time-proven nature.

-1:4-
Enlightenment is the process of transforming illusions into Truth.

This sutra simply declares what the following sutra has already stated in reaffirming that healing and enlightenment are synonymous terms. The word *enlightenment* has been used for millennia to describe a state of being that is free from suffering and is totally lit by the Truth. However, it is important to ask who this term enlightenment applies to. It is not used for cats, dogs, cows, birds, trees, mountains or stars; it is used for a human being—and a human being alone. A human being is the only creature on this Earth with the potential to reach a state of true enlightenment. Therefore, a human birth is considered as exceptionally precious indeed.

Knowing that suffering is removed by transforming illusion into Truth for a human being, then we must

The Sutras on Healing and Enlightenment

ask ourselves what part of a human being can transform illusions into Truth. It is not the feet, legs, arms, spleen or eyes that transform illusions into Truth. It is not the human body that does this, but the mind. It is only in mind that suffering arises, and it is only in mind that it can be transformed. However, mind alone cannot do this, because one who is in illusion can seldom discover Truth solely on his own. This is where the work of a healer comes in. For if healing and enlightenment are synonymous terms, then the healer is the one who assists in the enlightenment process.

It is in this process that healing occurs, and it is through this process that the symptoms of illusion fall away. The true healer works to enlighten his client to Truth in the best way that he can. He is not expected to be perfect. He is not expected to act as Guru. The healer who assists the enlightenment process is being enlightened himself in the process. He is allowing Guru to work through him and is made whole as well in the process. Enlightenment is therefore a term representing a final state where all suffering is transcended, as well as being the process involved in reaching that state.

The word *Guru* refers to the energy of God that works to transform illusions into Truth. Guru is not a person. It is the active aspect of God Himself that leads humanity from darkness to Light. A person who is fully enlightened can also be considered a Guru, yet the healer is not asked to assume such a role. A healer must be largely free from illusion, but is most often not a fully liberated being. The role of the healer and how he is also made whole through the healing process is stressed throughout the sutras. It is a sacred relationship when a healer and a client come together, for truly in that process each is enlightened to the Truth of his own being.

The Sutras on Healing and Enlightenment

-1:5-
Illusions are false beliefs, which deny Truth and have no basis in Reality.

Again, illusions that cause suffering are found only in the ignorance of a human mind. These illusions are false assumptions that appear real, yet they are not based on Reality. These illusions deny Truth but cannot change Truth. False beliefs are the thoughts within a human mind that are very painful lies denying who a human being truly is. These false beliefs are the cause of all negative emotions, all suppression and denial, all negative and destructive behaviors and the majority of what is commonly known as disease. The healer works to transform these false beliefs in himself and in his client through the Light of Truth. As this is the case, Truth is the healer's only real modality.

-1:6-
Truth can be experienced as Pure Existence, Pure Consciousness and Pure Bliss.

Because Truth is the healer's only real modality, we can see how important it is to thoroughly understand Truth. Therefore, the Sutras on Healing and Enlightenment use nine aphorisms to explain what Truth is. Yet it should be pointed out that Truth is never described as some abstract state, quality or philosophy. The perceptive reader of these sutras will notice that Truth is said to be able to be experienced. Truth can be directly experienced as one's True Nature, and in the healer's knowledge of the Truth he assists his client, and himself as well, in the process of healing and enlightenment.

The Sutras on Healing and Enlightenment

The first sutra describing Truth states that Truth is Pure Existence, Pure Consciousness and Pure Bliss. These terms come from the Yogic word *Satchitanand*, which can be broken down to mean: Sat–Existence, Chit–Consciousness, and Anand–Bliss. The word *Satchitanand* describes the absolute state of Godhead. The word *pure* is placed before each term because this describes a state of being untainted by any sense of "other." In Truth there is only one Absolute Bliss Consciousness with no sense of anything but this one Reality.

This Reality is the Only Reality, and therefore it is pure. It is pure of any sense of duality, disharmony, suffering or death. It is One Existence without any other, One Consciousness without any other and One Bliss without any other. It is one's True Nature and can be directly experienced. This state of being can be called God, but one should be careful not to associate the word *God* here with any sense of personality. Truth, as Satchitanand, is a nameless and formless state of Pure Divinity. Because it is the Only Reality, it can be considered the Source of All That Is. Yet stated even more accurately, it is All That Is, since nothing exists but this.

The well-evolved healer knows himself as this Truth and therefore cannot ever believe in anything but this one Reality. In this one Reality, there is no ignorance and no illusion and therefore no disharmony, sickness or death.

-1:7-
Truth can also be experienced as God the Unchanging Source, which is One Substance, One Power and One Love.

The Sutras on Healing and Enlightenment

Again, Truth is said to be that which can be experienced. Here it is experienced as God the Unchanging Source. The word *Truth* can only be applied to an unchanging Reality. That which changes cannot be considered as an Absolute Truth. The healer is empowered with Absolute Truth and never resorts to the relative field of changing phenomena. A healer knows himself as being One with God, the Unchanging Source, which is only Love. The scriptures all declare that God is Love and that God is the only substance and the Only Power. No power should therefore be given to anything else but God. This is the healer's only resource, because it is Source itself.

God is said to be the Source of All That Is. Yet it is important to understand that because God is one, there can be no two. God is non-dual, which implies that the Source and its Creations are one and the same. The healer understands that everything is God. Everything is God and is of God, and God is Pure Love—the Only Reality. The well-evolved healer cannot possibly see anything but God. By living in such a state, he gives no power to disharmony or disease. Empowered with this Truth, the healer becomes an exceptionally powerful force on this Earth to infuse the illusory world of humanity with the Divine Presence. Yet, it is once again stressed that the Divine Presence is All That Is. Only the illusions that cause suffering need to be transformed. Disharmony is not transformed, because it does not exist in Reality. Disharmony only appears to exist in the ignorant false beliefs of the human mind. Illusions simply do not exist. Therefore, disharmony is not transformed; it is simply seen to be nonexistent.

The Sutras on Healing and Enlightenment

-1:8-
*Truth is Absolute and is Immortal, Eternal and Infinite—
One without a second.*

The healer is empowered with Truth because Truth is Absolute, which means it is never changing and is always One Certain Truth. This Truth never dies and so is said to be Immortal. It never fades away, so it is said to be Eternal. It is everywhere, so it is said to be Infinite. Because Truth never changes, never fades and is everywhere, the healer always has access to it. The Divine is always present for the healer to work with and always present for the client to receive. We are again told that it is One without a second, and therefore it is the Only Reality that there is. The more enlightened the healer is, the more he knows that he is this One Absolute Unchanging Reality and that his very own True Nature is Immortal, Eternal and Infinite.

-1:9-
Truth also can be experienced as Pure Goodness, Pure Harmony and the Only Reality.

The beauty of a healer who truly understands God is that he knows that God is only Goodness and Harmony and that this is the Only Reality. Because God is One without a second, then being the Only Reality means just that, namely that God is All That Is and nothing exists except God. The word *pure* again is used to acknowledge that Truth is All That Is and that the healer can rest assured that he truly lives in a benevolent universe.

The Sutras on Healing and Enlightenment

-1:10-
Truth can be experienced as Soul, Spirit and Pure Light and even beyond Light.

Again, we are reminded that Truth can be experienced. The experience of Truth is often called Soul or Spirit. These words are relevant here. Because Truth is known to be All That Is, then Soul or Spirit is known to be All That Is. This statement implies that anything that appears to have birth and death, sickness or old age is an illusion that does not exist in Truth. Only Soul exists as Pure Light; and Soul and Spirit are synonymous terms. There is no sense of separation in God. The idea of a separate Soul is one of ignorance, not one of direct experience. Only the ego-mind creates the appearance that there are drops separate from the ocean. When Truth is experienced, it is nothing but Ocean, and one's True Nature is the Ocean. There is only Ocean, and this Ocean is Pure Light.

God is often considered to be Pure Light, and Pure Light is said to be All That Is. However, the human mind tries to conceptualize this based on its concepts or limited experience of light. The Pure Light of God is beyond words and concepts and can only be known through direct experience. Only the very mature and experienced mystic understands in this sutra that God is "even beyond Light." Only those who have taken the journey into Absolute Reality can know what that phrase truly means. When a healer does have the direct experience of this state of God Beyond the Beyond, then he truly is deeply empowered with the absolute knowingness that his Soul is none other than Truth Itself.

The Sutras on Healing and Enlightenment

-1:11-
Truth is Divine Intelligence, Mind and Life and is absolutely non-dual.

Here, Truth is given the attributes of Intelligence and Mind, yet the reader should be careful not to project the human qualities of intelligence and mind on to God. Divine Intelligence and Divine Mind are concepts totally beyond the limited conception of a human being. These qualities can best be understood by the healer through his faith that everything that exists in Truth is perfect, as it is governed by Infinite Love and by Supreme Intelligence. Although this state of being may be impossible for a human being to grasp, he can be assured that this aspect of God does exist and that it is absolutely non-dual within its creations.

To be non-dual implies absolutely no separation in any way. Therefore, anything that truly exists is not only one with Divine Mind, but is Divine Mind. As God is Life, Life is Mind. God is All That Is, and All That Is is Life. There is no other Reality but Life. In God there is no death. In God, there is only an Infinite and Loving Intelligence that is non-dual with its creations. God is always there for the healer and his client, and this implies only Infinite Intelligence, Love and Goodness.

-1:12-
Truth is the Whole, the All-in-All, the Great I Am.

This sutra is given here to remind the reader that nothing exists except God. The Whole is not the sum of the parts, for in God there are no parts. The All is the Great I Am. It is Pure Consciousness, and therefore we can see that nothing exists but Pure Consciousness. The Whole is the All, which is only God, Truth and Love. There is nothing else.

-1:13-
All true healing is mental healing, for God is All and All is Mind.

The previous sutras have clearly established the non-duality of God and that God is All That Is. With these basic premises established, the sutras now lead us into the nature of true healing. This is an important term because it is separated from any form of healing that involves using anything but Truth as its modality. The chapter entitled "Misconceptions about Healing" clearly explains what healing is not. Here, we can simply say that true healing is only of the mind because only Mind exists.

It is important at this point, however, to make a clear distinction between mind and Mind. The word *mind* as written in lowercase refers to the human mind, while the word *Mind* written with uppercase M refers to Divine Mind. The sutras make it very clear, however, that only Divine Mind exists, making the human mind nothing but an illusion. This illusion called mind does appear to cause suffering for a human being, but through Divine Mind, the illusions of human mind are annihilated and true healing then occurs. The symptoms that appeared to arise due to the human mind fall away when the Presence of Divine Mind transforms illusion back into Truth.

The profundity of this sutra only becomes apparent through actual experience. These Truths can be debated, but they cannot be changed. For once a person is healed through the process of enlightenment—where illusions

The Sutras on Healing and Enlightenment

become Truth and symptoms drop away—then no debate will ever ensue again. God is the only Healer. Throughout the sutras this concept becomes clearer and clearer as the nature of the manifest universe is explained. This sutra is placed early on in the thread of sutras because it boldly lays claim to the Healing Power of God. Yet the reader is not expected to fully understand at this point.

-1:14-
Symptomatic relief is not true healing.

After establishing what true healing is, the sutras say what it is not. Again, an entire chapter is given to this because human beings seldom understand the term healing. We can look at this sutra based on how the Sutras on Healing and Enlightenment use the terms healing and enlightenment synonymously. If we replaced the two words, this sutra would read, "Symptomatic relief is not true enlightenment." This statement will make sense to the reader who understands the nature of the spiritual path and its process of enlightenment. No one who has walked the path of enlightenment will say that to remove a symptom or one hundred symptoms will ever bring true Self-Realization. Symptomatic relief is not true healing because true healing is the process of transforming illusions into Truth, which is the process of enlightenment itself. The sutras go on to discuss symptomatic relief and its place, but never that healing is anything but enlightenment itself.

-1:15-
True healing comes from God and God alone.

The Sutras on Healing and Enlightenment

Since enlightenment is true healing, then we must ask from where does enlightenment arise? Enlightenment, which is the transformation of illusions into Truth, arises only from Truth Itself, which is God. Although the process of healing often involves facilitation by a well-evolved healer, it is important to remember that the healing process still only comes from God and not from the healer himself.

The first thing to understand here is that in Truth there is no separate healer as a human being, because in Truth, God is All That Is. An effective healer is a human being who knows that he is the Truth Itself and allows for his body, mind and emotions to be a suitable channel for that Divinity to express itself. When two people come together for healing, then God is there. God is All That Is and when two people unite to transform dualistic illusions into Truth, then the unifying presence of God is the healing force of the relationship.

In Chapter Five, Sutra 37, it is written, "True healing is only true if both the healer and the healed know themselves as Self in the end." It is therefore through the presence of the enlightened healer that illusions are transformed and the presence of God is revealed. God is doing the healing because the healer does not ever claim to be separate from God, and the healer knows that God is not a human being. A human being is a fiction, but God is the Only Reality. The healer is not living in the world of fiction but is deeply situated in the Truth. He knows that it is Truth that shatters the illusions that cause suffering, and nothing else. Therefore, all true healing comes from God, and God alone.

The Sutras on Healing and Enlightenment

-1:16-
True healing is not of the body, but of the mind.

It has already been established that true healing is enlightenment. Now it can be seen that true healing cannot be of the body, because the body does not become enlightened. The body can transform and symptoms can drop away, but true healing occurs on the mental level, which then transfers down to the physical level. Healing begins on the more subtle levels of being and manifests through the chakra system, not the other way around. The chakra system is explained throughout the sutras. Suffice it to say now, for true healing to occur, belief systems must be changed, which happens on the mental level—not the emotional, energetic, chakric or physical levels.

It shall be later established in the sutras that true healing requires forgiveness and that it is not the body that forgives, but the mind.

-1:17-
True healing is of the mind, yet the body may become healthy again in the process of true healing.

Sutra 16 establishes that true healing is of the mind. Sutra 17 goes on to say that the body may again return to health through the enlightenment of the mind. Note the word *may*. When the mind is returned to its Source and is enlightened as to its True Nature, this does not mean that the body will necessarily change in the direction the client desires. Most clients do not come to a healer seeking enlightenment, but rather wish for their symptoms to go away. They ask for their suffering

The Sutras on Healing and Enlightenment

to stop but do not realize what is causing their suffering in the first place. They do not understand that mind is that causative factor, and they usually are not willing to change their mind from its erroneous thinking. They ask for their symptoms to go away, but do not want to let go of the cause of their symptoms.

Even when true healing occurs, symptoms still may not go away. A body that is ravaged by disease and is at the point of ceasing to function most likely will not transform back into health even if the mind becomes enlightened. In the end, the client will appreciate the immense peace of knowing his Soul, far more than any repairs to his illusory vehicle with which he no longer identifies. Through skillful means, the healer can usually assist the body to return to health when true healing has occurred, but not always. Changes in the body are secondary, and the healer should never be disturbed if they do not occur. The primary work here deals with false beliefs and the return of the mind to Truth. Everything else is much less important.

Human beings exist to know themselves as the Divine. That is their sole purpose for existence. Any other focus is a diversion and a disservice.

-1:18-
All illness is psychosomatic because the body itself is psychosomatic.

This is a very powerful sutra that can only be understood from the point of view of the deepest metaphysical principles concerning the manifestation of mind into matter. The phrase, "All illness is psychosomatic," seems to go against what is typically termed "common sense."

The Sutras on Healing and Enlightenment

It appears in the world of matter that illness is real and that the manifestations of this world of matter are equally real, yet this is not the case. True metaphysics teaches us that matter is nothing but energy. Matter is not solid but is really mind-stuff. The order of manifestation shows that the body is the result of the mind and not the other way around. Consciousness does not arise from the body; the body arises from Consciousness and is nothing but Consciousness itself. Consciousness manifests as mind, and mind manifests as body.

Nothing exists physically that did not already exist on the more subtle levels of creation. A building, for instance, did not first exist and then become an idea in the mind of the architect. The architect has an idea arise in his mind and then that idea becomes manifest into form. The form is nothing but an idea. Things are thoughts and nothing more, and thoughts are Consciousness and nothing more. Consciousness is Spirit.

The word *psychosomatic* comes from the two Greek words *psukhe* and *soma*. The word *psycho* refers to mind or the mental level of a human being and comes from the Greek word *psukhe*, which actually means Spirit. The word *somatic* refers to the body and comes from the Greek word *soma*, which actually means body. The word *psychosomatic* refers often to a disease created in the body because of the mind. Taking the term in its most basic sense, we can see that the body itself is psychosomatic—meaning a body made of Spirit, or thought.

The body is nothing but mind-stuff. It is psychosomatic in and of itself; therefore, any disease that manifests in the body is also psychosomatic. The entire physical universe is in and of itself a macrocosmic psychosomatic manifestation. It is Spirit appearing as matter, yet matter is a mirage with only a relative existence. Spirit never becomes matter, just as a mirror never becomes what is reflected in it. All illness is just a reflection of a false belief made apparently manifest in the mind-stuff, which is the body.

-1:19-
Illness is illusion and can only be resolved through Truth, which is God.

So far, we have established that only God is real and that illness is an apparent disharmony arising from false beliefs in the mind. False beliefs are not real, and any apparent reality that they produce can only be considered as an illusion. A famous example from the Hindu tradition is in order here. Imagine a man walking to his teacher's house through the woods when suddenly he sees what appears to be a snake on the path. He becomes afraid and his heart starts pounding. Biochemicals are released, and the sympathetic nervous system goes into a fight-or-flight response. Blood and energy are pulled from the digestive and immune systems and sent to the muscles to prepare for some form of defense.

It is important to understand here that this entire so-called "physical" response, which is clearly measurable, is only the result of a thought. One thought caused an enormous chemical reaction in this person's body, yet can we blame the fear response on the chemicals or did the thought cause the response? It is obvious that the thought caused the response and not the other way around. The snake did not cause the response. As the story is often told, when the man looked closer, he realized that it was only a rope lying on the ground and not a snake at all. His

The Sutras on Healing and Enlightenment

the client by convincing him that his problem is other than mental. When we realize that only false beliefs create disharmonious realities, we are empowered to heal the root cause and truly liberate the being. When the root cause is eliminated, then the manifestation must fall away.

In the deepest sense, the root cause of all suffering is a false belief in a separate self. When a person thinks that he is a limited and finite body and mind, his thoughts reflect this erroneous conclusion in every way. Since everything is mind, when mind thinks erroneously, it manifests erroneous realities. To try to remove these erroneous realities without removing their underlying ignorance is very disempowering to the client. A person can believe he is healed if a symptom is removed, but if he does not know who he truly is through the process of so-called "healing," then no real healing has occurred. If the root cause of a problem is not eliminated, then it will simply manifest even more strongly in another way.

Pain is a communication. It is the body's way of telling the mind that it is thinking incorrectly and that some change must occur. If these communications are not heard, then the symptoms will have to become even more intense. If a person thinks that he is weak, which is a false belief, and this upsets his stomach, then medications that make his stomach feel better should not be considered a cure. If he still believes that he is weak, his stomach will eventually get an ulcer due to his underlying belief. If he somehow gets rid of the ulcer but does not change his false belief, then his stomach can manifest cancer. The body will keep screaming louder and louder until he gets the message.

The Sutras on Healing and Enlightenment

The body is communicating to the Soul all of the time. Once we truly learn to listen and remove the underlying cause of the disharmony, the manifestation easily drops away. This is true healing: remove the root and watch the illusory manifestation disappear.

-1:22-
Illness, which is disharmony, can only occur in the realm of manifestation, because Consciousness remains forever the same and is eternally pure, free and forever.

The importance of this sutra is that it makes a fundamental distinction between Consciousness and its manifestations. In Truth, there is only one Reality: Consciousness is All That Is. However, for the human mind, the manifestations of this world seem real indeed. A human being sees a tremendous amount of what appears to be disharmony and imperfection, yet this is only an apparent reality, similar to a mirage. A person in the desert may see an entire oasis. When the Truth is revealed, he can see that this mirage was just a false perception that had no true reality.

The manifestations of Consciousness are only apparent realities, which are illusions. To the human consciousness, illusions may be persistent but are still illusions nevertheless. Disharmony only occurs in the illusory manifestations that are seen through the five senses and the sense of the human mind. Pain, disease, birth, old age and death are not happening anywhere except in the human mind. Consciousness is the witness of all the mind's play. Consciousness is forever free and is never stained by the projections of the mind and its illusions.

The Sutras on Healing and Enlightenment

As the mirror is not tarnished by the objects reflected in it, Consciousness is also eternally unchanging and forever the same. The healer's role is not only to resolve the ignorance of the mind that causes the apparent disharmony, but, more importantly, it is to assist his clients in their knowing who they truly are. Healing is not healing if a person still believes that he is a person. Healing is only complete when one knows himself to be the Self. If a being is fully rooted in the Space of Pure Consciousness, he knows himself to be beyond birth, sickness, old age and death. This is the only freedom there truly is. Although the healer may help to alleviate symptoms, his primary role is to enlighten his client to his own True Nature. The beauty of this process is that the client is truly made free of suffering, and illusory symptoms may drop away as well.

-1:23-
Consciousness is unchanging and can never be disharmonious, yet it has an ability to manifest itself to appear as form while still retaining its True Nature.

This sutra continues the theme of Sutra 1:22. Regardless of the manifestations of Consciousness, the Consciousness itself remains forever the same. Consciousness itself is perfect and lacking nothing. It is Pure Awareness and Pure Peace. It does manifest into form, yet the forms in which it manifests are illusory. Forms, if any, do not ever change the Consciousness itself. Because the human being in his essence is this Pure Consciousness, what appears in the manifest world does not matter. Body, mind and emotions can manifest in an infinite number of ways, but the True Self remains forever unchanging and eternally free.

-1:24-

Consciousness is like a mirror in which the whole universe is reflected. The mirror remains forever the same even though the forms reflected in it are changing.

Here, the sutras explore the example of Consciousness as similar to a mirror. A mirror is a purely reflective surface that is unchanging regardless of what is reflected in it. The mirror can be seen as all-knowing in relationship to the forms that appear in it. Consciousness is like this: nothing that is manifest is separate from the underlying ground of being that supports the manifest forms. Consciousness, like the mirror, is the Knower of all the forms reflected in it; yet it is never disturbed by what it is watching.

Consciousness is always there no matter what is appearing in it. The mirror is always the mirror regardless of whether it is reflecting a happy or sad scene, a healthy or sick scene or a birth or death scene. To the mirror, nothing is ever really happening at all because the mirror really only knows itself. The mirror gives no reality to the forms reflected in it. In the same way, Consciousness is totally unmoved by the manifest forms and only knows its own Infinite Radiant Self.

Within the human being, awareness can be shifted from the object of Consciousness to the Consciousness itself. Once a human being is fully established in his True Nature, he comes to know that Self-Alone is. Regardless of the condition of the body, mind or emotions, the enlightened being rests in the Peace of the Self, knowing himself as eternally pure, free and forever. Just as the mirror never suffers because of the reflections in it, so too, the Self never suffers due to its illusory manifestations. If

The Sutras on Healing and Enlightenment

a being becomes fully rooted here, this can be said to be True Healing in its most absolute sense.

-1:25-
Understanding, experiencing and knowing one's Self as this Absolute Bliss Consciousness is the primary qualification of a true healer.

Because the essence of true healing is the process of transforming illusions into Truth, the true healer must be very well established in this Truth. The qualifications of a healer have nothing to do with credentials or modalities. If a person does not know the Truth, then he is no better than the blind leading the blind. A person who believes himself to be in disharmony is ignorant of his True Nature. If he asks for help from someone else who is also ignorant of his True Nature, both beings still exist in the realm of dualistic suffering, and no real healing will occur.

The healer who understands himself to be Absolute Bliss Consciousness is beginning to grasp the true essence of healing. The healer who experiences himself as Absolute Bliss Consciousness is getting even closer, but his experiencing is still dualistic. It is the healer who knows himself to be Absolute Bliss Consciousness who is truly empowered to do the real work of healing. The more deeply rooted the healer is in the Source of all Healing Power, the more effective his work will be. A healer who knows himself to be the Truth very easily shatters the illusions that cause suffering.

The Sutras on Healing and Enlightenment

Chapter Two—The Order of Manifestation

-2:1-
The order of manifestation from Pure Consciousness happens both macrocosmically and microcosmically.

The term *order of manifestation* refers to the emanations of the Divine from the most subtle aspects of being to the most dense. Manifestation does not imply separation in any way, because Pure Consciousness becomes the forms it creates, while still remaining itself. The infinite always remains the infinite, while projecting itself as the finite. God never changes but manifests as the changing forms of the Universe. Macrocosmic creation refers to the various planes that make up the entire Universe from Godhead into the physical plane. Microcosmic creation refers to the various bodies that the Divine will inhabit from Pure Consciousness to the physical body. The order of manifestation is explained more in detail as this chapter continues.

-2:2-
Macrocosmic manifestation refers to the various levels that make up the entire Universe, and its levels are called planes or worlds.

Planes or worlds are vast regions of manifested Divinity that are only distinguished by their levels of vibration. The physical world, which includes the entire physical universe, is the densest of these levels and actually the smallest. Each more subtle level contains the more dense ones that manifest from it and occupy the same space as these more dense levels. The Pure Consciousness

The Sutras on Healing and Enlightenment

of God is within and around each and every level that emanates from it, as the astral plane is in and around the physical plane.

The term *universe* used here is taken in its most literal meaning. The term universe comes from the Latin *universus*, meaning whole or all existing things seen as a whole. Therefore, various levels that make up the entire Universe include all phenomena that have a manifest and non-manifest existence. Anything that exists or does not exist—past, present and future—can be included in the term universe. While there may be multiple planes, levels or dimensions, there are not multiple universes. There can be no plural to the term universe by definition.

-2:3-
Microcosmic manifestation refers to the various levels that make up a human being, and its levels are called bodies or vehicles.

Bodies or vehicles are made out of their respective planes. A human being consists of far more than just the physical body. His entire existence is dependent on the more subtle planes that manifest into the physical plane and the more subtle bodies made from those planes that manifest into his physical body. It is important to understand these levels because nothing can exist physically without previously existing on the more subtle levels. Healing therefore is not about healing the physical body, because nothing physical is a cause. To heal a cause, we must understand the more subtle levels where the cause originates.

A human being is a microcosm of the macrocosm. Every single level of creation is found within his being, and his being is a hologram of the whole. The human body is more than stardust; it exists because of every aspect of the entire manifest universe and every subtle plane within the universe. A human body requires every single macrocosmic emanation from Godhead and every single microcosmic emanation of Godhead. The human being is truly created in the image and likeness of God based on a perfect sacred geometry and an exacting mathematical precision. There are no mistakes in God's order of manifestation, because it is all perfect geometry and perfect intelligence.

-2:4-
These levels are here based on the system of the seven chakras and relate to both microcosmic and macrocosmic creation.

It is commonly understood in esoteric and metaphysical sciences that the Divine has seven major levels of manifestation that result in the physical world. Because the human being is the microcosm of the macrocosm, these levels can be seen within his own being. Every level of creation exists independently of the human form and is not based on it, rather the human form is made up of and exists because of all levels. However, the human form is our focus here and our map for the entire universe.

The human body has seven major sections. These sections actually exist on the astral form of the human incarnation and not on the physical at all. These sections can easily be spoken of based on their physical anatomical locations as they run up and down the cerebral spinal axis even though they do not exist on the physical level.

The Sutras on Healing and Enlightenment

The chakras are discussed in depth throughout the sutras; however, a brief introduction is useful here.

The word *chakra* is a Sanskrit term meaning "wheel." A chakra can be considered any type of wheel, whether it refers to a cycle (like the wheel of birth and death) or a vortex of energy. Here, chakras are vortices of energy that act as transformers to step down the immense Divine Energy and to manifest the human form. Chakras allow the energies of the more subtle planes to become physical. Their importance in health and healing is crucial, because they are the portals through which physical realities come into being. If something appears in a physical body, it had to exist on the more subtle levels first. The chakras allow for this manifestation to happen.

Contrary to popular opinion, chakras do not ever close. If even one chakra ever fully closed, the body would die. Chakras can become blocked and out of balance. However, we must understand that chakras are never broken. They become blocked or out of balance because of the mind and not because they are machines that break. The causes of chakra imbalances are discussed in depth in the sutras. At this point, one should simply know that chakras do exist.

-2:5-
The seven chakras are known in Sanskrit as sahasrar, ajn, vishuddh, anahat, manipur, svadisthan, and muladhar.

Although the Sanskrit names are not important for understanding the chakras, their proper names are used here. The first chakra, muladhar, is typically associated with the most dense; in actuality, the first chakra is the one most closely associated with Source. The order

The Sutras on Healing and Enlightenment

of manifestation actually runs from sahasrar chakra to muladhar chakra and not the reverse. The order of microcosmic manifestation through the chakra system based on the human body is from the crown to the tailbone. However, most chakra systems speak of the tailbone chakra as the first, and end with the seventh chakra, sahasrar at the head. Because this is the common usage of the system, we have also adopted it here.

The energy of Godhead manifests through the chakras from seven to one to form the human being. This step-down system of energy is crucial, because the immense energy of God could never become a human body—it is simply much too powerful. The chakras enable this Infinite Light to densify itself into form. We must remember that there is no mistake in the order of manifestation. God does not manifest disharmony through the chakra system but only creates perfect and harmonious realities.

-2:6-
Sahasrar chakra is associated with the Absolute Reality of Godhead, which is Absolute Bliss Consciousness.

The nature of the Absolute has been already well established in the previous chapter. It is associated with sahasrar chakra, located at the crown of the head of a human being. However, it must be understood that God is not a chakra. The seventh chakra at the head is better considered as a gateway into Godhead rather than as Godhead itself. This chakra is often considered a thousand-petaled lotus flower and is more of a portal into Absolute Divinity; it is not the Absolute itself.

The Sutras on Healing and Enlightenment

When we place our attention at this chakra long enough, we come to experience ourselves as the Absolute Bliss Consciousness of Godhead. However, in meditation there is no sense of these chakras, because the focus on Pure Consciousness has nothing to do with the vibratory levels on which the chakras exist. When focusing on the Pure Consciousness found in the higher regions of one's being, the chakras have absolutely no meaning; therefore, often the seventh and sixth chakras are confused. Different systems exchange the location or role of one chakra for another.

In the sutras, it is very clear that the seventh chakra is associated only with the most absolute state of Godhead known as Pure Consciousness. Because the chakras also serve as our map of the order of manifestation, the placement of this chakra establishes a very clear and simple system that is easy to follow and will be familiar to most readers.

-2:7-
This is the seventh chakra and here there are no planes and no bodies as there is no movement or vibration.

The sutras explain that in the Absolute State of Godhead there is no vibration or movement; therefore, there are no bodies or planes. Godhead is described by the word *anahat*, which means "unstruck." This refers to the state of Pure Potentiality before it begins vibrating, just as a bell is in a state of potential sound before it is struck. When it is struck, vibration begins. Godhead is that state of being beyond all vibration and is therefore the Source of all manifested being. This chakra refers to the very essence of a man's being, which is not a separate soul, not a mind, and not a body.

The Sutras on Healing and Enlightenment

-2:8-

Its color is often seen as white, golden or violet light and it is associated with the crown of the head; yet in essence it is beyond all name, form, time, space and color.

This sutra basically explains itself. Although the chakra system usually assigns a color to this chakra, what it represents is beyond all color. Like all others, this chakra can be directly experienced. In Truth there are no words for it, because it contains all colors and the Light that is beyond color. Yet, when this chakra is transcended, we reach the underlying ground of all being where no color, light, name or form exists.

-2:9-

Ajn chakra is associated with the level of manifestation in its first movements as Light, creativity, the Vision of Oneness, Pure Ideas and the arising and movement of the subtle particles of creation.

From the State of the Absolute beyond time and space, we have our first emanation, which is Pure Light. This Pure Light is associated with ajn chakra, because this level of manifestation refers to the one becoming two. When the Pure Being of God becomes Light, the process of creating and manifesting the entire Universe begins; therefore, the sixth chakra here is associated with creativity. However, because this level of Reality is absolutely united by the Divine Light, it also represents the Vision of Oneness, as it is associated with the third eye point. The third eye is actually where the two physical eyes, which see only duality, become one in which the being sees only the Vision of Oneness.

The Sutras on Healing and Enlightenment

From the explosion of Light that emanates from the Absolute come subtle particles of creation that will make up everything within manifestation. These particles will eventually become form, based on the pure ideas held within the Divine Mind. This Divine Mind contains every idea for everything that will ever come into being, and it is on this level that all of creation already exists. From a relative perspective, we can see the order of manifestation evolving through time and space. But from the Absolute Perspective of Godhead, it all was instantly created and all exists simultaneously. These Creations of God as pure ideas are associated with the causal plane.

-2:10-
This is the sixth chakra, which is associated with the causal plane and the causal body.

The causal plane is associated with the first major emanation of Godhead, yet it can be considered a separate plane in and of itself. All aspects of the first order of manifestation can be broken down into many levels. For simplicity's sake, we have associated the causal plane with these first emanations of Divinity and the sixth chakra. The causal plane contains every pure idea of God. These ideas can be considered the Children of God, and they are perfect in every way. They are all created in His image and likeness as Pure Light. These ideas are the most subtle blueprints for all of creation, forming an entire plane or level of reality that is contained in the Pure Light of God.

In this world of pure ideas is the pure idea of a Child of God. This can be considered a causal body, but not necessarily human yet, for the Children of God can

The Sutras on Healing and Enlightenment

take on any form that they wish. Children of God are perfect and eternal creations, which can never change, yet they can re-create themselves in any way they wish. The Children of God are given the free will to re-create themselves as they choose. They cannot change who they are, yet they certainly can forget and create very disharmonious realities. The causal body is simply the idea of being a separate being. It can be considered ego in its purest sense of simply "am-ness." Ego is not bad in the way the word is often used. Ego simply represents those drops of water that can, if they wish, call themselves separate from the Ocean.

-2:11-
The sixth chakra, which is often seen as indigo, is associated with the third eye at the forehead region.

The sutras clearly state that this chakra is often seen as indigo in that chakras can be seen. This chakra is often experienced as bluish-purple and is seen in the space above and between the two physical eyes with the eyes closed. This chakra, however, is not actually only in the forehead because chakras have both fronts and backs. With the exception of the crown and root chakras, the other five major chakras have vortices of energy that come in from the front and the back and form a sphere relatively in the center of the body. Ajn chakra has its front entering at the forehead and its back at the occipital lobe associated with the medulla oblongata.

-2:12-
Vishuddh chakra is associated with the level of manifestation where the Divine expresses itself as mind, intelligence, ego-sense, and mind-sense.

From Pure Consciousness comes the Light of God and the causal plane of manifestation. As the Divine continues to express itself, it manifests in what Yoga philosophy is called *antahkaran*. Antahkaran can be considered the Mind and everything that will come to exist from Divine Mind. However, on a more microcosmic and human level, the term antahkaran refers to the inner instrumentality of the mind consisting of chitt, buddhi, ahankar and manas.

Chitt can be considered the lake of the mind itself, which includes within it buddhi, ahankar and manas. With the arrival of chitt in the order of manifestation, we clearly have with it a sense of duality—the sense of self and other. Buddhi is the intellect. Ahankar is the ego-sense, or the individual sense of "I." Manas is the mind-sense that will interact with the objects of sense. The distinctions between these four terms and the term antahkaran are subject to diverse interpretations, but here we can get a sense of what the mental level of vishuddh chakra entails.

-2:13-
This is the fifth chakra associated with the mental plane and the mental body.

Vishuddh chakra is the fifth chakra because it is the third manifestation out of Pure Consciousness, which is associated with the seventh chakra; whereas the sixth

The Sutras on Healing and Enlightenment

chakra is associated with the second wave of manifestation. Because this chakra is associated with the antahkaran, it is therefore associated with the mental plane and the mental body. In fact, one could say that macrocosmically antahkaran is the entire mental plane and microcosmically it is the mental body. We are reminded again that this is not necessarily referring to a human being. The mental body can exist clearly without a physical body in many different forms of its own choosing.

-2:14-
Its color is often seen as blue, and it is associated with the throat.

-2:15-
Anahat chakra is associated with the level of creation which vibrates at the density of emotions, the purest being love and compassion.

Anahat chakra is a very important energy center within the human body because it is the place where the higher and lower chakras meet. Every chakra has a symbol. The symbol for anahat chakra is the six-pointed star, which shows two equilateral triangles interlacing. This symbol represents the balance and harmony of the order of manifestation where Spirit and matter are one and the same reality. However, in the order of manifestation from Consciousness to form, when we are only at the level of anahat chakra, matter does not yet exist. Therefore, this chakra can be seen on a macrocosmic level as an entire plane vibrating at the density of emotion.

However, emotion is a very misleading word, because in the purest sense of manifestation the human emotions

The Sutras on Healing and Enlightenment

(for example, anger, fear, jealousy) do not exist. The purest emotions are love and its counterpart, which is compassion, yet these are not really emotions at all. Love and compassion are the truest sense of what anahat chakra truly is when it is functioning in its purest state. What are commonly known as human emotions are simply fluctuations in the flow of this energy. Love is All That Is.

-2:16-
This is the fourth chakra, which is associated with the astral plane and the astral body.

-2:17-
The fourth chakra, often seen as green, is associated with the region of the heart.

The astral plane and astral body in their purest essence are nothing but Pure Light; however, with the causal ideas and the sparks of creation, the astral plane is an immensely vast region dwarfing the physical universe. The astral plane contains everything that a human being could imagine in the physical world and an infinite amount more. This region is exceptionally well charted in esoteric literature and is often associated with astral travel in the vehicle of the astral body.

The astral body itself is nothing but Pure Light; yet when it is governed by the causal idea of becoming a human form, it takes the shape of this form as just Pure Light. It has arms and some semblance of legs, but it has no color and no detail. It is only when it continues to become more dense through the sparks of creation that its details begin to appear as it makes its way toward becoming physical.

When the astral body follows the pure causal idea of a human being, then it is perfect and without any trace of imbalance or disease. However, if the mind on the mental plane suffers from false beliefs, then these will manifest as negative emotions, thus affecting the formation of the astral body and the bodies that will subsequently manifest from it. The astral body being on the emotional level of manifestation is tremendously affected by the thoughts that create and sustain it. The astral body will form the blueprint for the bodies to come; and, if it is out of balance, then the bodies to come will be out of balance as well. However, we should understand that the order of manifestation does not create this imbalance, but only the false illusory beliefs that exist in the mind.

-2:18-
Manipur chakra is associated with personal power.

Manipur chakra is concerned with a slightly denser level of emotion and thought that is often called the lower astral, or lower mental, plane. It is not lower in a derogatory sense, but only that it is a denser region of the astral plane as the Divine makes its way into physical form. It is only associated with personal power on a microcosmic level of human manifestation, because the plane itself is simply a more substantial aspect of the astral plane, which may or may not contain aspects of personhood.

The Sutras on Healing and Enlightenment

-2:19-
It is the third chakra associated with the lower mental plane and lower mental body.

This chakra associated with the lower mental plane contains the lower mental body of the human being's microcosmic manifestation. The lower mental body can be said to deal with personal power as the aspect of manifestation where individuality truly comes into play. On a human level, a person must have a strong sense of self to function well. This must exist before the being even takes on human form. Its individual mind and emotional self must feel secure within itself; otherwise, its life experience on the physical plane will be quite challenging. Without the confidence and high self-esteem that come from knowing who one truly is, there will certainly be suffering.

In the order of manifestation, personal power, confidence and high self-esteem are natural as Pure Expressions of God. The lower mental plane is therefore not negative in any way. Its pure expression makes for a very functional and masterful human being. It is only through false beliefs and negative emotions coming from more subtle planes that this plane becomes out of balance.

-2:20-
The third chakra, often seen as yellow, is associated with the solar plexus.

-2:21-
Svadisthan chakra is associated with Consciousness, taking pleasure in its creations and in itself.

The Sutras on Healing and Enlightenment

The only real reason for creation is for the Self to take pleasure in its creations and eventually to know itself through its creations. The process is meant to be wonderfully joyful and pleasurable. In the perfect order of manifestation, there is no suffering; and life is meant to be a wonderful and exceptionally blessed experience. However, when there is imbalance in the more subtle levels, then svadisthan chakra also becomes out of balance, and life becomes a miserable and painful experience.

When the Children of God choose illusory beliefs over the Truth of who they are, these beliefs manifest down through the chakra system. Choosing error over Truth is a forgetting process that causes immense agony for the Soul. In its forgetting, the soul feels separate from God; and, for a Child of God, there is no worse suffering than to feel separate from its Source. The pain experienced then becomes a major impetus for eventually choosing Truth. Therefore, there is a reason for darkness and suffering, in that the Soul gets to fully appreciate who it is by coming to know what it is not. There is enormous Truth in such a concept, but it should be very clear that the order of manifestation will support false beliefs and allow them to manifest, but the suffering and imbalance that will appear are not the result of Truth but of illusions. When the Self comes to realize itself again and false beliefs are transformed back into Truth, then life becomes an intensely pleasurable experience, which is the reason for this second chakra.

The Sutras on Healing and Enlightenment

-2:22-
This is the second chakra, which is associated with the etheric plane and the etheric body.

The etheric plane associated with the level of the second chakra is the subtle blueprint that will eventually become the physical world. This plane looks exceptionally like the physical plane, except that it is not physical and is of a far higher quality. Everything on the etheric plane is a perfect mirror image of what will appear physically. This plane will reflect all of the more subtle planes "above" it. It looks and feels very much like the physical world and is often mistaken for it by semi-conscious disembodied souls. However, anyone who is conscious enough will clearly see the immense difference in quality while functioning on this plane.

The etheric body is made out of the stuff of the etheric plane and looks just like what the physical body will look like. Anything that manifests in the physical body exists here as the subtle blueprint for what the physical body will become. The etheric body is the feeling body, because it is the intermediary that communicates the physical body's sensations to the Soul. Feelings, which are not emotions, include hunger, thirst, tightness, itches, pain, or comfort. The physical body actually has no sensation at all in and of itself, for without the more subtle vehicles sustaining and animating it, the body is nothing but mere clay.

When the physical body ceases to function in what is commonly termed death, the more subtle bodies simply cease to associate with it. The body does not die, it simply transforms. The Soul does not leave the body, because the Soul is everywhere. The change that occurs is that the more subtle bodies move on to the dimension most

The Sutras on Healing and Enlightenment

suited for them, which is a very complex subject. The concept is mentioned here, because it is interesting to note the role of the etheric body in what is called the death process.

When the physical body "dies," the etheric body lingers for only a short period of time and then eventually "dies" as well. It simply transforms back into the etheric plane, just as the physical body transforms back into the physical plane. Sometimes the etheric body ceases to associate with the physical body before the physical body even dies. When this happens, the physical body is robbed of its life force and will soon cease to function. These more subtle bodies form the aura that is seen around the physical body by those who have such ability. The aura sustains the body. The body does not let off an aura; the aura lets off a body. A body may appear to be alive even when the more subtle vehicles are pulling away from it. When this happens, physical death is imminent. Not long after this separation, the etheric vehicle will soon cease to exist as well, because it was simply the blueprint to sustain and communicate with the physical vehicle.

-2:23-
The second chakra, often seen as orange, is associated with the region just below the navel.

-2:24-
Muladhar chakra is associated with Consciousness in its appearance in physical form.

Muladhar chakra is the energy center representing the densest aspect of the order of manifestation as Consciousness finds its way into the expression of itself

The Sutras on Healing and Enlightenment

as physical form. Anything that exists in the physical world is associated with this chakra; yet the boundary between what is physical, etheric and astral is not as clear-cut as many would think. It is important to realize that the physical plane is simply the more subtle planes that sustain and create it. Every single level of creation is found within the physical world. Therefore, ideas, thoughts, beliefs, emotions, feelings, light rays, gamma rays, x-rays, sparks of creation, atoms, etc. all make up what we call the physical world. The physical world is the conglomeration of every aspect of the order of manifestation.

This makes for an exceptionally dense and complex place that is tremendously subject to disharmony. Any imbalance on the more subtle levels manifests on the physical level, which is why the physical plane always appears in a state of constant chaos. The chaos of the physical plane is not chaos at all, but the perfect expression of everything that has gone into making it what it is. It is the result of every level preceding it. Because it is immensely complex and requires vast organization, it is consequently subject to infinite disorganization.

-2:25-
This is the first chakra, which is associated with the physical plane and the physical body.

The physical plane is so complex that it is quite challenging to keep it well organized. The human body, for instance, is far more complex than the bodies that create and sustain it. The numerous systems required for its functioning have an incredible capacity to become disorganized and to create a vehicle of tremendous

The Sutras on Healing and Enlightenment

suffering. However, we must be reminded that this is all perfect. Any disharmony, no matter how easily it can manifest, is simply the result of the levels that come before the physical. The physical plane of matter is inert and unintelligent. It has no will of its own, is not a cause and has no sensation. The physical plane is a total illusion of light appearing to be solid. It is not at all as it appears to the five senses. The physical body and the physical plane of which the body is composed are nothing but vibrating light held together by thought. Matter is nothing but Consciousness, because everything in the order of manifestation is Consciousness. The only substance is Consciousness. Therefore, the physical world, which seems so real, is really nothing but Pure Awareness made manifest. It is nothing but that.

Just as a gold ring is not separate from the gold itself, so too the physical plane is not separate from the substance of which it is made. You cannot separate the ring from the gold; likewise, you cannot separate matter from Spirit. Matter is Spirit, just as the ring is gold. The ring may appear to have a separate existence, but it really is nothing but gold. The physical world is therefore proof of the existence of God, because you could not have a physical world without the substance that makes this world. Just as the ring is proof of the gold, so too the physical world and the human body are proof of God.

The Sutras on Healing and Enlightenment

-2:26-
The first chakra, often seen as red, is associated with the region of the tailbone.

-2:27-
The order of manifestation, governed by Divine Intelligence, is perfect and harmonious in every way.

Everything that manifests from the Divine is itself Divine and therefore must be seen as being absolutely perfect. The Creations of God are based perfectly on Divine Order. All of the ideas and thoughts of God are perfect and of the highest intelligence. It is difficult for a human being to grasp how the order of manifestation is perfect and harmonious if there appears to be so much pain, suffering, disease, sickness and death. This common objection has been made for this sutra as long as mankind has had some notion of Deity. How could God have created this world and yet there be so much suffering in it?

There are many levels and answers to such a question, yet the first and most poignant answer is that God did not create pain, suffering, disease, sickness and death. In the order of manifestation, causal ideas manifest as perfect and harmonious realities, and the false beliefs of the ego manifest as disharmonious yet also perfect realities. The word *perfect* refers to that which lacks nothing essential, is complete, accurate, exact and completely suited for a particular purpose; being ideal. The word *perfect* comes from the Latin word *perfectus*, the past participle of *perficere*, meaning finish. We use the word *perfect* here to refer to that which comes directly through the order of manifestation based on the complete and exact laws

The Sutras on Healing and Enlightenment

of the system and "finishes" on the physical plane with exact certainty.

Thoughts that are attuned to Truth manifest perfectly on the physical plane as harmonious realities that do not cause suffering in any way. Whereas thoughts that are erroneous and not attuned to Truth manifest perfectly on the physical plane as disharmonious realities that do cause suffering. From the perfect ideas of God on the causal plane, there is no suffering for the Children of God. If the word *perfect* refers to a complete and finished manifestation, we can see the Perfection in how any thought can perfectly manifest and complete itself into creation. If such a thought does manifest physically and takes on a disharmonious reality, then this is a perfect experience for the one who manifested such a reality to reevaluate his thoughts and to choose again.

When sickness manifests in the body due to false beliefs, then that sickness is a perfect manifestation of a wrong thought system. The order of manifestation is infallible. Divine thoughts do not manifest disharmony. If Divine thoughts did manifest disharmony, then the order of manifestation would be imperfect; yet it is not. The system is by definition perfect and lacking nothing essential. The human mind has trouble with this and the next sutra, but in the end it is seen to be of the Highest Truth.

-2:28-
A human being—the Divine made manifest on every level of creation—is perfect in every way.

In the same way that Sutra 27 can be a leap for many, Sutra 28 may be even more so. The question arises, "How

The Sutras on Healing and Enlightenment

can a human being be perfect in every way and on every level when he is so full of fear, ignorance, anger, greed, pain, sickness and death?" The answer lies in understanding the perfect idea of a human being as created by the Divine Mind on the causal plane. The Divine Idea of a human being is perfect. He has no sense of sickness, negativity, suffering or death. When we understand the order of manifestation, we see that thoughts manifest as things. Things therefore are thoughts, and the thoughts of God are perfect and harmonious in every way. Therefore, when the order of manifestation is unobstructed by false beliefs, negative emotions and suppression, then it manifests as a perfect master who is free from the sufferings of humankind.

When the order of manifestation is filled with false beliefs, negative emotions and suppression, then what manifests in the human form are perfect manifestations of those qualities. If someone holds a belief that he is not good enough and inadequate, then this erroneous thought manifests as fear on the emotional level. This belief and emotion are usually held in denial by the being who does not want to admit such a thing and therefore it is suppressed. These suppressed energies block the perfect flow of the Divine Order of Manifestation and manifest as perfect but disharmonious realities.

These realities full of suffering and symptoms are communications to the mind that it is falling into error and needs to correct its thinking. These communications are perfect because they tell the being exactly where he is blocked. If the order of manifestation was imperfect and a human being was imperfect, then false thoughts would create pleasant realities where no suffering exists. To deny the Truth of who one is and to feel separate from that Truth are the only real hell that there is. If the being did not suffer because of its illusions, then he would never make efforts to awaken back to his True Nature. Likewise, if right thoughts created realities of pain and suffering, then the mind would choose illusions to try to avoid pain.

-2:29-
A human being is a self-conscious entity who is often unaware of his Divine origins and who can choose to become conscious of his True Nature, which is pure, free and forever.

The human form is the only form on Earth that actually has the capacity to contemplate its own origins. All sentient beings are conscious. Birds, dogs, whales, fish and apes are all conscious and exceptionally aware of the world around them. Yet they have not evolved to the level of Consciousness where they have become self-conscious and where they begin to question their own existence. However, the human being is intimately aware of his own sense of separation arising from the existential dilemma that screams, "I exist." In this declaration that "I exist" and that I feel separate and suffering, then true questioning begins. Yet, in the end, it is not the human being who is liberated at all, for the human form is limited and exists in a realm of creation where true freedom never exists.

The self-conscious entity struggles to feel safe and secure and free from all pain and suffering, yet this entity is not the True Self who is eternally pure, free and forever. In all of creation there is a misidentification with form. A bird believes itself to be a bird. A tree believes itself to be a tree, and a human being believes himself to be a human

The Sutras on Healing and Enlightenment

being. The Truth of existence does not lie in the forms, but in the Source of the forms, and it is only in a human incarnation that Consciousness can begin to question its origins and to find total freedom in those origins. The True Self manifests into form, yet still remains ever the same. Suffering arises when Consciousness misidentifies with its object of Consciousness, takes on false beliefs based on this object and then lives out of its illusions.

When the Soul wakes up to its Divine origins and stops identifying with its vehicles of Consciousness, then all false beliefs based on ignorance fall away and the truest sense of freedom arises in one's realization of who and what he always has been. The Eternal and Unchanging Reality is the Self, which the great sages declare is pure, free and forever. When this Truth is known, then liberation from suffering occurs regardless of the conditions of one's body or life situations. The process of healing and enlightenment is to assist a being in realizing this True and Divine Nature where all suffering ceases to exist. Symptomatic removal may occur during this process, yet it is not the goal of true healing.

-2:30-
Disharmony, disease, pain and suffering in the human experience are not based on the Divine Intelligence of God, but are an apparent manifestation of illusion, delusion and error.

The sutras are very clear: in the Divine Order of Manifestation based on the perfect causal ideas of God, there is no suffering anywhere in creation. Suffering is the result of illusion, delusion and error in that false beliefs manifest perfectly as a reflection of their ignorance. These are only apparent manifestations, like a mirage, where what is perceived appears to be real. Suffering is a very persistent illusion that is based on the error of believing one's Self to be a body, mind and emotions. When Consciousness identifies with its object of Consciousness and takes on false beliefs based on its misidentification with its vehicles, then it is bound to experience suffering. However, when Consciousness resides within its own being and knows itself as Itself, then false beliefs drop away and the order of manifestation appears as a harmonious and magnificent Reality based only on the Divine Goodness of God.

-2:31-
Through Truth, all disharmony, disease, pain and suffering are transformed back into harmony, health, comfort and peace.

Healing is the process of enlightening the client back into his True Nature as the Divine. Healing therefore is based on Truth and Truth alone. When the Bright Light of Truth dispels illusions, then one's life experience becomes one of harmony, health, comfort and peace. When the mind is calm and reflecting only the Divine Reality, then the body and emotions remain at peace, and life situations become very easy and natural. Every being knows this in his essential Self and that is why suffering, disharmony and pain are so disagreeable. Namely, the True Self is nothing but peace and joy and is very uncomfortable in experiencing its opposite. Yet Truth has no opposite, and therefore suffering is only the result of illusion and ignorance and nothing more.

The Sutras on Healing and Enlightenment

-2:32-
Enlightenment is the process by which a human being transforms illusions into Truth and realizes his True Nature.

Again, we must be clear that enlightenment is a process that can happen only for a human being and therefore it is a very blessed experience to have taken a human birth, which should not be wasted. There is no greater work than to assist another person back into the realization of his True Self—where all suffering is seen as nonexistent and illusions are totally dispelled. This is the only real work a human being is meant to do. It is his only task.

If a human being performs thousands of tasks for himself and others but does not perform this one essential task for himself and others, then his life is virtually wasted and is doomed to future suffering until he gets it right. There is only one agenda for a human incarnation and that is to realize the Self. Anything less for a human being is fraught with ignorance and therefore he cannot be said to be truly fulfilled and free.

-2:33-
The enlightenment process culminates in Absolute Self-Realization, which is a state of being totally independent of the health of the body, where Consciousness experiences that Self is All That Is.

The process of enlightenment is often confused with the liberation of a human being from the realm of duality; yet the human being is in the realm of duality and always will be. In the realm of duality, there will be harmony

The Sutras on Healing and Enlightenment

and disharmony. There always has been and there always will be. In the realm of duality there is birth, old age, sickness and death. Even the greatest of saints and sages have not escaped this. Through wisdom they lessened the sufferings of the body, yet they were not under the illusion that salvation would be found on a body level. Wise ones care for the body, mind and emotions, yet never think that their ultimate freedom can come on these levels.

To be truly free of the sufferings of time and space, one must know that they are never in—nor were they ever in—time and space. The Self was never the body, mind and emotions even though it pretended to be. The process of enlightenment is to slowly awaken to the realization that one's True Nature is Eternal beyond time and space and is forever free. When a being knows himself to be the Self, then regardless of the health of the body, he can be said to be totally healed and totally enlightened. Even on one's deathbed when the body is riddled with disease, healing can still occur and the being can be totally free. The body may cease to function, yet the Soul who woke up to his own Reality was healed and enlightened and forever knows himself to be eternally free.

Chapter Three—Mind and Matter

-3:1-
Pure Consciousness is the Only Reality, which is eternal, formless and forever unchanging.

Sutra 1 of Chapter Three simply reiterates the qualities of the Divine Truth as Pure Consciousness. This Consciousness is All That Is. It has no second and is therefore the Only Reality. Its manifestations are nothing but its own Self, and this Self always remains as it is—being eternal, formless and forever unchanging.

-3:2-
The manifestations of Consciousness, which are temporary forms, are always changing.

The manifest Universe is proof of God's existence. Philosophers have spent centuries trying to prove the existence of God because the Divine Reality cannot be experienced through the five senses. However, what the five senses perceive can only exist because of the Divine Consciousness, which manifests these forms. Just as a gold ring can only exist because of gold, so too, the world can only exist because of God. God is the substance of which the Universe is created. There is only one Reality, and therefore the forms of Consciousness are nothing but Consciousness themselves. In the eyes of enlightened love, there is nothing but one Eternal Sea of Light. However, even though this Light remains forever the same, it can be said that its forms are always in perpetual change and therefore temporary. The forms are proof of the substance of which they are made; yet they are not eternal and self-existing.

The Sutras on Healing and Enlightenment

-3.3-
Truth is that which is real and its manifestations are said to be unreal.

The word *real* can only be used when describing that which remains forever the same. The manifestations of Consciousness are always changing and are therefore said to be unreal. Consciousness is the Only Reality because it alone remains forever the same and is never changed by the manifested forms.

-3.4-
Physical form is a manifestation of Consciousness and has no absolute existence.

Only Pure Awareness itself can be said to have an absolute existence. Physical form is always changing and is not forever. Even though physical form manifests from Self and is Self-in-and-of-Itself, it is still a fleeting and temporary existence that has only a relative existence.

-3.5-
Physical form, which is a mirage, is said to be unreal, having only an apparent and relative reality.

A mirage is that which the five senses and mind-sense insist is real when in fact there is really nothing there. In true meditation, one comes to know that matter is nothing but an apparent manifestation of Consciousness and that Consciousness alone is. Apparent realities are not realities at all. Someone while walking could mistake a rope for a snake and become afraid, but there really was no snake. The physical world is not only said to be unreal because it is changing, but also because it is not as it appears.

The conscious mind of a human being can only process about seven units of information at one time. For example, while sitting at a table having a meal, the mind can be aware of breathing, eating, moving, smiling, the temperature and perhaps a sensation or two in the body, but more than that, it cannot take in. The mind can only process and take in a very small amount of the entire spectrum of Consciousness, yet we all know that the universe is far more than just the limited information that we can be aware of at any given moment. Not only does the mind through the senses take in exceptionally little information, the human form itself is not designed to fully grasp the nature of Reality. Millions of bits of information come into the senses every second, yet the conscious mind is aware of only about seven.

The human being cannot know Reality, yet the Divine Being, which is the essence of a human being, can. Even through out-of-body experience, one can enter into the core of a form and discover that it is nothing but vibrating light manifesting as an apparent reality. From the "outside," things look solid, but from the "inside" they are nothing but light. The human form may not be able to perceive this Truth, but that does not change the Truth. The physical world is like a stage prop on a movie set. The building looks real from the outside, but once you explore deeper, you see that it is only a facade. This is important to understand in the context of healing, because that which is not real is easily changed. Since the body and its diseases are not real, the enlightened healer never gives them any power and knows that they are easily manipulated through mind. Things are just thoughts and nothing more.

The Sutras on Healing and Enlightenment

-3.6-
All physical form is dependent in nature and is empty of any sense of being a separate self.

Physical form is not a separate self with its own substance that knows itself to be an individual entity. The world of matter is dependent on its source for its own existence, and each part of the physical world is dependent on each and every other part of the physical world. Nothing exists as a separate entity. A tree only exists because of sun, air, fire, water, sap, minerals and cells and so forth. A tree does not claim to be a tree, but is nothing but Consciousness made manifest. The form of the tree is dependent on every other form for its existence and is not a separate self in any way.

The problem with the self-conscious human being is that he believes himself to be a body, which is made up of some illusory substance called "matter." He feels himself to be separate from all other forms and barely knows that he is totally dependent on everything in the universe for his existence. His body is made up of fire, air, earth, water and sky; and these are made up of nothing but Consciousness itself. The human being, with his mind, walks around with a sense of being a separate "I," and this "I" is the cause of all his suffering. The world's great wisdom traditions aim at one goal in the end—to dissolve this false self and let what is left stand as Truth.

Truth is what is left when the ego fades away. The self-conscious human primate conceptualizes its perceptions and forms the concept of "I" as a separate entity. This fiction is dissolved through the process of enlightenment. When true healing occurs, this false self dissolves into its Source, and God-Realization is left. This is the truest sense of the term healing.

The Sutras on Healing and Enlightenment

-3.7-
Nothing exists in physical form that does not exist on the more subtle levels of creation.

The physical world is said to be unreal both because it is changing, relative and dependent and because it only has its existence due to the subtle levels that sustain it. Nothing can exist physically if it does not already exist on mental, astral and etheric planes of reality. A chair only exists because of the idea of a chair. This idea exists on the causal plane as a pure idea beyond all form. This idea becomes a thought in the mind of a carpenter. He begins to feel an emotional drive to make the chair, and then a clear etheric form comes to his mind. This etheric form is the blueprint of the chair containing the causal idea, the thought form and the emotional drive to make the chair.

Nothing on the physical plane has come into existence in any other way, because all physical realities have their roots in the more subtle levels that create and sustain them. When the order of manifestation flows unobstructed from the causal plane to the physical plane, then its manifestations are harmonious. Yet, if there are false thoughts, negative emotions and suppressions, then the physical manifestation will not be harmonious. The important point of this sutra is that disease is not a separate entity with its own reality and its own existence. It is dependent on the thoughts, emotions and suppressions of the more subtle planes that cause its existence. Nothing—disease included—exists physically without already existing on the more subtle levels of creation. Knowing this, the true healer never believes in the reality of illness. To give illness a reality is to say that there are two powers in this universe. It is to say that

The Sutras on Healing and Enlightenment

arthritis is a reality and God is a Reality. There is only one Reality, and that Reality never manifests sickness from its own pure ideas. Only the ego mind with its errors manifests sickness. Sickness is error. It is illusion. It has no inherent existence of its own and should not be given any power at all.

-3.8-
The physical world is a belief system, and belief systems are thoughts.

The physical world is nothing more than a belief, and all beliefs are false. To claim that matter actually has its own existence is to say that there are two realities—God and matter. God is One, and there is only God. If there is only God, then there cannot be matter. It is simply a belief in the mind that forms actually exist. In the order of manifestation, there are planes or worlds that are considered consensus and non-consensus realities. A consensus reality is where many beings with their own belief systems create a world around them and function within that reality. These consensus realities can be useful or not, helpful or not, and full of pain or not. These types of creations are mental constructs that are held together by a mass consciousness of beings who find their creations valuable. If a creation is not valued, then it is abandoned and given no more energy. The physical world is such a place. It only exists because it is valued and believed to be real. If no more energy were given to it from the more subtle levels of existence, then it would simply cease appearing to be.

A non-consensus reality exists whether it is believed in or not. A consensus reality exists because a group of beings believe it exists, whereas a non-consensus reality has its own existence regardless of belief systems. Nothing can change a non-consensus reality, yet everything that vibrates changes. Therefore, the only true non-consensus unchanging Reality is God (and God's Creations). Consensus realities depend on thought to manifest, but God is not dependent on thought. God is not changed by thought and exists regardless of the consensus realities of ego minds, which cause their own suffering.

-3.9-
Thoughts can manifest whether harmonious or disharmonious.

Any thinking being can be considered a Child of God, which is to say that anything that thinks has its origins in the thought-less. God is the thought-less. Pure Consciousness is only Pure because it does not contain any vibration in it. The Children of God are given free will to co-create with God, and anything they wish to create they can. It is the Will of the Divine that its Children be free to create anything that they want, therefore the Will of the Child is the Will of the Father. Whatever the child wishes to create, the parent is willing to allow.

Thus, the thoughts of the Children of God, whether Truth or error, are allowed. Thoughts can be in harmony with the perfect causal ideas of God, or totally fictitious and not based on Goodness, Love and Truth. Thoughts, which can be full of separation, division, greed, anger, hatred and vengeance, are all allowed. A Child of God is free to choose at any time which energies he wishes to invest in. He can choose to believe in sickness and give

The Sutras on Healing and Enlightenment

it a lot of energy, or he can choose Truth, which knows nothing of sickness.

For God to be All Goodness, there can be no disharmony in God. For God to be All Light, He cannot know darkness. Sickness is the result of blockages or what may be termed "darkness" in the aura of a human being. Then for God to be God, he could not possibly be aware of such limitation. The unlimited cannot ever be limited. Pure Consciousness is not aware of any opposite to its own being. Therefore, the Divine in its Pure Truth does not manifest disharmony. Only the false beliefs and choices of the ego mind manifest disharmony. All thoughts have creative power, and any thought can manifest harmoniously or disharmoniously if it is given enough energy.

It should be made clear that there is no opposite to God and that there is not any darkness in the sense of evil or disharmony in God. However, in Divine manifestations, the Reality of yin and yang, or simply stated feminine and masculine, does arise. These polar opposites are necessary and vital parts of the creative process. The yin or feminine energy is usually considered the receptive, nourishing and dark energy of God, but this concept of dark does not refer to an evil or disharmonious reality. Yin dances with yang, the masculine, bright and luminous energy, and is always in harmony with it. The terms "dark" or "darkness" in the context of "that which is not God" and "that which manifests in the human aura as blockage" are not synonymous with the yin, dark or feminine energies of God. In God there is no darkness, for God only knows Light. But in such a statement, both yin and yang, feminine and masculine are seen only as aspects of the one Light of God, and not as a disharmonious, negative darkness.

The Sutras on Healing and Enlightenment

-3:10-
Divine Mind only creates perfect and harmonious realities and has created the mind of a human being as perfect in its image and likeness.

    In the Order of Divine Manifestation, every causal idea is Perfect and Eternal and manifests as such. There is no disharmony, separation or division in Divine Mind. The mind as found in the state of a human being is not the way God created it. The confusion, limitation, doubts, fear and worry are not of God, but arise from the ignorance of the ego when it chooses to value illusions over Truth. The mind of man is the Mind of God. There is only One Mind, and this is the True Mind of the human being, just as this is the True Mind of everything. When a human being comes to know his Source, then he sees that his Mind is the Mind of God, because there is no separation in Truth.

    The so-called "mind" of a human being can be seen as a microcosm of the macrocosm. For some, it is too hard to grasp that there is only One Mind when so many people run around with their own thoughts in their own head. Yet this is only an illusion that a misidentified ego suffers from. In Truth even the microcosmic mind of a human being, which is a reflection of the macrocosmic mind, is One with it and is perfect just as it is perfect. A person may feel as if his mind is distorted and chaotic, but this is not the true state of mind. When a human being purifies his system and brings his mind to a state of quietude, then he comes to know what his mind and body really are. One comes to see that mind and body are not as they appear and are nothing but Consciousness itself. In that state, the order of manifestation in a human being

The Sutras on Healing and Enlightenment

is totally clear, and nothing but Divine Mind remains. This state is the true creation and condition of man, not the chaos that arises in the mind from illusions.

-3:11-
A human mind has the free will to choose between the real and the unreal, between Truth and illusions.

-3:12-
Choices based on that which is true and real create harmony; choices based on that which is untrue and false create disharmony.

The Children of God are given the free will to make choices to create their own realities. A Child of God cannot change who he is, but he can re-create himself as he chooses. Soul will always be Soul. Consciousness cannot be unconscious. Love cannot be anything but Love, and Peace will always be Peace. What God is and has created can never be changed, but the Soul does have the capacity to forget who it is, and through its thoughts, manifest realities based on who it does believe itself to be.

If the Soul chooses Reality and Truth as the basis for re-creating itself into form, then its experience will be in harmony with Divine Goodness. However, through its free will, if it chooses illusions and unreality, then it will suffer because its beliefs are not harmonious with Truth.

The experience of the Soul is a communication. If the experience the Soul is having is pleasurable and joyful, then it has chosen Truth. However, if there is suffering in any way, then illusion has become the basis of choice and can then be changed. Pain is just a communication to the

Soul that it is denying its own Truth. The experienced healer can use these painful communications to determine where the client is caught in false beliefs that are creating poor choices for re-creation. Once the illusion is made clear to the Soul that negativity or separation will never bring him what he truly wants, then a new choice can be made, a choice based on Truth.

-3:13-
One can choose to nurture false illusory beliefs, or at any moment one can choose Truth, which transcends beliefs.

This is a very important sutra because it speaks of nurturing false illusory beliefs. The only reason a person would nurture illusion is because he thinks it will bring him what he wants. For instance, someone could be choosing anger as a valid energy to give power to. The only reason such a painful energy would be valued and thus nurtured is if the person thinks that it will benefit him in some way. No one puts energy into anything that seems destructive to his or her well-being. Once it is made clear to the mind that it is investing its energy in places that cause it to suffer, then it can choose to withdraw its misplaced energy and invest it in a more beneficial way.

This sutra says that at any moment one can make another choice about what he will invest in. The only real option is to choose Truth as the basis for one's experience at every moment, and Truth has nothing to do with belief systems at all. When someone believes that he is bad, limited, shameful, stupid or unlovable, he can become aware of such beliefs and choose to let Truth be the guiding light for the basis of knowing who

The Sutras on Healing and Enlightenment

he truly is. All beliefs are false, and anything false will cause suffering. When we choose Truth, we transcend all beliefs and rest in who we truly are. When this happens, healing happens. This is enlightenment. It is to place one's attention on Truth rather than illusions. When Consciousness begins to know once again that it is and always has been Consciousness, then healing can be said to take place, regardless of how this shift affects the order of manifestation.

With the arising of Truth in the mind, the order of manifestation no longer manifests through false beliefs. In this case, negative emotions and their suppressions fall away, and the physical symptoms that arise from this blocked way of being usually fall away as well. However, the sutras are quite clear that even with the enlightening into Truth, the physical body may not heal itself. If one is on his deathbed, the body may not change. However, the Consciousness will be liberated and known to be forever free. This is healing in its deepest sense, and it all begins with the willingness of the client to let go of illusions and to choose Truth.

-3:14-
Illness is disharmony and is not of God.

The human body is always working to keep a state of homeostasis within itself and with its environment. In the Divine Order of Manifestation, this is the natural way of things and it happens easily and effortlessly. The manifested world of form when governed by Divine Intelligence is only harmonious. In it there is no separation, division or imbalance. When illness manifests due to false beliefs, negative emotions and their suppression, then this is not of God but of the ego mind and its ignorance.

Misidentification with the object of Consciousness causes the ignorance of the Soul about its True Nature. This misidentification causes false beliefs and their subsequent manifestations. When the Soul knows that it is God, then false beliefs drop away; and God is what is left. In the state of God Consciousness, matter is not only seen to be not real, but manifestation becomes exceptionally harmonious and healthy.

-3:15-
The physical world of matter has no inherent intelligence, sensation or power in and of itself.

The physical world is not a separate self and only derives its power from Pure Consciousness, which is All Power and the Only Reality. Since Consciousness is the Only Power, then matter cannot have any power in and of itself. This is also true of intelligence, since the Divine Intelligence is the only intelligence that there is. Matter has neither intelligence nor power, because it is only an apparent reality—a mirage. That which is changing and not real does not have its own energy; it depends on the energy that creates and sustains it.

If matter had power or intelligence, then a dead body could move on its own and work out the problems of where it will be buried or cremated. Matter is animated by the Spirit within it, which values it. By itself, it is nothing.

The Sutras on Healing and Enlightenment

-3:16-
Sensation is in mind and not in matter.

Matter has no sensation in it. Sensation refers to feelings, such as pain, discomfort, hunger, and thirst. Most people feel that the body is the one that feels; but without the more subtle bodies associated with the physical body, then no such feelings arise in it. Matter itself is inert and insentient. It only exists because of mind, and mind is where all sensation is felt through the medium of the astral and etheric bodies. During deep sleep no sensation is felt in the body. If the body were the cause of pain, then the pain would be eternal; but when mind is not there, then pain is not either.

Through hypnosis or other mind technologies, pain can be completely shut off from the experience of the Soul. Mind causes pain, and mind can remove pain. When the more subtle bodies are removed from their association with matter through out-of-body experience, near-death experience or death, then there is no pain in the body and no pain for the Soul. Pain arises in the mind only when it identifies with the physical body; yet when the mind is nonexistent in meditation, then no pain remains.

The world's great mystical traditions and their sacred texts speak of a condition where there is no longer pain and suffering. What good would these traditions be if they could not remove these things? And what would be their value if their words were just mere empty promises? When the Heart Sutra of Buddhism says that through the enlightenment process one comes to be free of suffering and pain, it means it. While this may be a lofty state that few human beings have ever experienced, it does not change the Truth. Matter has no sensation, and all sensation is in mind. When we know this, we are empowered to alleviate pain by simply offering the Truth to the mind.

Many of us have experienced within ourselves or others that when the body is injured, it does not hurt. It is only when we bring our attention to the afflicted area and believe that something is wrong that pain arises. When Consciousness is not placed on an object of Consciousness, then that object does not exist for the Consciousness. When Consciousness moves into the very essence of an afflicted area, it also realizes the same Truth, namely that matter is only an apparent reality and that there is no pain in matter. When Consciousness becomes so intimate with its object that the two become one, then one comes to see that there was nothing but Consciousness. In this state of Pure Consciousness, there is no mind; therefore, there is no pain. In the core of sensation, there is no sensation; because in the core there is nothing but God.

-3:17-
Matter is not a cause.

-3:18-
The world of form is the result of mind and not matter.

Just as matter is not intelligent and has no power or sensation, we can see that matter also is not a cause of anything. Matter is an effect, not a cause. It exists because of the more subtle levels that create and sustain it. Matter did not cause matter; therefore, matter cannot be the solution to problems. If a problem arises in matter,

The Sutras on Healing and Enlightenment

then matter cannot be its solution because the problem did not arise from matter but from mind.

This does not appear to be the case when we only know the world of matter. Because we are not aware of its cause, we think that matter must be its own cause. When we know that matter only exists because of mind, then we know that things are merely thoughts. Thoughts create the apparent reality of things, and things are not the cause of themselves. Any uncomfortable manifestation in the world of matter is not its own cause. One reason is that matter has no sensation in and of itself and so such discomfort arises from mind and mind alone. A second reason is that matter is not a cause of discomfort, because matter has no power or intelligence in and of itself to act. Nothing moves within the physical world without it moving on the more subtle planes first.

Take the example of a knife stab wound. One would conclude on the surface that the knife caused the wound and the pain, but this is not the case. The person wielding the knife could only move the knife because of mind. His body does not move of its own volition, and the knife does not move of its own volition either. Matter was not the cause of the stabbing, but rather mind was the instigator. The pain felt in the body of the one stabbed is not felt in the body at all, but in the mind; without mind, there would be no pain. Also, the person stabbed was not stabbed by accident, because nothing happens on the physical plane without first being initiated by both parties on the more subtle planes.

-3:19-
Things are thoughts, only apparent realities perceived through the limitations of the five senses.

The Sutras on Healing and Enlightenment

As should be clear to the reader now, things are thoughts and only apparent realities that are not as they appear. The five senses, also of the world of matter, can never perceive the energy that manifests as form. The underlying energy templates, planes and bodies that create the illusion of the physical world can be experienced, but not through the five senses. The five senses have a purpose, as everything in creation has a purpose. Fire is meant to be hot. Water is meant to nourish. Wind is meant to cool. Everything in creation has a reason for being in relationship to every other part of creation.

The five senses play the role of letting Consciousness experience physical reality; without these senses, Consciousness could not engage in the physical world. Yet the five senses are very limited and never communicate the Truth of existence to the more subtle bodies or to the Soul itself. The healer must have the direct experience that matter is not solid and real, or he will believe what his senses tell him. When one sees illness with the five senses alone, then one concludes that illness is a real and separate self that has its own power, intelligence and sensation. However, the Truth is that illness is only manifested thought, which has no separate existence, no power, no intelligence and no sensation. The manifestations of the world seem real indeed to a mind that trusts the five senses as a sole source of information, but the wise are never deceived by such illusions.

The Sutras on Healing and Enlightenment

-3:20-
The Consciousness of a human being identifies itself with the human form and the human mind and becomes misidentified with matter.

-3:21-
In the misidentified state, the mind concludes that it is the body and not Pure Consciousness.

There are two major problems facing the human condition. One is that the human being is ignorant of who he truly is, and the other is that in this ignorance Consciousness believes itself to be its object of Consciousness. This ignorance and misidentification is the cause of all suffering. Pain is not in matter and suffering is not caused by matter, yet a human being believes himself to be matter. His belief systems become based on his belief that he is a body; his pain arises from his mind, which says that he is this body.

When the mind concludes that it is a body and the Consciousness becomes fully identified with the mind, then the belief is that the being is its object of Consciousness and not the Consciousness itself. In this state of ignorance, suffering occurs; yet in Truth, when Consciousness resides within itself, then it comes to know that not only is it not a body, but also in Truth it comes to know that nothing else exists but Itself. Since only Consciousness exists and this is the true identity of all manifested beings, then a human being can come to know that he is—and always has been—pure, free and forever and was never bound by or to matter in any way.

Not only can Consciousness be totally free from the illusory pain and limitations of the world, but in its awakening to the Truth of its own existence, the order of manifestation becomes clear, and harmony manifests easily and naturally.

-3:22-
Its beliefs about who it is come from its self-created ignorance and illusion.

The beliefs held in the mind are not the result of matter but of Consciousness's misidentification with matter. This ignorance is not imposed from some external source, because there is no other source outside of Consciousness itself. Therefore, all ignorance and illusion are self-created, for only Self exists. There are no victims in the universe, because there is only one Reality. Nothing manifests without choice. Beliefs, which manifest disharmony, are chosen and never imposed.

The universe supports us in our beliefs. Therefore, it appears that the universe made us feel and conclude a certain way, but actually the opposite is true. When we believe something, we experience it. The saying, "I'll believe it when I see it," is not actually true in the deepest sense. The statement really should be, "When I believe it, then I'll see it." Matter does not cause mind. Mind causes matter. The ignorance and illusion of the Soul, which causes it to feel separate and limited, come by choice and nothing more. The healer must hold to this line of thinking or else he will support his client in the belief that he is a victim of circumstances. The belief of being a separate self and the uncomfortable consequences that go with it are self-created and nothing more. A healer must always keep this in mind and be largely free from such illusions himself.

The Sutras on Healing and Enlightenment

-3:23-
It concludes that it has the attributes of the body and the body's experiences rather than the attributes of Source.

Sutra 23 is the real essence of this work because it helps to explain the main reason for the false beliefs that create all of human suffering. When Consciousness believes itself to be a body, mind or emotions, then the mind draws conclusions from this false point of view. Consciousness is all-powerful. When it gives its power to a mind that is in error, then all of its manifestations will result in error. The attributes of a body are limitation, vulnerability, change and eventually death. When Consciousness believes itself, through mind, to be these things, then its conclusions are all wrong; and terrible beliefs, emotions, behaviors and physical manifestations arise. However, when Consciousness only knows itself to be Itself and mind is consciously used to re-create these qualities, then the experience is based on Truth—which is peace, bliss, joy, love, goodness, health and harmony.

When a person believes himself to be a person, then he will be full of lies. Yet when he knows himself to be the Divine Itself, then his mind will be full of Light and Truth.

The body and the body's experience do not dictate what the True Self is. The body may appear sick, old, ugly, dirty or dying, but the True Self never is. The healer must know this and only see his client as the Truth, as he leads his client into the Truth of who he is as well. This sutra can never be meditated on enough. It is the essence of true healing.

The Sutras on Healing and Enlightenment

-3:24-

These conclusions are false beliefs, which are thoughts; and these false thoughts do affect the order of manifestation.

Thoughts are creative. Every thought that was ever vibrated has creative power. It is in the nature of thought to manifest into form, yet not all thoughts find their way to physical manifestation. A thought must be held long enough and with sufficient emotional charge for it to manifest. The order of manifestation is governed by Divine Intelligence but has no discerning power in and of itself. Just as a pipe will let dirty or clean water through without preference, so too will the order of manifestation let through harmonious or disharmonious thoughts.

-3:25-

The order of manifestation is perfect, and false thoughts will perfectly manifest as disharmonious realities.

There is nothing in creation that is not perfect in the sense that nothing is an accident that just happened to occur. When a false belief is held for a long time with sufficient emotional charge, then this will manifest into form somehow and in some way. However, these beliefs and emotions manifest not by chance but as a perfect reflection of their vibrations. For instance, a belief that someone is weak will cause a feeling of fear that will manifest through the chakra system into the solar plexus region. The result could be a stomachache, a nervous stomach, ulcers, colitis, or irritable bowel syndrome; however it manifests, it is a perfect reflection of the underlying thoughts.

The Sutras on Healing and Enlightenment

Symptoms seem to be disharmonious, yet they are exactly what the Soul needs to see what it is denying about itself. In the case of the stomach issues, the manifestation of illness is a communication to the Soul. If the being can learn to listen to these communications and to understand what they are saying, then the false belief can be removed, the negative emotion will fall away, and the physical symptoms can drop away as well. It is perfect that they manifest as they do, and it is perfect how they fall away when they do. The wise healer must be there to assist the client in uncovering the cause of the disharmony and resolving it in the Light of Truth.

-3:26-
False thoughts are beliefs, which can appear as negative emotions, suppression, destructive behaviors, illness and disharmonious life situations.

The order of manifestation has already been made clear in the sutras, but now Sutra 26 discusses how false beliefs manifest through it into form. This is very important to understand, because the healer must learn to reverse this order within his client. False beliefs exist on the mental plane and then manifest into negative emotions, which exist on the astral plane. These beliefs and emotions are painful to the Soul and are often suppressed and denied from Consciousness. It is this act of suppression that causes these patterns to remain "stuck" in the more subtle bodies. Over time, these blockages end up manifesting through the etheric body into the physical body as destructive behaviors, illness and disharmonious life situations.

The blockages created in the more subtle bodies manifest as a vibration around the being that causes the outside world to become a reflection of the inside world. The outside world is the physical plane, and the inside world is compared to the more subtle planes. The outside is only a reflection of the inside and nothing more. When iron filings are sprinkled around a magnet, we can clearly see the magnet's invisible lines of force. The iron filings have no power of their own but take the shape of the magnet's energetic field. In the same way, a human being is an energetic being, and his aura pulls around it situations that reflect it. This concept helps us to see how there are no accidents and also how it is only through the energies of thought and emotion that we end up with physical realities.

-3:27-
The remedy for all disharmony on any level of manifestation is Truth.

This chapter closes with a reminder of the simple solution to all of mankind's sufferings. When the Light of Truth is brought to the mind and false beliefs are dispelled, then only Harmony remains. Harmony does not mean that things end up the way we want them. It only means that one is truly at peace with All That Is. Harmony is what is. Since God is Harmony, there can be nothing but harmony. Everything is perfect as it is for one who sees clearly. The eyes of dualistic ignorance still believe that there is actually pain and suffering in God's Universe, but there is not. All pain and suffering is an illusion arising from the ignorance of Truth. No one will believe these statements until they are made clear as to who they truly are. As long as ignorance remains, one will see problems and chaos. But when the Truth is revealed, then all suffering is seen for what it is— nothing.

The Sutras on Healing and Enlightenment

Chapter Four—The Manifestation of Illness and its Reversal

-4:1-
The essence of a human being is Pure Consciousness, which is often called I Am.

Chapter Four begins a series of sutras based on a more in-depth look into how illness manifests through the order of manifestation and how the healer is to reverse this process. It therefore begins with the Source of all manifestation, which is Pure Consciousness. The sutra declares that the essence of a human being is this Consciousness; while in Truth the essence of all manifested being is Consciousness. The important point here is that enlightenment, and therefore true healing, can only occur for a human being and so it is made clear that the essence of the human being is Pure Consciousness itself.

The words of this sutra are very clear: "…Pure Consciousness, which is often called "I Am." This is actually a slightly misleading term as Pure Consciousness does not declare "I Am." The real essence of the Universe is void of any sense of being a separate self and is beyond all vibration and causality. However, for the sake of healing and to give some basic concept of what the essence of a human being is, we use the phrase, "I Am." When thought, desire, intention, intellect, emotion, feelings and body are taken away from the human system, then the essence that is left is "I Am." It could be said that this "I Am" is ego-sense and not really Pure Consciousness itself, but for the sake of simplicity we use this term to imply the barest essential of existence, which is Pure Being and Pure Potentiality.

The Sutras on Healing and Enlightenment

The phrase "I Am" is often used to represent God. In Exodus 3:14, Moses asks God who shall I say hath sent me unto the people. God replies, "Tell them I Am that which I Am hath sent you." This "I Am" is the Source of the Whole Universe. It is the state of pure potential from which all manifested form will come into being. It is even more subtle than the phrase "I Am," yet this makes for a great starting point in understanding where disease comes from. The next sutra is very important concerning this issue.

-4:2-
Any thought placed after "I Am" that is held long enough will manifest into form.

This is one of the most important concepts to be grasped when we are attempting to understand why disease manifests in a benevolent universe. The phrase "I Am" refers to a state of pure potential that can become anything. "I Am" is a field of Pure Consciousness with the power to manifest into any form it chooses. Through the order of manifestation it unfolds itself into the mental plane where mind exists. Whatever thoughts the mind holds for a sufficient time will continue through the order of manifestation and become formed. There is no way around this because all thoughts with sufficient power and charge have to manifest.

If a human being, whose essence is "I Am," identifies with his body, mind and emotions and begins to say things like, "I Am stupid," "I Am unloved," "I Am worthless," "I Am limited," "I Am not good enough," then those false beliefs, which are thoughts, will eventually manifest into some form. Whether it be a negative form of emotion, negative life situations that support the belief or physical problems in the body, the manifestation is inevitable if the thought is held after "I Am" for a sufficient period of time. When Consciousness begins to bring its attention back to itself rather than identifying with its object, then it has chosen Truth over illusions and the order of manifestation will reflect Truth rather than error.

-4:3-
All thoughts have creative power.

Thoughts, which have no power in and of themselves, are only given power when Consciousness places its attention on them. What Consciousness dwells on, it becomes. When a thought is held over and over again, especially when this thought is charged with emotion and held in a suppressed state, then it has to manifest somehow and in some way. It is similar to pumping dirty water into a pipe and then trying to close up the other end. In time when the pressure gets too great, the dirty water will have to be pushed out. The dirt itself in a pipe has no power, but when the water pressure gets strong enough, the result must manifest.

The dirt here is analogous to negative thoughts. Alone, thoughts have no power; but when the water of Consciousness is applied, eventually thoughts take on form. Thoughts never exist on their own, because Consciousness is everywhere. Thoughts, which are only made of Consciousness itself, have creative power because their Source is pure creativity.

The Sutras on Healing and Enlightenment

-4:4-
In the order of manifestation in a human being, Consciousness associates with its mind, emotions and physical body and forgets who it really is.

Consciousness will always be Consciousness, and this can never change. Yet Consciousness can easily become identified with what it observes. In the unenlightened state, there is a total assimilation of Consciousness with its object of Consciousness. This process of misidentification is a forgetting process; because if you ask a human being who he is, you will get an answer that is associated only with one's life, body, mind or emotions. Only an enlightened being could answer the question with the full authority of realization and declare that who I Am is God—nothing more, nothing less.

-4:5-
Its thoughts then become based on the limitations of the object of Consciousness, which are body, mind and emotions.

In the ignorant state where Consciousness does not know itself and believes itself to be the body, the mind is in a relatively unconscious state and is often said to be asleep. The ignorant human being lives in a dream where he believes himself to be body, mind and emotions. Dreams are very plastic. They mold easily to the thoughts of the dreamer. However, when the dreamer believes that the dream is real and comes to value it, then his attention is placed on it and he forgets who he really is. In the forgetting process, the thoughts become based on the limitations of manifested form.

Not only is the Consciousness lost in an illusory world of its own creation, but also it begins to believe itself to be the vehicle it uses to experience this world. This creates a vicious cycle of Consciousness creating a world, and then Consciousness identifying with its own creations and simply perpetuating its own myths.

-4:6-
As a creative force, Consciousness will manifest realities based on the thoughts of the mind with which it is associated.

Sutra 6 takes us closer to the mind of the human being where a healer can look and see which thoughts in the mind of his client are causing disease. The healer knows that the essence of his client is creative energy and that whatever thoughts are held in the mind will become manifest. There is only One Consciousness, yet in humanity there appear to be separate minds; however, these minds that feel themselves to be individuals are simply illusions.

There is no separate mind anywhere, just as one thousand pots of water will all reflect the same moon. Each pot has a reflection of the moon. The moon is the macrocosm, and the reflection in a pot is the microcosm. The microcosmic mind has no identity of its own, yet it believes in its ignorance that it does. The moon, or mind, in the pot of water has the creative power of the moon behind it and is not separate from its Source. The Source is pure creative power. If the mind—which is in and gets its existence from this field of creative power—holds false beliefs, then these beliefs do manifest into form. It is therefore imperative in healing for the mind of

The Sutras on Healing and Enlightenment

the individual, which appears separate, to be addressed; because it is here that the source of all disharmony resides.

-4:7-
Thoughts of Truth and right knowledge are harmonious and manifest only harmonious realities.

-4:8-
Thoughts that are not true and not of right knowledge are disharmonious and manifest only disharmonious realities.

In the order of manifestation, thoughts attuned with Truth only produce harmonious realities, and thoughts not attuned produce only disharmony. This should now be obvious in our discussion. However, in commentary, we can go even deeper. When the mind is clear and quiet, it reflects the Divine Mind perfectly; and therefore one does not need to try to hold right and correct thoughts in the mind all of the time. The mind of a human being is a perpetual lie. Its words are maps of the terrain and not the terrain itself. Its judgments and descriptions of things are not the things themselves. For true healing and enlightenment to occur, the mind must return to its Source. When the mind is free of its incessant fluctuations, then Truth is what is left. This is a state of non-doership, where nothing need be done at all for Harmony to manifest, because Harmony is what is left when the ignorant mind is out of the way.

-4:9-
Thoughts that are not true are beliefs, and all beliefs are false.

Thoughts in themselves are not good or bad, because good and bad are simply judgments of the mind itself. The more important question is whether or not certain thoughts are beneficial or not. Some thoughts are helpful in producing harmonious realities, and some thoughts are not. Some thoughts are helpful in leading a person to the realization of who he really is, and other thoughts are not. Therefore, certain types of thoughts can be painful or not painful; however, one type of thought that is always painful is a belief.

Beliefs are thoughts held in the mind about things that are unknown. When something is known, a belief is no longer necessary. All beliefs are false by definition, because beliefs imply a lack of true knowledge. Whether a person believes that he is a good person or a bad person is irrelevant, because a person is not a person at all. The mind holding such beliefs does not know who it really is and identifies with its thoughts, emotions, body and behaviors. If the mind knew who it truly was as Pure Consciousness—free from all qualities—then it would not call itself a person at all, not good or bad, but would know itself to be God.

In Truth there is no duality; all beliefs are dualistic, and therefore false. Truth transcends beliefs, but in ignorance truth appears to become beliefs. Consciousness identifying with a system of beliefs empowers the beliefs, which will eventually manifest. The human being holds a very large list of negative beliefs that create tremendous suffering. All thoughts that are not true are beliefs, because that which is not true is not a known reality. When a human being comes to know who he truly is, then his thoughts only reflect that glory, and all false beliefs about Self drop away. However, when this is not

The Sutras on Healing and Enlightenment

the case, the false beliefs continue on through the order of manifestation.

-4:10-
False beliefs manifest as negative emotions, which are often expressed through speech and action.

False beliefs, which exist on the mental plane in the mental body, manifest into the astral plane in the astral body. The astral body is the level of vibration associated with emotion. The astral body has a very plastic form. If it is held together by false beliefs and negative emotions, then its form becomes less than desirable. Then the astral body, which is meant to be only Pure Light, becomes full of darkness and blockage. Beliefs and emotions are often held within the energetic system and claimed to be one's own. These blockages in one's energy field tend to govern one's speech and actions. Because Consciousness in most humanity is fully identified with the lower vehicles, it acts through them based on the mental impressions that reside there.

If a person holds the false belief that he is not good enough, his emotions may be anxiety, fear and frustration. These emotions will be held within and denied because they are too uncomfortable to fully feel. Denial and suppression block these feelings in the more subtle bodies, and then the misidentified Consciousness acts these out in daily life. Therefore, all disharmony is the result of these blockages in the energy field, which can be called mental impressions consisting of false beliefs, negative emotions and associated memories.

The Sutras on Healing and Enlightenment

-4:11-

Expression only reinforces negative beliefs and emotions.

The sutras in this section on suppression and expression go into the most important part of how disease manifests. False beliefs and emotions are not harmful in and of themselves. There is nothing wrong with anger, fear or hurt. These are simply energies that are floating in the universe. They are not right or wrong and should not be denied. However, these energies are often valued as useful by the ignorant mind, which actually lives its life based on them. All negative emotion comes from a false belief. Yet the ignorant human being will act on these emotions as if they are real and useful in getting him what he wants.

Every time an emotion is expressed through words or actions or acting out on these energies, the blockages that caused the emotions are only reinforced. A mental impression (memory, negative beliefs and emotions) often becomes associated with present-day events that remind the psyche of its past experiences. The past then gets projected into the present, and the ignorant being acts out on his emotions. For example, if a child was beaten by his father and often told that he was bad, then the child will take on beliefs that he is bad. He will be afraid of future hurt and perhaps angry with his father. The mental impression in Consciousness is a memory of the past events, the false beliefs and negative emotions. In the future when someone calls this person bad, his mind will instantly recall the past event when he was beaten and told he was bad by his father and will become angry again. His anger will be projected on the person who said he was bad, and this will only reinforce his lie about himself.

The Sutras on Healing and Enlightenment

The belief that any Child of God is bad is false. However, if the Soul believes that its beliefs are true, it will be affected by an event that supports this belief. The Universe supports us in what we believe about ourselves. If a person believes he is bad, he will always end up in situations where he is made to feel bad. He will become angry at these situations and the people involved and often act out his anger. He does not know that he is both the cause of the situation and the one who is angry at his own creations. Therefore, when an emotion is acted out, it only reinforces the pattern that fueled it in the first place. The sutras explain how to remove these mental impressions, and the first step is to learn that expressing negative beliefs and emotions only reinforces their existence.

-4:12-
In an ignorant state the human being often suppresses beliefs and emotions to avoid having to experience them.

-4:13-
These suppressed beliefs and emotions cause blockages in the energy flow of the subtle bodies.

If the cause of human suffering is summed up in one sutra, this is it. When a human being closes his heart to life and refuses to feel all of his feelings, then energy becomes blocked in the system. Mental impressions (memories, beliefs and emotions) become stored in the energy fields of the more subtle bodies and remain trapped there in holding patterns until released and transformed. A human being who suppresses his emotions is simply inviting disease and disharmony into his life in his vain attempt to avoid such things.

The Sutras on Healing and Enlightenment

In the ignorant state, the Soul becomes misidentified with its body and terrified of the things around it. The fear of death arises because now the identity is associated with what is not eternal. Therefore the will power is used to either push away or to cling to uncomfortable energies. Using will power to block the flow of life in any way is sure to manifest disease because, once life is blocked, death begins to set in. Death is a lack of life, but there is no death in God's creations. Death is an illusion that appears due to the ignorance of the Soul that believes there is a reality other than God. Nothing is born and nothing dies in Truth. Yet in the Soul's illusion of birth and death, life force energy is blocked in an attempt to avoid feeling bad. In blocking vital energy, the only possible result is darkness and disease. Life is everywhere, because Life is God. When any energy is shielded from Consciousness, Life appears not to be there and all that can be left is darkness and death.

The physical universe without the attention of Consciousness obeys the Law of Entropy, which holds that any system that is not maintained returns to its original state. If a building is not properly maintained, it will return to the earth and decompose. The opposite of entropy is Life, and Life is Consciousness. If Consciousness can fully embrace the experience of Life, there is no duality, no darkness, no disease and no death. There is no death in Consciousness or in matter. Matter is not born and never dies because it does not really exist. It is in a constant state of change, and what is called death for the body is simply a transformation. When the body transforms into a state that is no longer useful, then the more subtle bodies leave it; however, nothing dies.

The Sutras on Healing and Enlightenment

The problem with suppression is that the mind as a subtle body cannot escape its physical world experience and so concludes that the only way to be safe is to close down the heart. When this act of suppression occurs, life force energy gets blocked and entropy begins to set in. The body begins to decay when robbed of Consciousness and energy. Emotions are energy in motion. When their motion is inhibited, they remain trapped in the aura as darkness. When these energies are not given attention, are left lying dormant for years, and are constantly held down, the areas where they exist become imbalanced. If a human being does not suppress his emotions, then energy is allowed to flow again, emotions are purified, and health and harmony result. Suppression should never be underestimated as a huge cause of human suffering; and it should never be considered a valid option for health, healing and wholeness.

-4:14-
These blockages, which are mental impressions that cause disharmony in the physical system, must be removed for healing to occur.

The Sanskrit word *sanskar* refers to the mental impressions that the sutras frequently mention. A sanskar is the result of life experience imprinted on Consciousness as a memory. Simply reading these words is creating sanskars. Every single life event and every impression from that event can be considered a sanskar, and there is nothing wrong in any way with these mental impressions. Sanskars occur due to the Soul's interactions with the manifest planes, and that is perfectly fine.

The Sutras on Healing and Enlightenment

The problem does not lie in the sanskaric patterns—which every human being has from life experience—but in the suppression of the patterns. Sanskars consist of memories, the beliefs developed during past events and the emotions that arise from those beliefs. A sanskar then is a mental impression filled with memories, beliefs and emotions. We draw conclusions about an event and therefore ourselves and have certain feelings. This is perfectly fine and necessary for us to function in the world.

Sanskars have an interesting method of associating their past memories with present-day realities in order to make sense of things based on past experience. For the child who was beaten and told he was bad, a very big sanskaric imprint was made. The sanskar has stored within it the memory of the beating, the belief that the child is bad, and the associated emotions: hurt, fear and anger. When the child is grown up and told that he is bad, the sanskaric pattern is triggered as the mind associates the present with the past. The emotions of hurt, fear and anger arise; and he usually will act in one of two ways. Either he will act out his emotions and only reinforce his sanskars, or he will suppress these emotions and pretend that he was not bothered by them. In either case of suppression or expression, sanskaric patterns are reinforced and the blockages are strengthened.

The process of healing involves several factors. The first is that a person must be taught how to stop creating more suppressed sanskaric patterns. The second is that blocked sanskaric patterns must be removed. The third is that the client must come to know who he truly is so that further sanskaric patterns are not created. When

The Sutras on Healing and Enlightenment

the Consciousness knows Itself to be Consciousness and not the objects of Consciousness, then, for it, sanskaric patterns do not exist. However, on the relative plane where healing is involved, suppressed sanskars must be removed for healing to occur. With the release and transformation of a blocked sanskar, negative beliefs are removed, negative emotions are removed, destructive behaviors fall away, and the darkness of the suppression that was causing imbalances in the subtle bodies becomes once again full of light. Through this process, the being is awakened to who he truly is, and disease usually falls away in the process. Throughout the sutras, the process of releasing and removing sanskars in therapy is discussed in detail. In the chapter on empowering the client, the teachings on how the client can transform his own sanskars on a day-to-day basis is discussed.

-4:15-
Healing does not occur from the dense levels of manifestation inward, but from the more subtle levels outward.

As the sutras have made clear, nothing can exist physically without existing on the more subtle planes first. When a person tries to heal another person by only removing a physical symptom, then true healing cannot be said to be occurring. The order of manifestation is very simple. Thoughts become emotions and emotions become matter. Therefore, things are thoughts. To truly resolve a disharmonious thing, one must remove the disharmonious thought. Sanskaric patterns are always residing within any physical symptom. Without the release and transformation of the sanskar, healing cannot take place.

Sanskars are held together by the beliefs they contain. When these beliefs and their subsequent emotions are suppressed, then these blockages manifest as disease. Disease or "dis-ease" occurs only through false beliefs; and without their transformation, no real healing occurs. For instance, a tension headache that is caused by a tightening of muscles or a constriction of blood vessels occurs from the emotion that is contained within this pattern. The emotion of perhaps fear, worry or anger comes from a false belief. False beliefs are not real. In the order of manifestation, a false belief in Self—not knowing who one truly is—causes an emotion. This emotion is usually suppressed; and the holding pattern creates tension in the body, thus manifesting a headache. The headache is not a separate self and is not its own cause. It results from the more subtle levels of creation as these manifest through the order of manifestation. To remove the symptom is actually a disservice to the client. Beliefs, emotions and suppression not released will manifest more seriously later.

-4:16-
Suppressed beliefs and emotions manifesting as physical symptoms or negative behaviors must be resolved through Truth.

-4:17-
Truth shatters false beliefs and their associated emotions and symptoms.

Sutra 15 clearly establishes that true healing occurs from more subtle levels down, and Sutra 16 continues with

The Sutras on Healing and Enlightenment

the means for this healing to occur. Because false belief is manifesting as emotions, suppression and symptoms, it is Truth that will set the person free. Another word for Truth is *God*; therefore all true healing is of God. It is not the individual mind that truly heals, because the notion of an individual mind is an illusion. Therapies, which all use the power of the individual mind to heal the body, miss the point because they acknowledge another power outside of God and give this power to a mind that has no basis in Reality. There is only One Mind and that is God. The ignorance of false beliefs is transformed with Truth and Truth alone.

Healing is not the process of replacing negative sanskars with positive ones. Positive sanskars that are suppressed also create problems. When a person believes that he is a bad person, and the therapist through whatever means convinces him that he is a good person, then the therapist simply re-programs the sanskaric pattern and does nothing to truly free the client. Only Truth sets us free because it shows us that we always have been free. The bondage of false beliefs is an illusion, because false beliefs do not exist. If a person comes to know that his illusions were never there in the first place and he wakes up to Truth, healing can be said to have taken place. This happens from the more subtle levels downward and never from the more dense levels upward, and it only happens with Truth.

-4:18-
To treat physical symptoms and emotions alone is not true healing.

It should be clear at this point that treating physical symptoms is not true healing, but it also must be made

The Sutras on Healing and Enlightenment

very clear that treating emotions is not true healing either. All emotion comes from belief. If a person is sad because he believes that he is unlovable, removing the sadness cannot be said to be true healing. The person must be made aware of his false belief first. He must admit, for instance, that he feels unlovable. In this process of bringing the false belief to Consciousness, it is no longer suppressed or denied. Once it is brought to the Light, then the person can be awakened to who he truly is through Truth. With the awakening to Truth, the unlovable person realizes that he is more than simply lovable and that he is Infinite Love. With this dawning of realization, sadness falls away instantly.

Now if the belief that someone is unlovable causes him to be sad, and this sadness is held long enough to create some disease in the physical body, then it would be absurd to remove the physical or emotional symptoms without addressing the root cause, which is the belief. If a certain modality is used to remove these symptoms and Truth is not brought in as the True Healer, then the client learns that matter is more powerful than Mind. The attempt to remove the symptom actually again becomes a disservice. Not only will the reappearance of the symptom be even worse, but power will be given to modalities and not Mind. The person will suffer again in the future. In his ignorance, he will keep looking for new ways to relieve his symptoms. He will never know who he truly is, never honor God as the true healer and believe that matter has more power to heal him than his own Mind.

The Sutras on Healing and Enlightenment

-4:19-
The mechanism of suppression must be reversed.

The sutras have clearly explained the dangers of suppression. It must also be clear that reversing suppression does not mean expression. Neither suppression nor expression works to remove sanskaric patterns. We now must clarify the requirements for true healing. If an emotion is not suppressed or expressed, then we must ask what happens to it? When an emotion is not allowed out but also not denied, then it is not given any power. What does not have power slowly transforms. What is not given attention becomes subject to entropy. A guest who is ignored does not stay long. Emotions that are not given any reality do not last long and never again return in the same way.

More ways to remove sanskar will be discussed throughout the sutras and commentaries. For now, the healer and client should be made aware that when energy is pulled out of emotions without suppression or denial, the emotions quickly go away. Transformation is the only answer, not suppression or expression.

Only three things can be done with energy suppression, expression or transformation. Only transformation fits the category of true healing, and the means of this transformation will unfold as the sutras unfold.

-4:20-
Emotions and beliefs must be brought to the Light of Consciousness.

The process of suppression keeps beliefs and emotions in blocked holding patterns that cause disease. It is very clear that these patterns must be unblocked. A sanskaric pattern brought to the Light of Consciousness begins to unravel. It no longer has the power afforded to it by suppression or expression, but is revealed for what it truly is. A sanskar is not Reality; it is an impression of an interpretation of Reality. Sanskars are not video cameras recording exact information, but are based on all sanskars in the system. Thus, nothing is experienced or remembered as it truly is. The subconscious mind, the repository of sanskars, does not hold historical memory but subjective memory. There is no truth in the information that the sanskars hold. Sanskars consist only of false beliefs and can never tell the truth of who one is. Sanskars brought to Consciousness can then be transformed in the Light of Truth.

-4:21-
Truth must end up replacing negative beliefs.

For the order of manifestation to allow the symptoms of false beliefs to drop away, then Truth must be brought in as the real healer. How this is done is the important part of the healing process. To know conceptually that Truth, which is Love, heals all is not enough. The healer must be empowered with his own realization of Truth, or he cannot be said to be a true healer. If healing involves bringing to the surface and transforming false beliefs, the healer himself must not buy into the beliefs of his client. If the healer is still under the illusion that he is unworthy and his client expresses this belief, then both will feel that this is true and will not be able to let it go. However, when the healer knows that he is a Divine Child of God and worthy of all Goodness, Love and Grace, then he

The Sutras on Healing and Enlightenment

can help to impart that Truth to his client. If the healer understands that all pain and suffering arise from false beliefs, then even if he has the same beliefs as his client, he can heal along with his client if he is willing to let his own beliefs go and to let Truth be his guiding light. This theme is discussed much more throughout the sutras.

-4:22-
The heart must remain open.

This short yet poignant sutra is the real key to all successful and lasting healing. A client must be taught to keep his heart open to all life experience. A closed heart blocks life force energy and can only lead to sickness, premature old age and death. A closed heart—a dead and depressed heart—is not capable of feeling all its pain and therefore is not capable of feeling all its joy. When the heart is closed, we do not have all our tears and all our laughter. The heart can open and close, but the heart is meant to be open. A human being is meant to experience all of the seasons of his heart without shielding himself in any way.

Transformation in the human psyche and physiology never truly occurs if the heart remains shut down. The true healer must be empowered with many ways to assist his clients in opening their hearts, and his must be continually opening as well. The most difficult part of healing is to get the heart open. False beliefs, negative emotions and physical pain are easy to release, because the person does not want them. However, the person does want the walls that he put up to protect his heart, and their roots run very deep. The healer should always be aware that his client is protecting himself and that

The Sutras on Healing and Enlightenment

he does not really want to change whatever makes him feel secure. He must be made to see that these walls are actually harming him now and do not serve him any more.

The process of dismantling protective walls is a true art. Helping people to see that these walls are not bad is the important part of helping walls to come down. When most people come up against the closed heart, they pretend to be a victim to these walls. They even get angry with the walls for not letting them into their emotions and causing them to be depressed!

This is pure ignorance and only creates further division. A closed and blocked heart is already seriously divided, and anger at this fortress only makes it worse. The secret is responsibility, compassion, forgiveness and understanding. The person must take responsibility for putting up these walls in the first place. He must have compassion for his reason for doing so and acknowledge that he did the best he could with his given resources to feel safe when he felt threatened or in pain. He must forgive himself for closing his heart and realize that he truly did the best he could do. Then he must understand what a closed heart does and how to live with an open heart.

If the client does not feel safe enough to live with an open heart, then he will not let down his walls. He must be empowered to be fully open to life, and yet at the same time know that his true liberation and freedom will only come from this total surrender. This work of opening the heart is vital to the healing process. Like many other themes, it will come up time and time again in the sutras.

-4:23-
Forgiveness must occur.

Without forgiveness, there can be no healing. Forgiveness is the key to truly opening and releasing the sanskaric patterns in the heart. When a person is angry with himself or herself or with another, then forgiveness is the only real answer. When we are dealing with a closed heart, we must understand that this person has been hurt in the past. From their hurt they have become afraid, and from their fear they have become angry. This usually all gets suppressed into the heart and then walled off to prevent future hurt and attack. These suppressions manifest as illness. Without forgiveness, these patterns cannot be released.

With enough suppression, the heart closes so much that a person becomes depressed. Even though this person may seem to be just lacking energy and life force, it should be understood that one can never lose power, and all this energy is lying dormant and locked away in sanskaric patterns. Such a person is most certainly angry. If he is angry with others, then he is also angry with himself. This is simply called guilt, and it must be resolved. As long as the guilty punish themselves, then sickness will occur as a form of punishment for one who feels he deserves it.

The only real hell, or punishment, for a Child of God is to feel separate from God. When the heart is closed and full of hurt, fear, anger, separation and guilt, there appears to be a huge separation for such a being between himself and his Source. This separation is only resolved through the release of the bottled-up emotions and then through the process of forgiveness. Once a person

The Sutras on Healing and Enlightenment

forgives himself and others, the separation that was being made can be resolved, and Oneness can be found again. When we separate ourselves from any aspect of creation, we separate ourselves from God. Even a thin veil of anger or guilt will create division. Forgiveness is the only real answer when the healer is working on the level of mind, beliefs and emotions.

-4:24-
Consciousness must be re-established in its True Nature.

For true union to occur, Consciousness must be re-established within Itself. Once a being awakens to his True Self again, he realizes that unity is all that there is and ever was. After the release of negative emotions and the transformation of false beliefs, combined with the letting go that comes from forgiveness, a person can truly transcend his lower sense of self and discover who he really is. Any form of healing that does not take this leap into Source for the healer and the client is not true healing. For the union is enlightenment, and without enlightenment there is no healing.

-4:25-
The mind must learn to see itself as a manifestation of Divinity on all levels.

During the process of waking up to who we truly are, we must acknowledge that there is nothing but God. God is the Only Reality. The mind must come to understand that every single level of the order of manifestation is nothing but the Divine and that in Truth there are no levels because there is no separation. In a formless field of

The Sutras on Healing and Enlightenment

Consciousness, there is no form. However, for the mind that is waking up to its Source, there must be no division between the Soul, mind, emotions, feelings and body. These exist on their various levels, and the client must come to know that it is all Divine Perfection. This sutra deals with the need for understanding, so that the client can see that he truly does live in a benevolent universe where there is nothing but God happening.

-4:26-
Consciousness must learn to know itself as Itself and to avoid identifying with the new positive self-image established in the mind.

-4:27-
Enlightenment, which is the process of establishing the Self within Itself, has nothing to do with physical or emotional well-being.

During the therapeutic healing process, a new self-image will be the inevitable result. This new self-image will replace the old model of self, which did not serve the client. The one who is healed will inevitably shift from seeing himself as bad or "less than" into being good and worthwhile. The new self-image will be based on a shift from negative beliefs to positive beliefs. He will feel a new surge of positive emotion and a whole new mental self-portrait to go along with the healed state. The body will feel better. The person's life will begin to improve—but this is not true realization.

Consciousness must come to know itself as it is and not become identified even with the new positive self-image. Consciousness, in its essence, is not body, mind or

The Sutras on Healing and Enlightenment

emotions. It must be assisted to avoid identifying with these lower vehicles, no matter how pleasant they are. Therapy can pave the way for enlightenment by helping to free the client of his sanskaric patterns and to build a new healthy self-image. In the end, only the realization of the Self can be considered true healing. The body can be healed and also the emotions and mind. However, without mental healing and Self-Realization, healing is not complete.

-4:28-
Healing can assist in the enlightenment process, but perfect harmony on any level is not required for full realization.

-4:29-
Harmony on the lower levels assists in the enlightenment process.

The term healing in this sutra is used in the sense of seeing change occur on the lower levels of manifestation. The core theme of this sutra says that when a person is healed of some disharmony of the body, mind or emotions, this healing can assist in his awakening to who he truly is. It is very difficult to contemplate and meditate on one's True Nature as Consciousness when discomfort from the body, mind, emotions or life situations are constantly demanding attention. Although it is helpful to relieve these imbalances, it is not a prerequisite for full enlightenment.

The lower levels of creation do not define who and what the Soul really is. No matter how disturbed the body, mind or emotions are, it never can affect the True Self. Once a being has become established in his True Nature, he is free regardless of his body, mind and emotions. On

The Sutras on Healing and Enlightenment

the level of manifestation, there is constant change. One day a person will feel good, and the next day bad. Duality is always shifting between polar opposites, and this will never change. The mind will always find something to complain about, and the emotions will always fluctuate. Freedom is not found in making these things still or nonexistent. Freedom comes from knowing who one truly is and in that state of complete unity, there is no dependency in any way on the things of the world for one's peace, bliss and joy. The wise being takes good care of his vehicles, but his realization is not dependent on them.

When there is harmony on the lower levels, one can much more easily engage spiritual practice. When the body is comfortable, meditation on the True Self becomes much easier and enjoyable. Therefore, it is recommended that one take excellent care of his body, mind, emotions, and life in general so that his ability to dedicate more time to Self-Realization can be used to the fullest.

-4:30-
A strong and flexible body, an open heart, a clear mind, a good memory, high energy and a well-evolved intellect all assist in the enlightenment process.

A strong and flexible body is able to sit in meditation for long periods of time. An open heart affords every opportunity for sanskaric patterns to burn away. A clear mind allows for the Light of Consciousness to be much more apparent. A good memory helps one to recall his True Nature and the teachings that are leading him toward that. High energy is vital for being able to engage in long periods of meditation, exercise, study and service to others. A well-evolved intellect is crucial to understanding the deeper philosophies and teachings given by the saints and sages to assist in the enlightenment process. In short, one must do everything he can to make the body, mind and emotions suitable vehicles for effectively navigating the spiritual path.

-4:31-
There are many modalities, exercises and techniques that can assist in creating harmony on the lower levels of reality.

Over many centuries, mankind has sought ways to be free from suffering. Some methods relieved physical suffering, some mental, others emotional and others behavioral. Each modality has its place in making the life of a human being more pleasant and should not be overlooked. Modalities like Massage, Yoga, Tai Chi, Reiki, nutrition, weight-lifting, cardiovascular training, Acupuncture, Chiropractic, and even at times traditional allopathic medicine all have their place. These modalities should simply be understood for what they are and used when necessary or desired. The Sutras on Healing and Enlightenment simply work to transcend these modalities into a truer sense of what healing is and do not exclude anything. Spirituality must be all-inclusive and recognize that every aspect of creation has some value. Sometimes things that no longer serve a person are valued. Sometimes the only value of a thing is that it is communicating the errors in the mind. Nothing is to be suppressed or denied or considered as invalid and useless. Anything that can bring harmony can be adopted as long as wisdom keeps it in its proper place.

The Sutras on Healing and Enlightenment

-4:32-

However, true healing and enlightenment occur only through Divine Mind, which is Truth.

When all man's creative ideas have been exhausted and true peace and freedom still elude humanity, perhaps man will truly turn to the Divine as the Source of everything that was ever needed. Every human method of healing is fraught with illusion, delusion and error, but the Divine Mind and the Truth that it brings are all that is needed for true healing and enlightenment. The surrender to the Divine is the only real requirement for true healing. When one lets go of his ego and all of his means and modalities, the Truth can really begin to work in his life.

When a human being plans his life, he leaves God out. When he desires for things to be a certain way, he does not allow for Truth to be as it is. When the individual mind gets out of the way, then the Divine Mind can come in. God never goes against the will of his Children but is always there ready and waiting to come into their perceptions. When a person has suffered enough, he turns to God. In enlightened understanding, we come to know that God should be the first and only real choice where true healing is concerned.

So little power is given to God, when God is All Power. So little attention is given to the immense healing power of Love because so few humans truly know what Love is. It is only when we truly wake up to who we are and begin to grasp the Infinite Goodness of Truth that we can then begin to see the ever-present assistance of the Divine in our lives.

The Sutras on Healing and Enlightenment

-4:33-

Once a being is fully established in Truth, then he is free from all misfortune and pain regardless of the condition of the physical body.

In Truth there is no suffering, misfortune or pain. These concepts and their apparent realities exist only in the illusory world of mind where negative thoughts appear as things. Things are only thoughts. In Divine Consciousness, there are no things and there are no thoughts. There is only Pure Existence, Pure Consciousness and Pure Bliss. For a being established in the Absolute Truth, there is no suffering, because there is only the Space of Pure Love and Freedom. Therefore, a being who has reached such heights knows that nothing but God exists and that in God there is no misfortune or pain. It is only in illusion that suffering has any place, but because illusions do not exist, then suffering also does not exist.

The Sutras on Healing and Enlightenment

Chapter Five—The Healer and the One Healed

-5:1-
Truth is the only healer there is.

The sutras have thus far clearly established that all disharmony is illusion and that Truth is the only means of truly rectifying illusions. This chapter goes on to discuss how the healer can be empowered with the Truth to help another person in need and ideally lead him back into God Consciousness.

-5:2-
A human being fully established in Truth becomes an exceptionally powerful healing force, because his True Nature is known as being one with Truth.

This sutra is the essence of what it means to be a great healer. The more established in Truth a healer is, the more easily he can dispel the illusions of his client. When a healer has taken an immense plunge into the Glory of his own Divinity, then he walks this earth with the full realization of Truth, seeing nothing but God. He is no longer deluded by the illusions of the masses and can walk among them as a totally free being. He is not limited to the use of mystic powers or the laying on of hands, but trusts implicitly in the Divine to work through him in all situations. The absolute conviction he holds concerning the Absolute Goodness and Grace of God is his greatest healing modality.

The Sutras on Healing and Enlightenment

-5:3-
A true healer can see only Truth and knows that all disharmony is a manifestation of a deluded mind.

The true healer knows God and knows that God is All That Is. He knows that God is Pure Harmony and that God's creations are perfect and without suffering, disease or pain. He sees any disharmony as the result of ignorance and nothing more. A deluded mind manifests illness, but the healer knows that a thing is just a thought and that a disharmonious thing is just a disharmonious thought. It was not created by God and therefore does not exist in Truth.

-5:4-
A true healer knows that illness does not exist in God's Order of Manifestation and that God did not create illness.

The order of manifestation when aligned with Truth does not produce negative behaviors, sickness or even so-called death. The true healer cannot buy into the reality of anything that is considered as illness, because he knows God did not create it. Anything that was not created by God is a temporary and fleeting thought that can easily be changed through the Light of Truth. The order of manifestation will allow for negative thoughts and false beliefs to manifest, but the healer knows that these are not of God.

-5:5-
A true healer does not believe in illness because he knows that only the Creations of God are real and all else is unreal.

The Sutras on Healing and Enlightenment

We have already seen that what is unreal does not exist except in a relative and dependent way. An unreal reality constantly changes and has no inherent self of its own. These are not the Creations of God but merely the manifestations of ego-mind. That which is real is of God, and such creations are Eternal and can never be changed. The perfect causal ideas are God's creations, and these ideas only manifest as perfect and harmonious realities. Illness is not a perfect causal idea of God, but simply a manifestation of a deluded and confused mind. No real healer would ever believe that such a thing was real.

-5:6-
A true healer does not see his client as sick or support the client in his beliefs about illness, disharmony, pain and suffering.

True healing never occurs if the healer supports his clients in their illusions. True healing actually finds its genesis in the Space where the healer knows who the client truly is and does not believe in his illusions. If the healer supports his client as being sick, then both the healer and the client empower the reality of the illness. A true healer will never even see the sickness of his clients. The clients's problem is their own, and the healer does not even know that the problem exists. If the client has no complaint, the healer has nothing left to do. It is only when a client believes that he is ill that the healer can help to free him of his false beliefs. However, the moment the healer honors his client's beliefs as real, then in that moment both become bound by illusions.

The Sutras on Healing and Enlightenment

-5:7-
A true healer must be healed himself.

-5:8-
In true healing both the healer and the client are healed simultaneously.

If a healer attempts to work on a client and still is under the illusion of being a separate self, then he will project that on to his client and will only support the client's illusions as well. The more established in Reality the healer is, the more he can easily free his client of his own illusions. A healer must constantly work to heal himself and must understand that in true healing both the healer and the client are healed simultaneously. When a client's negative beliefs are removed, then such beliefs are also removed from the healer. Even though the healer may not invest much energy in his client's beliefs, he still is healed when his client is healed, even if only to a small degree.

-5:9-
The one being healed is referred to as a client because they must offer some form of compensation for the healing that is being done.

-5:10-
Compensation need not be monetary, but there must be some form of giving and receiving, no matter how small.

Any sacred relationship is based on a mutual giving and receiving, and healing is the most sacred relationship that exists. The healer is a healer because he is empowered

The Sutras on Healing and Enlightenment

with Truth to assist his client in coming to know the Truth. The client is a client. He is not a patient, because the doctor-patient relationship has proven to be one of separation and disempowerment. A client is someone who simply comes asking for help, but the healer sees the client only as God. Because he cannot call his client God, he calls him a client. Because the client must offer some form of exchange for the healing, he is called a client. The healer who makes healing his sole profession is entitled to a healthy monetary income like anyone else. What he offers is more valuable than perhaps any other vocation, and his client should pay him well. However, no one should ever be turned down for lack of money, yet there must be some form of compensation to show that the client does indeed value the healer's time and expertise.

A client is never brought to a healer by accident. The relationship is formed because of the intention of both parties to be free of suffering and to come into a Space of Truth together. Thus, the healer should never turn down a client for any reason, but should trust in God to manage his client load and to remove those people who will not be suitable clients. If a client is difficult for the healer, the relationship is meant to heal not only the client but the healer as well. The healer, usually the more conscious force, should be able to use the relationship for his growth as well as his client's. The more evolved the healer becomes, the less he feels himself to be the doer and the more he finds himself surrendered to God. When this occurs, he trusts completely in the Divine and knows that whoever comes through his door was brought there by God and is none other than God. Therefore, all clients are treated as God, for in Truth they truly are.

The Sutras on Healing and Enlightenment

-5:11-
In true healing the healer must see the client as already healed.

When a healer meets his client, he cannot believe in his client's illusions. The client is already healed, because the client is always God. There is no division in the true healer's mind and therefore what he sees is only the Consciousness that he is. Consciousness is never sick, never out of Harmony and never suffers from birth or death. In Truth there is only One Love, One Light and One Peace, and that Peace is only Divine Perfection. The moment the healer comes to realize this Truth, at that moment both he and his client are truly healed. However, because the realization of Truth does not change the Truth, then regardless of the healer's or the client's perceptions, the client is already healed whether he knows it or not. It is the healer's role to simply show the client who he always is, and in that knowledge, for the client to realize that there has never been anything wrong with him.

-5:12-
In true healing the healer must know that the client is not and can never be sick.

The concept in this and the previous sutra cannot be stressed enough. True healing involves only the healer getting out of the way and allowing for the Divine to do its perfect work. There is no formula for healing in Truth, because healing is of God and God is not a formula. The healer cannot conceptualize God or the healing process, because God is not a concept that can be labeled or

The Sutras on Healing and Enlightenment

defined. Because in Truth the client is God, he can never be sick. The healer must know this and not buy into his client's concepts of sickness, suffering and death. The healer who has become Whole himself will never believe in anything but the Infinite Goodness of God. To see anything but Perfection is to see illusion from a mind filled with ignorance. When a true healer sees his client with the eyes of Enlightened Love, he cannot see anything but God. A client will come to the healer after healing has occurred and ask if the healer has noticed a change in him. A true healer could only reply, "No, you were God when you walked in and you are God as you walk out." The true healer cannot possibly see anything wrong with the client in the beginning of therapy, because there is nothing wrong with a Perfect Child of God. They are perfect before and after therapy. Ideally after therapy they know this fact as well.

-5:13-
The true healer must see illness only as a fleeting mirage.

As we can remember from earlier sutras, the physical world is not as it appears. It is an apparent reality whose essence is nothing but Light and Consciousness. To the five senses, it appears to be solid and real, but in Truth it is nothing but empty space. Therefore, all matter is nothing but a fleeting mirage that is neither here today nor gone tomorrow. Consciousness is All That Is, and manifest forms do not exist. Therefore, sickness does not exist. In the dream of the manifest world, nothing is as it appears, and nothing is real or eternal. Anything in the dream can change and must change. Only the Divine remains forever the same. When the healer knows

The Sutras on Healing and Enlightenment

this to the depth of his being, he is empowered to dispel illness because he knows that illness cannot possibly exist in God.

-5:14-
The healer should know that he is absolutely one with his client, even if the client does not.

Nothing can ever be expected of a client. A client only comes to the healer because of his state of ignorance and illusion. Clients are not expected to be anything but what they are and should be honored with love, respect, compassion and kindness. The healer is not superior nor inferior to his client. Being one with his client, the healer must know that he and his client are the same One Being.

All true healing must be rooted in Spirit or it is not true healing. The healer who himself is deeply rooted in Spirit knows of his Eternal Oneness with All That Is. He could not possibly imagine himself as a separate entity from his client and must always know that there is only one Reality. When the healer knows who he is, then he knows who his client is. Because the healer must know that he is God, he also knows that his client is God. Because there is no sickness, error or illusion in God, there can be no sickness, error or illusion in the client. The client will manifest an apparent reality of disharmony, but the healer is never to believe that this has any basis in Reality.

-5:15-
The client must come to the healer asking for help; the healer should never try to convince a client to begin therapy.

The Sutras on Healing and Enlightenment

True healing is instigated by the will of the client who has come to a place where he has suffered enough and is willing to change. Without this willingness to change, healing cannot occur. God Himself never goes against the will of His Child, and therefore how can the healer? All Children of God have the free will to create their own realities. If they are pleased with their creations or find them useful or valuable, they are not going to be willing to let them go. No one can go against this, because God Himself does not go against this. A person is free to create whatever he wants for as long as he wants. When his creations no longer serve him and are causing suffering, he can choose to let his creations go.

A person who has suffered enough with a willingness to change is ready for healing. True healing is of God and does not require a therapeutic relationship per se, but sometimes a person is led to a healer through God to facilitate the healing process. If the healer is rooted in Truth, there is no separation between God, the healer, the methods used and the client himself. However, if the so-called healer is acting as a doer and using techniques that merely remove symptoms, he is not a healer at all but only a manipulator of matter. Any monkey can manipulate matter, but only the true healer, who is united with God, can facilitate true healing. Thus, the true healer would never convince a client to do therapy, because he knows how sacred the healing relationship is.

Since the true healer is not a doer, he would not make efforts to solicit clients or encourage them to return to his office. He trusts completely in the Love of God for his well-being and for the well-being of every other Child of God. The healer acts through effortless action and only lets energies come to him. He never goes out to energies.

The Sutras on Healing and Enlightenment

-5:16-
The healer must evaluate whether or not his client meets certain criteria or healing cannot occur.

Although certain criteria must be met before healing can occur, the healer should not be too concerned with criteria, because anyone who comes for healing must be accepted openly. The healer is not a doer and does not decide who will be healed and who will not. A healing relationship is a sacred relationship, and both the healer and the client are made whole in the process. If a healer dismisses a client for any reason, healing cannot occur. If the relationship is meant to end, God will end it. The client will simply stop coming if it is not harmonious for him to come. The healer does not need to be concerned about who is healed, but simply trusts in God.

However, the healer must be aware of what is necessary for a client to make progress in his therapy. The healer should not dismiss a client if he does not meet these criteria, but can help to point out to the client what he needs to be able to heal. Perhaps the healing will simply be that the client realizes that he is not willing to change or that he still wants his problem and is not suffering enough to be willing to let it go. Even if such a client did not work with the healer, the healer still understands the perfection of the relationship—no matter how short-lived—and knows that service was rendered perfectly as it needed to be.

The following sutras deal with the nature of these criteria and how the healer can work with them to best help his client. These criteria are not the basis for accepting or rejecting clients, because this is not the healer's role. Rather, the criteria are useful means to help the client make the most out of his time with the healer.

The Sutras on Healing and Enlightenment

-5:17-

However, if the majority of the criteria are met, then the healer can help to nourish the criteria lacking in his client.

If most criteria are not met, the healer need not worry, because this client will not last long in therapy. However, if the client has what it takes to make it through the healing process, success will be easy. Yet, no client meets all the necessary criteria or he would not be a client. Clients come for healing because they are suffering and cannot be expected to be in the perfect state of mind for healing to occur. They are afraid of opening up. They are afraid of change. They still think their problems are necessary to some degree, so they value their problems and are not willing to let them go. They are not willing to accept being fully whole. They feel they deserve their problems and should be punished by them. The list is enormous and goes on and on, but the wise healer can discern where his client is not meeting the necessary criteria for healing and can help to nourish those qualities in his client.

Many criteria are necessary for healing to occur, and no list can exhaust this topic. An experienced healer knows intuitively what it takes for a client to transform, and he trusts in God during the healing process to point this out. During healing, the healer learns to listen very well and knows that his client will tell him everything he needs to know. When the mind of the healer is out of the way and he is not pretending to be the doer, whatever the client needs to hear to help prepare him for therapy will be heard.

The Sutras on Healing and Enlightenment

-5:18-
Not only must the client meet the criteria, but the healer as well.

The healer is not separate from his client. He must understand that anything that he asks of his client, he too must be willing to live up to. If the client must meet basic criteria for healing, the healer must have already met those criteria. He cannot ask his client to open his heart if he is not willing to do so himself. He cannot ask a client to release self-sabotaging behaviors if he still clings to his own. If the healer is in Truth, he will meet these criteria without any effort on his part. The healer knows that Truth is the only healer. If he is in Truth, he can rest assured that he meets the requirements for facilitating the healing process. Humility is all that is required on the part of the healer to ensure that he will continue to meet the needs of his clients.

-5:19-
The client and the healer must both have a willingness to heal.

The sutras now discuss the necessary criteria for healing. The healer and the client are both addressed, because the sutras are written primarily for the healer and not the client. The word *they* is used when saying who must meet these criteria, because they both must, or healing cannot occur.

The most important point is that they both must have the willingness to heal. If the client, and of course the healer, are not willing to change, then nothing can change them. You can never go against another person's will. If they refuse to change, that must be allowed. The

The Sutras on Healing and Enlightenment

healer can point out this fact to his client. The healer can make sure that they both understand that healing is up to them and that it is fine if they are not willing to make these changes. Healing will have occurred even if the interaction only helped the client to acknowledge that he is not willing to heal. The healer can trust that his role may have only been to point out this key factor to his client. Even if formal therapy never begins, if the client realizes that he needs a willingness to change, healing has occurred.

-5:20-
They have to be ready to let go of their suffering.

If a suffering person finds value in his suffering, it will be difficult for him to heal, because he wants to keep what he wants to be free of. A person who is punishing himself through guilt comes to the healer to be free of the symptoms of guilt. If he will not stop punishing himself, he is caught in a very thick illusion. The client must be made to see the absurdity of wanting to be free of pain and yet still holding on to what is causing the pain. When someone has suffered enough, he will be willing to change. The healer can actually amplify his client's symptoms—if that seems appropriate and safe—to show his client how harmful his actions toward himself are. When he comes to see that his symptoms and their cause do not serve him any more, he will easily let the symptoms go.

The Sutras on Healing and Enlightenment

-5:21-
They must believe they can heal.

Both healer and client must believe that healing can occur. It seriously hinders the therapeutic process if either client or healer doubts the ability of the client to heal. Remember that healing is simply the movement from illusion to Truth. The healer must know that anyone can heal—no matter how serious the disharmony appears. Healing is not based on degrees of difficulty. The shift into Truth is possible for anyone, because if a Child of God could not be healed, that Soul could never know itself as the Divine Truth again. Every Child of God who feels separate from God will eventually wake up to the Truth of who he is again. The healer must remember this and never believe that his client cannot return to his Divine origins.

When the client comes seeking help, it does not matter on which level he wants to change, because the healer knows that true change only occurs on the mental level. The healer must believe that change can occur because he understands the Divine Truth of his client. The client must be convinced that he can heal, and he should be helped to know what true healing is. The more he can believe that healing can occur, the better.

-5:22-
They must believe that the healer can heal them.

If the client doubts the healer's abilities, or if the healer doubts his own abilities, then healing will be seriously limited. It is actually more important that the healer believes in his abilities than the client. The healer's confidence will always assist tremendously in building up the client's faith. The true healer who understands true healing knows that through God all things are possible and that anyone can be healed. The healer should always maintain an honest attitude about what healing entails, but he should also have a very confident, "Yes, I can" attitude. If there is doubt, then there is a lack of faith. Faith in the healing power of God is a must in true healing. The client may not understand or believe in God and most likely will put his trust in the healer, and this is fine. However, the healer must know that God is the real healer and that he is not separate from God.

-5:23-
It is very helpful for them to believe in God and to have a strong spiritual viewpoint; otherwise, a desire for discovering the Truth is imperative.

The more evolved the healer is, the more he will experience his Oneness with the Divine Truth. He does not have to call this God and does not need to believe in some personal deity, but he must honor that there is Truth and that Truth is the only healer that there is.

As far as the client is concerned, he does not need to believe in God at all; however, the stronger his belief is and the more faith he has, the better. Because disharmony arises from false beliefs, the client must have a desire to know the Truth, or he will not become free. If a client clings to his false identity, beliefs, guilt and anger, then he will not heal. When a client is willing to let go of his illusions, he comes to Truth. It does not matter what he calls this, but in the end it will be his salvation.

The Sutras on Healing and Enlightenment

A strong spiritual viewpoint is very helpful for both healer and client because understanding, love, forgiveness, compassion and surrender can facilitate a very powerful healing session. The more evolved the healer and client are on the path of love, the more powerful the healing sessions can be. However, because healing is simply a movement into Truth, some of the most powerful healing actually happens for the most ignorant of clients. Those who have been most deeply caught up in illusion who become free of their symptoms and sufferings, by discovering their Divine Self may have profound breakthroughs. When a room is very dark, it does not take much light to notice a huge difference. However, when a room is very bright already, it takes a lot of light to notice the difference.

-5:24-
They must want to heal and to be healed.

The healer must want his client to be healed and should have no ulterior motive for the client to remain ill. Doctors and psychologists make fortunes on keeping people sick. Their exceptionally strong belief in illness only creates more illness, and their desire to make money from sickness perpetuates it even more. A healer must work to bring clients to their goals in the shortest time possible. This not only should be his ethical agenda, but he must not believe that it takes time for healing to occur. He must want his client to be free in the shortest time possible.

However, the client must be willing to do whatever it takes to be healed—no matter how long it takes. When the healer works to make healing occur quickly and the client is patient, then healing works very well. If deep down the client does not want to heal, he will sabotage his healing. Many people do not want to be healed. They believe that their problems actually serve them. They should be helped to see that they are suffering enough and want to get rid of their problems. Sometimes the healer needs to amplify their symptoms to get the client to see the need to want to heal. Of course, this is done only when it seems safe and appropriate.

-5:25-
They must be willing to accept being healed and the responsibility of being Whole.

The client comes to the healer believing that there is something wrong with him, yet the healer must know that the client is always perfect as he was created. The client is already whole in the healer's eyes. He was God when he walked in, and he is God when he walks out. The client therefore has been living in an illusion that there is something wrong with him. He has become accustomed to living with this sense of lack and limitation. It will be a whole new world for him to live out of his Divine Truth. Therefore, the healer must assess if the client is willing to accept the responsibility that comes with being free.

The state of Divine Freedom is every Child of God's inherent birthright. There is no lack in God. There is no suffering in God. In Truth there is no real responsibility in God, because this is God's Universe and no one individual is responsible for it. However, the client may feel that he is a separate doer who will have to live differently when he is healed. If he is not willing to accept being complete, he is not ready for the therapeutic process.

The Sutras on Healing and Enlightenment

A client comes in feeling depressed. He wants to be free of his symptoms of sadness, fatigue, gloom and misery; but he does not want to let go of the supposed benefits that he derives from believing that he has these problems. This is called a secondary gain, or a negative payoff. In secondary gains, a Child of God pretends to be something he is not and actually believes his illusions serve him. By being depressed, the client may avoid his supposed responsibility of having to: go to work, shop for himself, shower, get dressed, make love, take care of the kids or other things he may wish to avoid.

All suffering is self-created, and no Child of God invests power in anything unless he believes that it will serve him. The healer must help the client to see that he has suffered enough and that his problem is not beneficial in any way. Once the client is willing to let go of his issues and is willing to take responsibility for being Whole, healing occurs very easily.

-5:26-
They should be made to expect that healing will occur and that it already exists in Truth.

Both client and healer must expect that what they are about to enter into will be successful. What a person expects tends to be realized. The healer's confidence is therefore essential and must be imparted to his client. The healer's confidence comes from knowing that his client is already healed, for a Child of God is never incomplete. The healer only sees the final result of the healing process in his client because he knows that the final result already exists. The final result is Love, Truth and Bliss. There is nothing but Love, Truth and Bliss; and the healer should know that his client already is that. The client simply does not believe or know this Truth, and that is why he is a client. Because the healer never sees his client as sick, his client can truly experience himself as whole. The healer's point of view imparts an enormous amount of positive expectation in his client that healing is inevitable.

-5:27-
They both must be committed to the healing process.

If either healer or client is unwilling to do what must be done to heal, healing simply does not occur. Commitment says that healing is a process and that the process must continue to its very end. This requires that neither healer nor client stop the process when things become difficult. The client must be made to feel that his own personal well-being is the highest priority in his life and that he should do whatever it takes to become whole. The healer should always evaluate how committed his client is to the process. When taking on a new client, the healer should seriously reinforce this very important quality in him.

-5:28-
They must both surrender the outcome of the healing work to God and be non-attached.

If the ego of the healer or client gets in the way of therapy, the Divine does not come fully through. If either healer or client brings in a rigid goal of how the healing process should unfold, they limit the process tremendously. Unnecessary stress comes about when either party is attached to a certain result. When the

The Sutras on Healing and Enlightenment

healer knows that the client is already healed and that everything is in Divine Order, he easily surrenders the outcome to God. Healing is only of the mind, and the physical body may not change much through the healing process. The healer should understand what true healing is and not be attached to how that healing will manifest through the order of manifestation. When there is attachment to the outcome, there will be suffering in the end. In non-attachment and surrender, the Divine Mind can do its perfect work, and the outcome will always be for the greatest good.

-5:29-
The healer should work within the client's model of reality, while always holding the Space of Truth.

How much the healer should impart his view of Reality to his client is a very delicate matter. There are two major ways of working with a client that deal with the issue of models of Reality. In one case, the healer never ever compromises his knowledge of Truth and never buys into his client's illusions. This must happen no matter what, but in this first instance, the healer only speaks the highest Truths and trusts in the Divine Wisdom of his client to grasp what is being said. The client may not understand the words that are being used in this way of being; but his Soul will know, and he will feel comfortable. By never leaving the top of the mountain, the healer pulls his client to the pinnacle of Truth. Illusions are brought to the Truth, but Truth is not brought to illusions.

The second way of being is to meet the client totally in his reality and to speak only at a level that he can understand using only his model. This is an art that

The Sutras on Healing and Enlightenment

requires a deep rapport with the client as well as the ability to not forget Truth while diving into illusions. Here the healer remembers what the top of the mountain is while going down into his client's illusions. Once he climbs down, he then leads his client back up one step at a time.

Of these two ways, the first is by far the best for the healer and the client. When the healer never leaves the Truth, he becomes an exceptional healing force which tends to attract only those who are ready to join in at the top. When he leaves the top and begins to vibrate at a lower level of reality, he may work better with the masses, but he will not affect the truest sense of healing. There is never any reason to compromise the Truth, but the healer should also know how to dance with his client's model of reality without losing rapport.

The healer works in his client's model but never leaves the top of the mountain. This is done through compassion and understanding, but also with a firm sense of never believing in illusions.

-5:30-
To a great extent, the healer must be freed from false beliefs or he will not be able to free his client from such beliefs.

A healer who is still caught in the realm of illusion cannot be called a healer at all. The sutras clearly begin by showing that healing and enlightenment are synonymous terms. Therefore, we could say that an enlightener who is still caught in the realm of illusion cannot be called an enlightener at all. How can one who does not know who he truly is lead another to the knowledge of his True Self. The healer need not be completely enlightened; however,

The Sutras on Healing and Enlightenment

the greater the degree of his Self-Realization, the greater his capacity to be of service.

False beliefs are what separate the human being from his Divinity. These beliefs, if unquestioned, simply are the statement of who the person is. Yet when a person begins to heal, he is led to question his assumptions about who he is. He comes to know that he is limiting himself through illusions and that these illusions based on ignorance are the cause of all suffering. The healer who is free from these false beliefs can easily see where his client is caught. Those who know the Truth never buy into the lies of those who do not. A healer who is empowered with Truth is truly an exceptional force on this earth.

-5:31-
A healer's modalities and credentials are entirely secondary to his degree of enlightenment.

A healer is one who promotes healing. He can be anyone and need not have any training at all. Healing occurs through Truth, and Truth is not something that can be taught. Truth is who and what we are, and the healer who knows himself as Truth has not gained this knowledge intellectually in a university. The knowledge of the Self can never be book knowledge. Those who only know of Truth through books and classes can never claim to be enlightened to the Truth. If a person has not completely gone through the fires of Divine Transformation, then he is still holding false beliefs about himself. Such a being can never be a true healer until he has become thoroughly cooked.

Many people spend years and years in medical schools and still have no real healing power at all at their disposal. Modern psychotherapists and psychiatrists

The Sutras on Healing and Enlightenment

can have many degrees, but without the knowledge of Truth, then they are not true healers. Many doctors and psychologists are not healed themselves. They live in an illusion where sickness is real and God is a theory to be studied or rejected. Their modalities are human constructs and only manipulate matter or mind, but never bring about the enlightenment of mankind. Some healing can work its way into their interactions with others because the Divine is present in all relationships, but they themselves are not truly facilitating healing if they are not healed themselves.

The healer's modalities are only deeply attuned to the ways of God. These modalities may differ from healer to healer and their range of application can be vast. But in the end, it is only Truth that is working through the healer, and the modalities are entirely secondary. God is the healer, because Truth is what sets a person free. A lever may be used to shift a boulder, but gravity sends it rolling down the hill. Training in the use of levers becomes less and less important to the healer who simply understands how gravity works and operates in harmony with natural law. Said another way, the healer who can simply get out of the way and let the Divine Law of Love enter his relationships becomes a very powerful force that heals by doing nothing at all.

-5:32-
A healer is to be used by Truth to free a client from illusions, and therefore the healer must be a clear channel for Truth to come through.

If we could look into the mind of the healer we would simply see a clear mirror. We would not see a

The Sutras on Healing and Enlightenment

clever intellect and ego who is doing anything at all. The mind of the healer is free. It is not filled with the false beliefs of mankind, and it is not full of the belief in being the doer. The healer is in Truth because he is empty of the notion of being a separate self. He is One with All That Is and knows himself as the Whole. This knowledge is not intellectual, but his very own True Nature, which he lives and loves. Empowered with the force of Truth, the healer cuts through illusions with the double-edged sword of knowledge and compassion.

It is easy for an enlightened healer to work with his client because he is free. He is free to be what the moment needs. Being one with Love, his actions are spontaneous and wise. His words, which are only words of Truth, therefore do not allow for illusions to remain. Being a clear channel, he exhibits a power unlike physicians, psychologists and others who remove symptoms. The healer goes right to the root of suffering, because he knows that only the ignorance of Truth can be its cause. As a clear channel, the healer is simply God in action. The clearer the healer is, the more Divine Power can come through.

-5:33-
A healer must know that healing does not take time because false beliefs can be transformed in an instant.

There is a false belief in the world that healing is a process that takes time. This belief exists because symptom removal has become synonymous with healing. In fact, healing and symptom removal are two very different things. A person suffers when he believes himself to be a separate self and lives out of this illusion. The belief in being a separate self is just that—a belief. When a person believes himself to be his body, mind and emotions, then he holds many false beliefs in his mind. A false belief is a thought, and only one thought can be held at a time in the mind. When the mind releases one thought, another comes in. Therefore, when the mind releases a false thought, then the Truth can come in. A false belief can be instantly released, and the suffering that this belief causes can easily fall away. Symptoms can sometimes take time to transform, because symptoms exist in the world of manifested form, but healing is instantaneous. A person may spend years and years working for enlightenment, but enlightenment itself happens in an instant.

The more the healer is empowered with the Truth of this sutra, the less he will rely on techniques that rely on time. Time is an illusion that God does not buy into. Truth transcends time and is ever-present. There is no illusion in Truth; therefore, there is no time in Truth. The healer has transcended time and space and has come to know that matter is an illusion sustained by mind. Mind can change instantly, and therefore so can matter. Often it appears that symptoms are taking time to transform, but usually this is because healing is taking time. Healing does not need to take time, but because the healer and the client are often working out their illusions together, then it does take time. When a healer is exceptionally free and his client is very ready and willing to change, healing can be instantaneous and symptoms can fall away in their first meeting together.

The average person is filled with negative beliefs, and it is a lifetime process to remove them and to wake up to the Truth. Healing is a shift from ignorance to Truth, but this must happen countless numbers of times until

The Sutras on Healing and Enlightenment

a person is truly free. There can be a dozen or more false beliefs sustaining a symptom, and all of those beliefs must be removed for the symptom to totally fall away. This only takes time because in the client's illusion it took time to create and so it takes time to unravel. However, to the degree that the healer is truly free, healing can occur exceptionally rapidly.

-5:34-
Physical symptoms may take time to change because they are in the realm of time.

This sutra should be carefully read because it states that physical symptoms may take time to heal, but it does not say that physical symptoms always will take time to heal. The order of manifestation is exact. Nothing manifests by chance, and nothing changes by chance. There is a mathematical exactitude behind all manifested existence and a perfect geometrical order to all things. When disease manifests, there is a cause behind its appearance. The false beliefs, negative emotions and suppressions all lead to the arrival of the symptoms that best reflect their cause. When the cause is removed, the symptom is also removed. This takes time only because the order of manifestation becomes more and more based on time because its planes become more and more dense.

On the mental plane where true healing occurs, change happens instantly; therefore, true healing does not take time in the deepest sense of the word. However, often it takes a long period of time to get a client to open up and to let go. Healing is a process because people are far too afraid and conditioned to be able to fully open up and release all error during one meeting with a healer.

The Sutras on Healing and Enlightenment

The process can be slow and requires patience. Getting the body to respond to the mental changes can be an even slower process. However, these statements only exist in the realm of possibility. Again, the word *may* comes in. It may take time, but it may not.

Miraculous healings occur all the time. When these spontaneous and instant healings occur, it is not that the healer has gone against the laws of nature. The laws of nature are laws of illusion, whereas Divine Law is Eternal and always based on Truth. The healer does not go against God's Laws but helps to fulfill them. Harmony and balance are laws of God. A Child of God can appear to get out of balance, but Truth will always bring him back into balance. When a healer assists in this process and allows a miracle to occur, he has simply brought the deluded mind back into Truth and allowed for that mental shift to manifest itself physically as health. A miracle is not a violation of God's Laws; it is God's Laws fulfilled.

When the healer understands this, he simply knows that the more he gets out of the way, the more he can work miracles. Physical healing does not need to take time, but there is really no such thing as physical healing. All healing is mental healing, which is not bound by time. Miracles are therefore not bound by time. Divine Law, which is not bound by time, governs the order of manifestation. Profound cases of rapid physical healing, which are brought about by the Divine Mind alone, occur all of the time. In fact, all healing is of the Divine Mind, and healing is happening at each and every single moment. God is always bringing His Children back into balance and working with them to remind them of who they truly are. God's Law of Adjustment is Eternal and always there for His Children.

The Sutras on Healing and Enlightenment

-5:35-
Once the cause of a symptom is removed, the symptom has no more power and cannot last long.

When the cause of a thing is removed, that thing cannot last long. When a balloon is floating due to the helium inside, its lift depends on how long the helium lasts. When the cause—which is helium—runs out, the upward lift ceases to occur. The balloon itself has no power of its own to move and to rise. In the same way, when an illness is manifesting, if the healer removes the cause, then the illness will soon fall away. Matter is not a cause. When iron fillings are sprinkled around a magnet, they form the shape of the magnet's lines of force. The fillings have no will or intelligence of their own. The force that organizes them into specific patterns is necessary for them to have any sense of order at all. Without this cause, the fillings eventually fall away.

The lines of force of the human aura are perfectly geometrical, and the iron fillings of the sparks of creation that form the body have no will of their own. The sparks of creation form a perfectly healthy and lovely body when the underlying energetic fields are balanced and aligned. When this alignment goes out of balance, then the sparks of creation are also out of balance. When the energies of the human aura are aligned and flowing, the body remains healthy. We should remember, however, that healing is not about manipulating these lines of force, energy fields or sparks of creation as manifested as the physical body. The mind is what misaligns energy fields, and it is the mind that must be healed.

When the mind is healed, which is to say when the mind is aligned once again with Truth, then the order of manifestation automatically adjusts itself back into Divine Order. The physical disharmony is removed, because the underlying grids that held the disharmony in place are allowed to balance themselves out naturally based on the geometry of Truth. When the healer understands Truth, its order of manifestation and its perfect geometry, he is incredibly empowered to remove causes and relieve symptoms. However, the healer understands that he is not a doer and that when causes are removed through Truth, symptoms fall away on their own. God is the healer, not man.

-5:36-
True healing can occur regardless of a change in physical symptoms.

The sutras stress again that mind is the only thing that needs to be healed and that once mental healing has occurred, physical healing is largely irrelevant. Sometimes the physical body is no longer useful for the Soul in its continued interactions with time and space, but the body itself helps the Soul to look at its denials while it is still functioning. A person on his deathbed can experience such a profound healing where peace, love and openness are finally allowed in. Even if the person's entire life was spent being closed down and living with fear, anger and separation and even if his body is totally wasted on his deathbed, as long as this person opens up and learns to forgive and love, then healing can be said to have occurred.

Physical symptoms do not define who the Soul is. The Soul is always perfect, whole and complete. False beliefs would tell it otherwise, but the Truth is simply not that

The Sutras on Healing and Enlightenment

fragile. When illusions are replaced with Truth, healing occurs. The Soul is eternally free and will know this freedom only through true healing. This is the goal—not a change in the body. The body will eventually end and often that occurs because the subtle fields that sustain it are pulling away. When Consciousness stops placing its attention on something, then that something will not remain long. When the body no longer serves the Soul, then the Soul will pull its energy away from this dense vehicle. When this happens, the body will begin to decay. This is perfect and natural. It is during this time that the healer should be sure that mental healing is occurring, and little attention should be given to trying to remove symptoms. Of course, pain can be alleviated in any way that it can, but a true healer is more concerned with the liberation of the Soul rather than the simple removal of disease. One way or another, the body will suffer from entropy the moment Consciousness begins pulling away from it. What happens to the body at this point has nothing to do with healing, and the healer should focus most of his attention on mind and not body.

    It is not important for the healer to discern whether the body should remain alive or not. His mission is always the same: to bring the client back to Truth and let the order of manifestation take care of itself. Symptoms fall away when they do. The physical body is a symptom. When it falls away, that is perfectly fine and a welcome relief for the Soul.

-5:37-
True healing is only true if both the healer and the healed know themselves as Self in the end.

The Sutras on Healing and Enlightenment

True healing is only true when the Self is known, but if healer or client is lacking this knowledge, then healing simply has not occurred. It is impossible for healing to be complete if the client ends up knowing who he is, but the healer does not. Healing is mutual and is only real if both healer and client end up in a place of unity. If there is separation between healer and client, then healing is not complete. If the client knows that he is eternal and immortal through the healing process but the healer still feels separate, isolated, alone and identified with his mortal frame, then healing has not fully occurred. Both the healer and the client are rejuvenated in true healing. They are both made whole when they realize their unity in God.

When both healer and client discover themselves in One Light, One Truth and One Love, then healing is real. This is a sacred moment when a client who was in illusion is brought to Truth. At the end of such a session, when the healer and the client have eye contact, then God is truly looking at God. The healer ideally was looking at God the moment he walked into his office, but the client himself did not know who he really was. Through the healing process, the client is made aware of his True Nature and is set free. In that freedom, both parties are made whole. Healing occurs for the healer as well as the client. The glory of the process cannot ever be put into words, because when one Child of God assists another Child of God in knowing God, the entire purpose of creation has been fulfilled in this most sacred of relationships. This, without a doubt, is true healing as it occurs in the most holy of relationships.

The Sutras on Healing and Enlightenment

Chapter Six—Understanding Illness

-6:1-
The body communicates to the mind the mind's denials of the Self.

Sutra 1 of Chapter Six is a profound statement that begins an in-depth look into the nature of illness. The body is truly put into its proper place here in this sutra where we come to see that the body is always communicating to the mind in a way that is perfect in helping the mind to wake up to its Divine origins. When the mind holds a false belief, this becomes a negative emotion. These beliefs and emotions, when suppressed, block the energy fields of the more subtle bodies that create and sustain the physical body. The immense importance of the physical body in this process is that the mind can get by with suppression, but when disease manifests because of suppression, it is forced to address its denials.

Many of the world's great wisdom traditions say that only a human being can come to know God. Animals do not have the capacity or level of Consciousness, and angels are simply too much in bliss to acknowledge that they are still not fully realized. In the human incarnation the Soul gets to deal fully with its denials of who it really is. All false beliefs are a denial of the Truth of the Self. Without a body, these beliefs are not that painful for the Soul—not pleasant but not bad enough to force change. Negative emotions as well are not necessarily bad enough to cause a profound transformation in the psyche. Yet when these disturbed energies are causing cancer, arthritis, migraines or asthma, then the psyche is forced through the body's communications to look at its illusions. The belief that

The Sutras on Healing and Enlightenment

one is his body and that he could suffer and die from illness is a huge wake-up call. There is no accident in God's creation. The human body is therefore incredibly valuable as a means of communicating to the mind where it has gone astray. The body is also the perfect platform for the Soul to fully come to know who it is, because the body itself is designed to make enlightenment possible. The human body is a geometrically perfect vehicle for Self-Realization; therefore, the human incarnation is incredibly blessed and should never be denied or underestimated.

-6:2-
The body is a metaphor for the beliefs and emotional patterns of the mind.

A metaphor is a linguistic term for the use of a word or a phrase that ordinarily designates one thing but is used to designate another. "To flower into joy" uses the word *flower* to designate an opening or a blossoming. "Flower" is usually a noun referring to a specific thing. The word communicates more to us than what we ordinarily associate with it. A metaphor then has many meanings and levels of understanding. Just as the word *flower* communicates so much more to us, so too does the body, as a metaphor, communicate so much more than most people ordinarily perceive.

Deeply listening to the body reveals an enormous amount of information about the psyche that inhabits it. Nothing manifests by accident, because there are no accidents. No matter what is happening in the body, the healer can listen carefully and gain exceptionally relevant information about the beliefs and emotions underlying

The Sutras on Healing and Enlightenment

the physical manifestations. Each chakra has a specific body part that can be affected when it is out of balance. Each organ or organ system can be affected by certain emotions. Meridians can get blocked based on certain psychological patterns. Sensations in the body can reveal so much to one who learns to listen.

Imagine a person who comes to the healer with a right arm that cannot move well. The arm is swollen, and the elbow is in pain. The client complains that the elbow feels blocked, limited, hurt and hot. She suffers from arthritis in her hands and feet, and her knees also hurt. She feels helpless in her situation and is very scared. The body is manifesting major issues in the hands and feet, which are associated with the first chakra representing issues around security. The elbows and knees represent issues associated with the fourth chakra, dealing with issues of love. The right side of the body is usually associated with masculine energy in most systems of thought. Now if you asked this person if she felt insecure and lacking in love as a child and helpless to get that love, most likely from her father, which caused her a lot of fear and a closing down of her heart, you would most likely get a resounding "Yes."

If the healer comes to understand the body as a metaphor for the mind's denials, then he is exceptionally empowered to help his client find the root cause of illness. The body is used to trace the order of manifestation back to its mental origins of disease. The body exists because of the etheric body, which deals with the feelings of the body. The etheric body exists because of the astral body, which deals with emotions. The astral body exists because of the mental body, which deals with thoughts and false beliefs. Nothing exists in the body that does not have its origins in the mind. The body is a metaphor for what is

The Sutras on Healing and Enlightenment

held in the mind. The healer must know that this is true in all cases. He should never be convinced otherwise, no matter what the client may say.

-6:3-
The body is a three-dimensional reflection of one's thinking.

Thoughts are not three-dimensional, and neither are emotions. Thoughts and emotions cannot be seen, but they do manifest physically through the order of manifestation. Therefore, the physical body is simply the three-dimensional reflection of one's thoughts and emotions. Sickness is a three-dimensional image of a thought. Imbalances in the body are imbalances in the mind. There can be no exceptions to this rule, because mind is the creator of matter. Things are thoughts, and there are no exceptions to this. If there were exceptions, some parts of matter would be their own creator, but this is not the case. Matter is not its originator, but mind is. Again, nothing manifests physically that does not already exist on the more subtle levels.

We should understand, however, that when Consciousness places its awareness on something, then that something is given power. When negative beliefs and emotions are given power, they manifest physically, and the body becomes the reflection of these energies. This is perfect, because it communicates very loudly to the mind its own errors. However, when Consciousness has had enough of using its physical body, it begins to withdraw its power from it. The body then begins to suffer from entropy and begins to decay back into the ground. At this time, blocked sanskars can manifest very powerfully, and profound healing can occur; yet we must understand

The Sutras on Healing and Enlightenment

that the body is being dropped and that symptom relief is not our aim. Sanskars that appear physically in the three-dimensional world are exposed and can be seen and dealt with.

If the mind has evolved sufficiently to understand the power of listening to communications from its vehicles, then it can respond before the whispers become shouts. A false belief hurts, but not always enough to act. A negative emotion arises from a false belief, but this is also not bad enough to act. The etheric body begins to manifest feelings of discomfort, but this also is usually not enough. Eventually the physical body manifests some symptom, which arises from the imbalance in the etheric template. This also is usually not enough. It is only when the symptom is very strong that it gets the attention of the mind. The more evolved the being is, the sooner he can catch this process and reverse it.

Here is an example of how this works. A person believes that he is not good enough, which is a false belief existing on the mental level. This belief becomes the emotion of fear on the astral level. This emotion of fear becomes constriction on the etheric plane, which is felt as a dull ache in the solar plexus. The chakra being affected is the third chakra because the belief is associated with personal power. Now the person holds this belief for decades and suppresses the feelings when they come up because they are uncomfortable. He lives out his belief that he is not good enough and always lives and acts from fear. In time the ache in the solar plexus begins to become irritable bowel syndrome. This too is ignored or suppressed with allopathic medicines, and the beliefs only become stronger. He feels more and more that he is not good enough to heal himself and feels more and

The Sutras on Healing and Enlightenment

more powerless. Now the irritable bowel syndrome turns to ulcerative colitis. He still does not get the message, and then this turns to cancer. The communications simply keep getting louder and louder until we are forced to listen. The body is not bad, and neither are its communications. The body simply is a vehicle that reflects the thoughts of its owner. If its owner does not acknowledge his denials and heal them, the body will continue to get sicker and sicker. Only Truth is the cure, because only Truth eradicates the root cause, which is a simple ignorance of Self. The person in our example is not "not good enough," he is a Perfect Child of God who is not only good enough but is Pure Goodness Itself. Only the enlightenment to one's True Nature heals beliefs; therefore, God is the only Healer there is.

-6:4-
The body does not cause false beliefs and emotions, rather false beliefs and emotions cause the illusion of the body.

-6:5-
Many believe that sickness causes negative feelings, but the reverse is true: negative feelings cause sickness.

This sutra is one of the most important sutras to understand, because it lays the foundation for the formula for uncovering the cause of illness. Most people believe that their sickness makes them feel certain beliefs and emotions about themselves; however, we have come to see in the sutras that beliefs and emotions cause sickness, not the other way around. The way a client feels about his problem is actually the cause of his problem. If a healer makes a list of the negative beliefs and emotions

The Sutras on Healing and Enlightenment

associated with the person's illness, then he will actually be holding a list of the causes of this illness. If the healer then transforms those negative beliefs and emotions, the illness will drop away. Healing is often not quite this simple, but many times it is. We need to understand what the word *transformation* really means, that emotional blockages are truly released, that forgiveness occurs, that the heart remains open and that the beliefs are truly brought back to the Light of Consciousness and enlightened to the Truth.

Understanding the way a person feels about his problem is very relevant for how to heal that problem. A person may say his headaches make him feel depressed, anxious, angry, frustrated, jealous and scared. He may say that they make him feel useless, incapable, unlovable, weak, sick, small and unworthy. The healer must not accept this. He must understand that headaches do not cause such beliefs and emotions but that the body is communicating the exact denials of the mind. When the beliefs and emotions are acknowledged, instantly both the healer and the client have uncovered the cause of the illness. How the transformation occurs and how to draw out the beliefs and emotions in the first place is a skill that the healer must bring. There are countless numbers of ways to transform beliefs and emotions. As long as the Divine is leading the process, success is guaranteed.

-6:6-
Pure Consciousness identifies with body, mind, emotions and life experiences and defines itself as such.

The biggest reason for illness is ignorance, and the greatest ignorance for a Perfect Child of God is to believe

The Sutras on Healing and Enlightenment

that he is a body and a mind. If Pure Consciousness misidentifies itself with its object of Consciousness, then it begins to define itself as what it is observing. The mind, therefore, under the power of the deluded Soul, begins to hold beliefs about itself based on the body and the life experiences that the body has. The body is limited, mortal and temporary. If the Soul identifies with it, the mind begins to think that it is limited, mortal and temporary. This causes tremendous fear and the whole range of negative emotions. Because of this ignorance that results in so much suffering, the person tries to close down the heart in order to feel comfortable.

The result is a human being who is totally ignorant of his True Self, who is closing his heart, bottling up negative emotions, believing himself to be a mortal body and living out of these illusions through all sorts of destructive and self-sabotaging behaviors. This is truly a sad state of affairs but it is inherently perfect, because when the Soul has suffered enough, then it begins to long for Home. Without knowing this extreme degree of darkness and delusion, the Soul would never come to fully appreciate the Light and Truth that it is.

-6:7-
Instead of knowing itself to be Perfect Divinity, Pure Consciousness takes on belief systems based on life experience.

In the ignorant state of the Soul, its Perfect Divinity is lost to it, and the Soul begins to define itself based on its experiences. This is important to understand because life events will therefore reinforce negative beliefs, which will create negative emotions, which will create life

The Sutras on Healing and Enlightenment

patterns. This is a viscous cycle for the ignorant Soul who through his beliefs manifests situations and then defines himself again based on those situations. The events and beliefs create emotions, and these create behaviors. The behaviors create more and more imbalance, and the cycle simply keeps repeating itself. Ignorance creates illusions, and illusions create ignorance. Without the healer, such a person can become deeply lost in the wheel of pain and suffering. The awakened healer can put the proverbial wrench in the spokes and help to break this cycle once and for all.

The Soul enters its incarnation as a human being with many sanskars all wound up in its bodily vehicles. These vehicles manifest the physical body as a reflection of who the Soul believes itself to be. Life unfolds, and the events that occur are the result of the beliefs held in the psyche. Life supports the Soul in what it believes about itself. The Soul, through the vehicle of mind, concludes the same things about itself that it already believes and simply ends up confirming its illusion that life is exactly as he thought it was. These beliefs create emotions. The emotions create behaviors, and the cycle goes on and on. The most detrimental part of this ignorance is suppression. When the Soul denies its own denials, then it is really becoming lost in an illusory world of its own creation. When the Soul has suffered enough in this, then the desire to be free will manifest situations and healers who will be of service to lead the Soul back to Truth. Again, Truth will be the only healer. As the Soul manifested its own dream of hell, so too now will it begin to manifest its own means of awakening.

The Sutras on Healing and Enlightenment

-6:8-

The range of false beliefs is proportional to the infinite experiences that a Soul can have.

The references to "a Soul" in the sutras are actually references to the ignorant state of mind, because in Truth there is only One Soul, and this Soul is not ever caught up in any way. Soul is eternally free and is never bound. However, when we refer to "a Soul," we are referring to a being who believes himself to be something that he is not. There is no separate and eternal Soul, and the True Soul never suffers in any way. Suffering is an illusion, and illusions do not exist. Yet the realm of illusion holds an infinite range of experience for the ignorant Soul to have. Since ignorance, illusion and experience are infinite, so too are the beliefs that can be developed. The mind can conclude anything, and any conclusion that it comes up with is a belief.

This sutra is important, because trying to heal all beliefs would be impossible and would never bring the Soul to come to know its True Nature as an eternally free being. Soul is not bound, and in Truth it can never suffer. It is eternally free, even if—through the power its gives to the deluded mind—it believes itself to be something that it is not. A separate Soul, an individual mind, personal emotions and a mortal body are all illusions. We are reminded again that in Truth illusions do not exist. The truest sense of healing then is not to bring up every single illusion and think that they all can be erased. The Soul simply must come to know who it truly is. The Soul comes to know the Soul. Beliefs, like experience are infinite and can never be exhausted. Only through self-knowledge can freedom be obtained.

The Sutras on Healing and Enlightenment

When a client comes for help, he is under the illusion that something is wrong with him. The true healer knows that there is nothing wrong with him and has nothing to offer. Only when the client complains of an illusion can the healer address this illusion. For the healer, illusions do not exist, and he is not under the impression that freedom will come for a client by removing all illusions. The healer knows that the client is already Perfect, Whole and Complete and that he is Forever Free. Only those beliefs that cause the client suffering are dealt with as means of bringing the client back to Truth. This may have to happen hundreds of times, but the true healer is never shaken. He knows his client is God when he walks in, and he knows that his client is God when he walks out. Problems do not exist except in the deluded mind. If you look for problems, you will find them, for false beliefs are infinite.

-6:9-
The Universe will always support a person in what he believes.

This sutra is a very powerful statement because it acknowledges the nature of the Soul and the Universe and how they work together. In Truth there is no Soul separate from Universe and no Universe separate from Soul. In Yogic Philosophy, two words help us to understand this apparent duality: *Purush*, which is Soul, and *Prakriti*, which is Universe. Purush, Pure Consciousness, is the Source of all manifested being. Prakriti, the energy of the Universe, is therefore the Universe Itself. Prakriti has no intelligence or will of its own and exists in the service of Purush.

The Sutras on Healing and Enlightenment

When the Soul has chosen to take the plunge into illusion, Prakriti supports these illusions. Whatever the Soul chooses to believe, Prakriti will support those beliefs. If the Soul thinks it is bad and deserves punishment, Prakriti will create situations that support this belief. This goes on and on until the Soul has simply suffered enough from its own illusions. When the Soul decides to wake up, Prakriti, in its service of Purush, begins to create situations that help the Soul to wake up. Prakriti has no power of its own and only follows the dictates of Purush.

With no intelligence or will, Prakriti is impartial about what it is asked to become. If the Soul believes it is unlovable, Prakriti will continue to form itself into situations where the Soul gets to feel unlovable. Prakriti is inexhaustible. As long as the Soul holds this belief, the drama will go on indefinitely. Only when a being has suffered enough is he willing to let go. The beauty is that Prakriti is simply energy and can change forms instantly. When false beliefs are dropped, Prakriti in the service of Purush can instantly manifest into a form that best supports Purush's new agenda.

On a more basic level, we should understand that people will always support a person in what he believes about himself. If he believes he is a victim, people will treat him like one. If he believes he is unworthy, he will be treated as such. Until these beliefs are changed, the person will only experience a world of his own creation. Prakriti will support whatever the Soul believes. Only in the True Healer does this not occur. Most people are so caught up in Prakriti that they are lost in the illusion. The True Healer knows that he is Purush, the Soul, and is not caught in the illusion. He therefore will be the only person who will not support his client in the client's false beliefs about himself.

The True Healer never supports illusions. When he sees his client only as perfect, Prakriti begins to work in the service of the healer, and the client is healed because of the healer's enlightened perspective. A True Healer knows of the inherent Goodness of the Universe and that Prakriti is on his side. He uses the power of Pure Consciousness and Love to direct Prakriti to manifest only as goodness for his client. Truth then begins to act in the world of Prakriti and brings freedom to those who are blessed enough to be in the healer's awareness.

-6:10-
These false beliefs create negative emotions.

The fact that beliefs create false emotions is a major theme of the sutras, but here we can look at the real reason why. The mind is a very powerful substance because its power comes from Pure Consciousness itself. Thoughts held long enough begin to gather the sparks of creation around them. When dense enough, they begin to form the astral plane and the astral body. An emotion is energy in motion, and energy in motion is a thought. Emotions therefore are thoughts placed into motion that have been given a sufficient amount of energy. Thoughts first manifest as emotion.

The belief that someone is incapable manifests as fear and anxiety. Fear and anxiety are simply the thought "I am incapable" manifested on the astral level. The astral body actually begins to form based on this thought. When made as dense as the astral plane, this thought now becomes an emotion. These beliefs and

The Sutras on Healing and Enlightenment

their manifestations as emotions suppressed and held long enough eventually form the etheric template based on their vibrations, which eventually forms the physical body. When there are no negative beliefs, there are no negative emotions. When negative beliefs and emotions are gone, psychosomatic illness cannot possibly arise.

-6:11-
The range of negative emotion is proportional to the number of false beliefs held in the mind.

As long as there are false beliefs, there will be negative emotions. The more false beliefs a person holds, the more negative emotions he will have. Most human beings live under the illusion that it is necessary to have the full range of emotions to be fully alive. It is necessary for someone to feel whatever they feel without suppression, but it is not necessary to suffer day in and day out with sadness, fear, hurt, insecurity, jealousy, anger, rage, lust and guilt. These emotions are only the result of false beliefs, and false beliefs can be eliminated through Truth. To the extent that a person holds on to negative beliefs, to that extent he will be filled with the negative emotions that follow. The important point to remember here is that there is a state of freedom where these energies simply cease to exist. If the negative beliefs are exceptionally few, then the negative emotions will be few as well.

-6:12-
Experiences of love, joy, peace, bliss, ecstasy and true happiness are not emotions, but are direct experiences of Truth when not clouded by beliefs and emotions.

The Sutras on Healing and Enlightenment

When a person receives the information from the last sutra, he is often shocked that a human being can live without emotions. They consider such a person to be dead, lifeless and passionless, yet that is because they have never cleared out their hearts and discovered what is left. People value their negative emotions because with them they feel alive. Most people live with a closed and virtually blocked heart and when anger does come through they feel alive. The anger is actually far more conducive than their depression, which results from their suppression; and when the anger is expressed, then they usually feel that they have gotten what they want. Anger never brings someone what he or she truly wants; however, they only like it because it is better than their depression.

If the heart is purified and negative beliefs are eliminated, the True Nature of the Soul shines through. The resulting experiences of love, joy, bliss, peace, ecstasy, true happiness and passion are not the result of beliefs but actually what is left when beliefs are gone. Negative emotions are disturbed fluctuations of Pure Energy. However, if the Divine Energy flows smoothly and freely through the chakra system, what is left is Love. Love is not an emotion; it is what Is. Love is Pure Consciousness, and it is not a vibration. It is the state of a human being who has only chosen Truth and was willing to let go of ignorance. The healer and client should both know that when negative beliefs and emotions are no longer present, the person will not be lifeless but rather full of life, passion and joy. The natural state of the human being is boundless Love; anything else is just a false belief.

The Sutras on Healing and Enlightenment

-6:13-

Depression is not an emotion but the result of suppressed emotion.

The ignorant mind hears statements that it can be free from emotion and usually translates this as suppression. Most human beings only know how to feel better through the denial of their pain. The suppression of emotions is perhaps the most significant cause of sickness and imbalance. To deny one's feelings, beliefs or thoughts is a certain way to a miserable life. If energy gets blocked, then disease will surely manifest. Depression occurs after so much suppression that emotion simply cannot come through the heart with ease.

It is helpful to see the average human being as a series of layers. The first layer is the Consciousness, which we can imagine to be located at the crown of the head, although in Truth there is nowhere that Consciousness is not. The next layer is the will power and decision-making ability of the Consciousness. Below that are the mind with all its thoughts and then the heart with all its emotions. Finally, the Divine Energy is pushing up those emotions in an attempt to make it back into Pure Consciousness. The average human being is taking his will power and pushing down on the emotions that are trying to come up. Another layer develops and acts as a wall between the head and the heart, usually manifesting in the throat.

The head is associated with consciousness, willpower and mind. The throat region usually acts as the barrier between the head and the heart; and the heart deals with the entire torso, which houses the heart and solar plexus chakra, which deal with emotion. When the head is

The Sutras on Healing and Enlightenment

unwilling to feel all seasons of the heart, then it closes down and a barrier is placed between the mind and body. People like this are quite lifeless—they are dry. They live in their heads and usually value their intellect very highly. Although now this is an intellect robbed of Divine Energy, so it is not an enlightened intellect at all. The thicker the wall, the more depressed a person will be.

Depression is not a disease. It is a result of someone who was not willing to fully live because life was too uncomfortable at one point. Such a person either consciously or unconsciously closed down, and in this closing down he blocked vital life force energy. When the heart closes, the Divine Energy cannot make it through. Therefore, Love and fear are cut off from the psyche. It is important to understand, however, that a person can never fully close down or he will die. Chakras can never fully close or physical death would be instantaneous. However, through an excessive use of the individual willpower, the heart can be virtually shut down.

The healer should never be misled. Such a person with a closed heart is not free from emotions. He is full of emotion but has simply managed not to have to feel too often. Underneath, depression is an enormous amount of guilt, anger, fear and hurt. A person does not close down due to excessive amounts of Love. They close down when it gets to be too much. However, they will also desperately cling to positive feelings and the people, places and things that appear to bring about those positive feelings. This only leads to more blockages. Holding on to positive emotion is also a very effective way to further close the heart.

When a person is closed down and depressed, they will do anything to feel better. They do not understand

The Sutras on Healing and Enlightenment

why they feel so sad and lifeless, but they certainly can easily fall in love with anything that gives them a ray of light and happiness. Such a person has no idea what real Love is, but instead they only know of a love that is filled with attachment, dependency and jealousy. They are exceptionally conditional in their ability to love and will be devastated if they lose what they claim to have loved. Such a heart and mind is in a deep state of ignorance and will suffer tremendous grief, sadness and loss when a loved one passes away or leaves. This is not natural. It is typical, but it is not natural. The natural state of a human being is his True Nature, which is unconditional Love, Light and Peace. If the heart is closed to any degree, then one's True Nature will be veiled accordingly. Just because most of humanity lives this way does not make it natural. It is quite normal but not natural, and it can be changed.

-6:14-
False beliefs and negative emotions in and of themselves are not the cause of illness; when these are suppressed and unresolved, they truly create disharmony.

This sutra speaks to the ability of a human being to be truly free and quite healthy while still having negative beliefs and emotions. When energy is flowing freely, it is perfectly fine no matter what condition it is in. Feeling anger in and of itself is not that harmful. It is the result of illusion, but it is not all that destructive when it is allowed to be felt fully. When anger is suppressed or expressed, then it can be harmful, but by itself it is perfectly fine.

Any emotion that is fully felt and not suppressed or acted out can easily transform itself and simply burn away.

The Sutras on Healing and Enlightenment

It is when these emotions are blocked that they truly cause disharmony. When the heart is open, the person will feel the full spectrum of his feelings and that is perfectly wonderful. This is what it means to be fully human. It is to fully feel with a completely open heart. When the heart closes, disease is eventually going to follow. Blocked energy is the cause of physical manifestations of illness, not free-flowing emotion. The other sutras explain how to deal effectively with emotions. The main point of this sutra is that emotions that are not blocked are no problem; but suppressed emotions will wreak havoc on the bodily systems.

Blocked energy is the cause of physical manifestations of illness, not free-flowing emotion. The sutras go on throughout their verses to explain how to effectively deal with emotions, and so that will not be addressed here. The main point of Sutra 14 is that when emotions are not blocked, then they are not a problem; but when suppressed, they will wreak havoc on the bodily systems.

-6:15-
Suppressed beliefs and emotions combined with the memory of the events that created them are stored in the mind and called mental impressions.

In earlier commentary we have discussed mental impressions with the use of the Sanskrit term sanskar—an impression placed on Consciousness from an event usually with a set of beliefs and emotions. Of course, certain impressions are quite mild and an infinite number go totally unnoticed by the conscious mind. Therefore, here we are only concerned with mental impressions, or sanskars that are filled with charged negative emotions, false beliefs and accompanying memories.

The Sutras on Healing and Enlightenment

In Yogic Psychology, the topic of sanskars is huge; and in Yogic Philosophy, the topic is even more vast. The important point in healing is simply to understand that a sanskaric pattern—what we find in a closed heart—needs to be released and resolved. Sanskars, which are like dark spots on the aura that can manifest as disease, need to be purified and are best removed through Truth. However, their emotional charge must be released first, and forgiveness must occur for the past events and the people involved. Healing sanskars is the main topic of the sutras. As the aphorisms unfold, the process of sanskaric purification will become clear.

-6:16-
Mental impressions that remain suppressed form the subconscious mind and are blockages in the energy flow of a human being, which can eventually manifest as disease.

-6:17-
In Truth there is no subconscious mind.

Our simple model of the human being shows the possibility of a major division between head and heart. The head is associated with the conscious mind in most people, while the heart is associated more with the subconscious mind. Sub-conscious simply means 'below conscious awareness.' This is a mind that is not fully integrated with the conscious mind, and the conscious mind only feels like a separate individual mind because of the wall put up between it and the subconscious. In Truth there is no subconscious mind, as in Truth there is no division of any sort. In Truth there is only One Mind, and this division of conscious mind and subconscious

The Sutras on Healing and Enlightenment

mind is only the result of the apparent duality within the human psyche.

This duality is the result of the suppression of mental impressions, which get stored in the heart. These memories, beliefs and emotions, which were not allowed to fully pass, become stored in a place where they become subconscious. The subconscious mind is also called the unconscious mind, yet this mind is not unconscious, because nothing in the universe is unconscious. The subconscious mind is fully conscious, yet it is held below conscious awareness. It is the repository of unresolved energies that the conscious mind felt unable to deal with. The walls between subconscious and conscious must be torn down. The separation between head and heart must be resolved. Without the integration of head and heart, a human being will always feel divided.

In Chinese, the word *Shen* refers to the Spirit. Yet the Shen is housed in the heart and is often referred to as heart/mind. During trauma, the Shen dissociates from the heart because it is too sensitive to deal with extremes. What happens then is that Consciousness pulls up into the head and leaves the heart with all its pain, creating a division. Consciousness hides in the conscious mind, which is only considered the conscious mind because that is where Consciousness is focused. Because Consciousness has withdrawn from the heart, the heart seems to become the subconscious mind. All unresolved memories, beliefs and emotions are left in the subconscious, and the Consciousness tries to be free of these.

This division must be resolved, or the unresolved sanskars—which still remain in the heart—will keep getting worse and worse until they are dealt with. The

The Sutras on Healing and Enlightenment

subconscious sanskar, which is left in the heart, is held there by the power of the Consciousness itself. This power gets invested in keeping the sanskar in a subconscious holding pattern where it does not have to disturb the conscious mind. However, not only is energy being wasted here when it could be used for immunity and digestion, but this energy is actually feeding the sanskar. The sanskar keeps gaining more and more power the longer it is suppressed. As a blockage of energy flow and a dark spot on the aura, the sanskar will eventually, through the order of manifestation, appear as a physical symptom if it is not released and transformed.

The psychological theory of the conscious and subconscious minds is based on observing a human being who is still in illusion. The average human being has been the study of psychologists, but the true model of the human being should be the enlightened saint, for in him there is no division. The enlightened being has no conscious or subconscious mind, for he is nothing but Consciousness itself. In him the head, heart and Spirit are one. There are no unresolved memories with negative beliefs causing negative emotions. There are no unconscious behaviors that stem from illusions, because such a being is perfectly whole and complete. The healer should only see his client from the highest Truth and should never believe that such a division as conscious and subconscious exists in Truth.

Models of psychology that honor this division always keep their clients divided. The true healer knows that Infinite Consciousness is All That Is and there is nothing about a human being that is truly unconscious. Suppressed sanskaric patterns form the subconscious mind. The belief that this mind has some function that

The Sutras on Healing and Enlightenment

is important for the human being to exist is absurd. The subconscious is often considered as the storehouse of beliefs and emotions in psychology; yet there should not be a storehouse for beliefs and emotions. It is often considered that the subconscious mind runs the human body and directs energy, but only God should run the human body and direct energy. No valid theory explains the need for the subconscious mind, because its very existence implies that there are two minds. There is only One Mind, which is God, and this Infinite Intelligence is more than capable of maintaining the human organism. When the subconscious runs things, there can only be disharmony.

Trying to reprogram the subconscious mind to do a better job is not Divine Healing. The subconscious should not be manipulated—it should be transformed back into the Self. Using therapeutic modalities to make the subconscious a "good" mind instead of a "bad" mind is like trying to make a "bad" murderer into a "good" murderer. Any mind that causes division and harbors suppressed beliefs, memories and emotions is not beneficial for the human being. Any notion of mind that creates separation simply needs to be brought back to Oneness. Its existence should never be taken seriously, and all models of the human mind should only be based on the enlightened Mind. The theory of the subconscious mind as a part of the human anatomy is like saying that cancer is a part of the human anatomy. Psychological and physiological theories should not be based on illusions.

The Sutras on Healing and Enlightenment

-6:18-
The heart is the root of the mind because whatever the heart is feeling, the mind will talk about.

-6:19-
When the heart is pure, then heart and mind are seen as one.

The heart, or the supposed subconscious mind, is the root of the mind, or the supposed conscious mind. Whatever the heart is feeling, the mind will think about in an attempt to make the heart feel better. The mind tries on thoughts like a person tries on new clothing. If an article of clothing does not feel good, it is discarded. Over and over again, a person can try on new garments until one feels just right. When this happens, the item is purchased and made one's own. The mind is also like this. It tries on many thoughts. When it finds one that makes the heart feel good, it settles on that one and makes it its own.

The heart may be hurting from too much suppressed sadness. Because the heart is the root of the mind, the mind will try to find a way to make the heart feel better. The mind will talk about how the heart feels and always look for the solution that best creates comfort. A more evolved being brings in spiritual teachings to heal the heart adequately, but a more unconscious being will do whatever feels best regardless of the consequences. Factors that motivate behavior in the less evolved being are false beliefs and negative emotions of the heart and the mind's thoughts that try to make the heart at peace. If the heart therefore is full of sadness due to false beliefs and

The Sutras on Healing and Enlightenment

negative emotions from past events, the mind will try to make this feel better.

Whatever the mind comes up with that brings a moment of peace will become the determining factor for behavior. If the mind finds that overeating can make the heart feel better, it will constantly turn to food when the heart is in pain. Many will argue that the mind does not cause disease, but that things like drugs, alcohol, smoking, overeating or excesses of any kind cause disease. Yet we must understand what motivates these disharmonious behaviors. No behavior exists from its own power. Nothing exists physically that did not exist mentally first. The thought is always the motivating factor, and thoughts rooted in the disturbed heart will always lead to imbalance in one's life.

People often tell others to listen to their hearts, but the human heart is not a reliable source for guiding our actions. The heart is full of false beliefs and negative emotions. The unconscious human being listens to his mind, which is rooted in his heart, and says that he is simply following his heart, as if this is some holy and sacred way to live life. The average human heart is the worst thing to listen to, because it is deeply wounded and will only act in ways that help it to feel better, based on its past. People who follow their heart are only attempting to avoid what felt bad in the past or to get what felt good in the past. They are never living in harmony with the Divine Will of the present moment and are always going to find disharmony in their lives. God leads one's life, not the neurotic human heart. When the human heart is purified, then it is not separate from God. Only then can it be considered a reliable source of information. When the heart is pure and the mind is undivided, the

The Sutras on Healing and Enlightenment

human will and the Divine Will are absolutely the same. In Truth there is no division or duality; and the heart then is not the root of the mind, for heart and mind have become one.

-6:20-
Where and how disease manifests in the body is very relevant because the body is telling the story of the mental impressions stored in the heart.

As we have seen before, the body is the three-dimensional reflection of one's thinking, and the body is constantly communicating to the mind its denials of its True Nature. The body is a metaphor, and nothing that manifests within it manifests by chance. The order of manifestation is exact and perfect in every way, as it is based on the perfect geometry of God. Therefore, the healer must be aware of where and how disease manifests in the body. Through chakras, meridians or organ systems, the body is telling the story of the mind. The skilled healer learns how to listen to his client's body through the client's beliefs and emotions. Once the beliefs and emotions that are manifesting in the body are uncovered, then true healing can really begin, because now the root cause has been exposed. The body, therefore, should not be neglected in mental healing, but should be totally included in the healing process, no matter what level the healer feels he needs to work on. In Truth, all healing is of the mind, but the body is not a mistake. It is the perfect means for communicating to the Soul and should always be listened to.

-6:21-
How a person feels about his symptoms is an exceptionally good indicator of the mental impressions causing these symptoms.

As we have seen before, a person can be asked how he feels about his problem, and the answer he gives is actually the cause of his problem. The body may house certain symptoms, but the mind feels a certain way about those symptoms. A person may be terrified, confused, afraid and lonely because of their illness. They may feel as if they are betrayed, abandoned, unloved, bad and deserving of this illness. The healer must know that illness is not the cause of emotions and beliefs, but the emotions and beliefs are the cause of illness. When this is understood, the healer simply needs to ask his client how he feels about the problem and who he concludes himself to be because of the problem. The answers that are collected become the basis of the healing process.

-6:22-
Through skillful means the healer can determine which false beliefs and emotions are causing the illness and through which chakra the illness is manifesting.

In Sanskrit the word *uppayah* can be translated as "skillful means." Uppayah—the methods used to help to bring a person to wholeness—are vast and infinite in number, and the skillful healer will have many at his disposal. Healing with skillful means alone is not true healing if God is left out of the equation. However, if the healer relies only on God without knowing how to work with his client, he is virtually useless. Healing involves

The Sutras on Healing and Enlightenment

the combined use of skillful means with absolute self-surrender. In the end, God is the only Healer, but if that is all that is necessary for healing, then everyone would already be healed. In Truth, everyone is already healed, because God does not know His Children as sick in any way. However, many of His Children still believe that they are not perfect, whole and complete. The healer is the means through which the Divine helps to liberate His Children from their illusions of suffering. If God worked directly on the client, then the healer would not be necessary. The healer uses skillful means to help pave the way for Truth to enter the client's mind.

How the healer works to expose negative beliefs and emotions is largely based on his training and personal experience. There is no one way to do this, and the sutras are only here to act as a guide book for the basics of what must happen in therapy for true healing to occur.

-6:23-
Where an illness manifests in the body is related to a specific chakra and its energetics.

-6:24-
A chakra's energetics are complex, and only the most general and practical explanation is given here.

Because the chakra system is the step-down system that the Divine used to manifest as the human form through the order of manifestation, then a problem in a certain area of the body can easily be related to a problem in the energetics of a certain chakra. Each chakra's energetics are explained in the following sutras. This sutra shows us that this basic model only begins to explain the system. The practical information given here forms the basis of a true understanding of the importance of the body in communicating mental blockages to the mind and to the healer.

-6:25-
Problems in the hands, feet or tailbone region deal with muladhar chakra and are associated with issues of one's security.

The first chakra is located approximately at the tailbone region; therefore, any symptoms that manifest in this general area are usually associated with its energetics. Problems with the hands and feet also tie into first chakra energetics, which deal with issues of security. The phrase "standing on my own two feet" relates to this energetic. When a person feels secure within himself and his life in general, then this chakra is functioning well. If a person feels insecure about anything in life, there is an issue in this chakra. Insecurity around housing, food, clothing, relationships, sexuality, personal power, love, expression, creativity or spirituality all have to do with first chakra issues.

Any chakra can manifest through or with any other chakra. For instance, the first chakra, which deals with security, can manifest through the fourth chakra, which deals with love. The skilled and intuitive healer begins to see connections between chakras and begins to understand the larger picture of his client through the ways the chakras interact.

The healer must understand that a chakra itself is never the problem, even though we may say that a person has a first chakra imbalance manifesting through the fourth chakra. The problem is not in the chakras, but rather it is in the mind. When the mind believes itself to be unlovable, the first chakra will manifest the insecurity and the heart will manifest the false belief around love. The chakras always work perfectly. A false belief manifests perfectly through the chakras, and the body reflects the imbalance.

-6:26-

Problems in the wrists, ankles and sacral region deal with svadisthan chakra and are associated with pleasure and sexuality.

The second chakra is associated with the region just below the navel; any problem in this area will most likely be associated with it. The sacrum, wrists and ankles are all second chakra areas and problems with pleasure will usually manifest here. Pleasure can be seen through any chakra. First chakra pleasure is feeling secure. Second chakra pleasure is usually sexual. Third chakra pleasure is usually through the use of personal power. Fourth chakra pleasure is love. Fifth chakra pleasure is expression. Sixth chakra pleasure is creativity, and seventh chakra pleasure is the True Love of God. Second chakra energetics can manifest through any chakra, for example, through the heart, where sex and love are confused.

A woman who does not feel the love of her heart may use her body to get love through sex. It would not be uncommon for such a person to develop some disease in the sexual organs or in the bladder eventually. The breasts are also sexual organs and should be considered when looking at second chakra issues. Also a weakness in the sexual organs, wrists or ankles relates to this chakra as well. The connections between the chakras and their manifestations are complex, but even this limited amount of knowledge can empower the healer to understand his client better.

-6:27-
Problems in the forearms, lower legs and solar plexus region deal with manipur chakra and are associated with personal power.

The third chakra deals with personal power in the sense that the person is now dealing with his own sense of being an individual as apart from the tribe. He is concerned with his confidence, self-esteem and ability to use his power to get what he wants and needs. If there are problems of low self-esteem and a lack of real power in handling emotions well, problems usually develop in the solar plexus area. The internal organs of this area include the digestive and eliminative tracts. Issues in the forearms and lower legs also are associated with the use of personal power. Again, the healer should know that the third chakra could manifest through each and every other chakra simultaneously. Imbalances in the use of power create disharmony, while its proper use only creates balance and goodness.

-6:28-
Problems in the elbows, knees and heart region deal with anahat chakra and are associated with love.

The heart is a very important chakra. Its main imbalance will be around issues concerning love. We can see, however, that as the heart chakra manifests through other chakras, love can be quite a complex issue. Love manifests in the

The Sutras on Healing and Enlightenment

first chakra as feeling secure in being able to love. Love manifesting in the second chakra is associated with being able to feel the pleasure of love and being able to bring love into one's sexuality. Third chakra love is associated largely with human emotions and their ability to be infused with love as well as with the ability to use power in a loving way. The fourth chakra deals with love in its purity, largely with self-love. Fifth chakra love is about the ability to express love through any chakra. Sixth chakra love is about loving being creative and often deals with devotional love of God, and the seventh chakra deals with Love in its most absolute sense as the Love of God.

Problems in the elbows and knees are usually associated with heart chakra issues and problems with the physical heart, and often the lungs deal with fourth chakra issues.

-6:29-
Problems in the upper arms, upper legs and throat region deal with vishuddh chakra and are associated with expression.

The throat chakra is important as it deals with expression on every level. A person can have trouble expressing in his first chakra and finding it hard to do what he needs to do to feel secure. Second chakra expression issues deal with trouble in expressing one's sexuality or pleasure. The third chakra deals with expressing personal power. The fourth chakra deals with expressing love. Fifth chakra expression usually deals with expressing one's own voice, which includes personal thoughts and feelings. Problems with the throat area may indicate a closing of this energy center in order to protect head from heart.

The Sutras on Healing and Enlightenment

Sixth chakra expression deals with expressing creativity, and seventh chakra expression with expressing one's spirituality. Problems in the upper arms and upper legs are usually related to this energetic.

-6:30-
Ajn and sahasrar chakras do not manifest in the body directly, but problems in these chakras will manifest as poor creativity, lack of purpose and a lack of spirituality.

Problems in the sixth and seventh chakras do not manifest directly; but when a person is not in touch with his own Source as Spirit and its guidance and creativity, of course, many problems arise. These chakras, which do not have exact anatomical locations where disharmony manifests, can still seriously affect a person's life. The greatest hell for a Child of God is to feel separate from God. Ignorance of one's True Nature is the biggest cause of suffering. When a person believes that he is his body, mind and emotions rather than knowing himself as Pure Spirit, then he is destined to suffer from false beliefs, negative emotions, destructive behaviors and suppression.

To wake a person up through the healing process to his True Nature can only benefit the lower levels of his being. The real secret to spiritual growth is simply to focus on the Highest Reality and to surrender all other energies of the Universe to the Divine Intelligence. A person who is not in touch with his higher chakras is living totally in the lower self of body, mind and emotions. Such a person is in very deep ignorance and misidentification and will always be afraid, in doubt and deeply confused.

The Sutras on Healing and Enlightenment

-6:31-
Problems that arise in the region of the head are often the result of the suppression of emotions through the closing of the heart and throat chakras, causing a lack of energy flow to the higher chakras.

Ajn and sahasrar chakras do have physical components in relationship to the pineal and pituitary glands respectively; however, for most cases where healing is required, the healer should look to the other chakras when problems manifest in the body. He should always remain aware of working to open these higher energy centers through bringing his client into self-knowledge all of the time. There is never a healing session where these chakras are not involved. Problems that manifest in the head are usually the result of closing the throat and blocking energy above and below the throat chakra itself. When blockages of the first five chakras are removed and ignorance of one's True Self is removed, then energy flows very freely through the entire chakra system. Health and healing are the result.

-6:32-
Each chakra functions through each and every other chakra; problems can manifest in multiple chakras simultaneously because much larger patterns are all interconnected in the system as a whole.

Many chakras can become imbalanced simultaneously; each chakra can and does manifest through each and every other chakra. The system is relatively complex; yet a simple knowledge of each chakra's energetics and how they relate can be very empowering to the healer in understanding his client.

The Sutras on Healing and Enlightenment

Here is an example of how this system manifests in the healing setting. A client comes in with what has been diagnosed as rheumatoid arthritis. Her hands, feet, elbows and knees are most seriously affected. The right arm is swollen much larger than the left, and she complains of constriction in the throat. Here, we see the hands and feet as first-chakra issues. The elbows and knees are fourth-chakra issues. The throat is a fifth-chakra issue. We therefore have problems in security, love and expression respectively. Each chakra manifests through the other chakras. This person therefore has a problem expressing herself in ways that bring her love and security (chakra five manifesting through four and one.) She does not feel secure enough to express her true feelings and therefore could never get the love that she wanted (chakra one manifesting through five and four). Because her heart has been closed to some degree, then she never feels that she can adequately express herself (chakra four manifesting through five).

During the healing process, while this client was walking outside between sessions, she tripped and fell (first chakra.) She landed on her elbow and hit her chin on the ground as well (fourth and fifth chakras.) There are no accidents in this Universe. This client manifested problems in her body through her false beliefs, negative emotions and suppressions through the related chakras. The right side of the body usually deals with masculine energy and this client's swollen arm was communicating to her that she could never feel safe enough with her father to express her feelings and get the love that she wanted. People are complex, but healing is quite simple. When this client released her negative emotions, resolved her false beliefs, forgave her father, stopped suppressing her feelings and moved into her True Nature of peace, power and love, then symptoms started dropping away at a very rapid rate.

The Sutras on Healing and Enlightenment

The point then of this sutra should never be underestimated. The healer must acknowledge how the chakras manifest through each other to get a complete assessment of his client's conditions.

-6:33-
The mental level of a chakra must be healed, because chakras are not a cause of disharmony but are only the channels through which disharmony can manifest.

In commentary, we are here reminded again that the word *Sutra* means thread and that sutras are pearls of wisdom joined together by one essential theme. Here our theme is Absolute Self-Realization through the healing and enlightenment process. We have clearly come to see through our journey along this thread that all true healing is mental healing. Chakras are therefore not the cause of disease but can be said to be blocked or out-of-balance. These blockages and imbalances are the result of mind— and nothing more. Damaging the physical body does not damage a chakra, and energetic blockages do not damage chakras. Nothing manifests in the lower levels without already existing on the higher levels. False beliefs manifest suffering through the chakra system, and these beliefs must be resolved. Chakras, which are channels through which disharmony can manifest, are not the cause of disharmony itself. The so-called healer who only rebalances chakras is like the car mechanic who tries to balance the tire to stop road vibration while the driver is taking the car over a pothole-filled brick road. In healing, there is nothing wrong with the vehicle (body) or the vehicle's systems (chakras); there is only something wrong with the driver (mind).

-6:34-

By knowing the underlying beliefs and emotions of a symptom and its corresponding chakra, a healer can begin a true process of healing for his client.

By collecting a list of the client's complaints, along with the beliefs and emotions that manifest these complaints plus a list of the corresponding chakras, then the healer has all that he really needs to help to empower, enlighten and heal his client. Whatever modalities are used to bring about change are entirely up to the healer as long as those modalities allow for Divine Power and Intelligence to be the true healer. Regardless of how it happens, once false beliefs, negative emotions and suppressions are resolved, then profound healing can occur. When the appropriate chakras are addressed, the healer can direct his client into the appropriate expression of that chakra so that each respective energy center remains open and properly functioning. In essence, mind was the cause of the problem; Divine Mind is its solution; and the healer's skillful means assist the process.

-6:35-

If the underlying cause of a symptom is not brought to the surface, then it will manifest again in an even more powerful way.

This sutra speaks to all would-be-healers who only remove symptoms and do not work on the level of mind. Even modern psychiatry—which claims to work on the mind but gives medications for so-called "disorders"—is not even close to true healing. A person is not a person but a Divine Being who is fully capable of expressing his

The Sutras on Healing and Enlightenment

Divinity on this Earth. Every Child of God can heal. As long as the healing occurs through an awakening to Truth, symptoms will drop away and not reappear. Symptom removal is often simply symptom suppression. The client may not suffer from his symptom, but he is still suffering within. If his ignorance is not removed, he will manifest an even greater problem.

The healer must understand the body and its communications. Doctors, psychiatrists and the like believe in accidents, but the true healer living in a Universe governed by Divine Intelligence does not believe in accidents at all, but only in Divine Order and Freedom. The healer must know that symptoms are simply communications showing that the mind is in error. Therefore, he knows that the ignorance of the mind must be healed and that symptoms will drop away on their own. When this happens, these symptoms never come back, and the person remains forever free in the knowledge of his True Self. Because this is the Soul's only real agenda, to remove a symptom without removing ignorance will only lead to an even more powerful symptom that will get the mind's attention. Patterns of suffering eventually wake the client up to his need to find their cause.

-6:36-
There is nothing wrong with treating symptoms to relieve another's pain and suffering, but a true healer should never call this healing.

The word *healing* is a very special word that is often misused. The real purpose of the sutras is to put this word into its proper place so that human suffering can be truly relieved by healing the human condition of its ignorance

The Sutras on Healing and Enlightenment

about its Divine origins. However, this in no way implies that a person should ever be left in pain and suffering. Any healer whose heart is open knows that he will do anything to help another being in pain. There are certain religions and schools of thought whose practitioners have been denied medical care because they were trying only to rely on God for their or their children's healing. True healing is a very sacred relationship that happens only when a person is truly ready to heal. For instance, many children are not even close to being ready for true healing, and therefore their symptoms must be relieved.

Every being who lives with a body is entitled to a life where comfort can be found. No one should live with pain and suffering while waiting for God to heal them. Healing is a process that often does not come directly from Source but occurs in the sacred relationship between the healer and the client. Even during this healing relationship, symptoms may not be removed for many months. During that time a client should not go on suffering unnecessarily. Certain ways to remove symptoms can suppress symptoms even more and fool the client that they have healed. Therefore, the healer should understand what the client is doing to feel better and gently suggest certain ways of being that allow for true healing to occur during the removal of symptoms.

A client comes in suffering from bad headaches. If it takes four sessions ranging over two to four weeks to completely heal this person and remove his symptoms, during this time the client should not be asked to suffer from his pain. When the beliefs, emotions and suppressions that were causing this pain are removed, the symptom will be removed whether the client took an occasional aspirin or not. This is a very important point, because the healer should never suggest that a client not get the medical care that he feels he needs. The healer is not a symptom remover. If a client breaks his leg, the healer should not try to change negative beliefs to heal the leg. The leg should be taken care of through the appropriate means, and then the client can begin to look at the belief systems that caused the break. Through mental healing, the break may heal quicker. Through Divine Mind, it may heal instantly. However, the healer should humbly respect his place in the process and not think that he should be able to make the leg better with simply the touch of his hand. Healing, in its trust sense, is a process. To simply mend the leg through mind-power would not necessarily be true healing.

The healing process may require this client to walk on crutches for many weeks to help him amplify his mental conditions and work through his false beliefs. The healer cannot pretend to understand the way the Soul is working out its karma. He should never interfere with this process. He only serves if he is asked to help, and he never pretends that he understands the complete life picture of another person. He simply does what he can to bring a client to God-Consciousness through the healing process, and he surrenders the outcome to Divine Mind.

-6:37-
Symptomatic relief is not true healing because the negative beliefs and emotions that manifested the problem still remain intact.

-6:38-
Once negative beliefs and emotions are transformed, Truth will take their place, healing will occur, and harmony will be restored.

The Sutras on Healing and Enlightenment

Chapter Seven—Misconceptions about Healing

-7:1-
Negative beliefs and emotions combined with the act of suppression block chakras and energy channels and cause illness; chakras and energy channels do not get blocked by themselves.

This chapter begins with a recapitulation of the major causes of illness and leads into some misconceptions that accompany health and healing. The first sutra simply restates what the sutras have been constantly emphasizing: namely, that false beliefs cause negative emotions, suppression of these emotions blocks chakras and energy channels, and as a result the body falls into disharmony. The important point to remember here is that chakras and energy channels do not have their own intelligence or will. Chakras do not block themselves and do not get blocked on their own. The human system, which is Divine, only falls into imbalance when the mind, through the power of Consciousness, uses willpower, suppresses emotions and behaves in ways that are unfit for the bodily temple.

-7:2-
Chakras, energy channels, energy and matter are not the cause of illness.

The cause of illness is ignorance. The component parts of the human physical and energetic anatomy are not the cause of illness. An imbalance in one part may lead to an imbalance in another part, but the true cause of illness resides solely in the ignorant mind. The healer may find it useful to rebalance chakras, energy channels, energy or the physical body to help to relieve pain and

The Sutras on Healing and Enlightenment

suffering; but true healing is only of the mind, because the true cause of illness is only of the mind.

-7:3-
Modalities that simply manipulate these lower levels of reality never provide true healing.

The sutras are quite clear about what true healing is and never deny the need for manipulating the lower levels of reality to bring comfort to a person. However, the sutras do stress that the order of manifestation demands that nothing exists physically without already existing on the subtler levels first. When the mind is healed, the levels below heal themselves. The term lower levels is not a derogatory term but refers to more dense levels of vibration. Mind is not the subtlest level, but it is the root cause of disease. Therefore, to change mind is to change the levels that manifest from it. The healer must know this to understand what true healing really is.

-7:4-
Any form of healing that does not put its full faith in God is a disservice to the client in his spiritual growth.

-7:5-
Any modality that does not lead one back into a true knowledge of Self only supports ignorance and illusion and does not honor God as the Ultimate Healer.

Any form of healing that does not put its full faith in God is not healing at all. Healing is a shift in Consciousness from ignorance to Truth. If a client finds symptomatic relief from any modality, yet does not learn that only God is the healer, he is done a disservice. When

The Sutras on Healing and Enlightenment

a client puts power in anything except God, he believes that there are actually two powers in this universe. There is not medicine and God, because there is only God. There is not homeopathy and God, because there is only God. There is not disease and God, because there is only God. When a client learns to put his full faith in God, he is empowered to heal his mind through Truth, and in Truth he is made free. This does not mean that the client should never use medicine, homeopathy or other modalities. It simply says that true healing only occurs through God, and the rest is only symptomatic relief.

To grow spiritually, a client must come to know himself as Spirit and deepen that connection daily. Spiritual growth implies living in Spirit and modalities that call themselves alternative, holistic or spiritual that do not enlighten a client to his True Nature are not healing modalities at all. Any healer who truly understands the process of how illness manifests could not possibly rely on anything but Truth as his primary tool for transformation. When the client also begins to do this, he is empowered. When he does not, he loses his power because he has put it somewhere other than in his Source.

-7:6-
Chakras, beliefs, emotions, energy channels, energy and matter have no power in and of themselves except for the power given to them.

-7:7-
God is the Only Power and the only true healer.

The true healer understands that there is only One Power and that is God. Nothing exists in the universe that is not given its relative existence except through that power. When Consciousness puts its attention on something, that something comes into being. When Consciousness is withdrawn from something, that something returns to its Source through dissolution of its constituent parts. Love is the force within the Universe that unites and holds all things together. When there is no Love, there can be no union; and when there is no union, then there is a disuniting of energies. Nothing exists that is not given value. Whatever is valued is loved and given conscious attention.

When we value something, we put energy into it. When something is not valued, energy is withdrawn from it and it ceases to exist. When this principle is applied to healing, we can see that nothing has the power to heal unless it is given that power. However, true healing is the removal of symptoms. If a substance is given the power to heal, actually what has happened is that this substance was empowered by mind through belief; and this belief caused symptom removal.

An example of this was found in the conception of hypnosis or mesmerism, as it was called then. Franz Anton Mesmer, an Austrian physician, began using magnets to heal his patients. He found great results through what he called magnetic passes where magnets were gliding over the patient's body and afflicted areas. Mesmer eventually began using only his hands without magnets and still got the same results. In time, he and those around him learned that it was not magnets or hands that healed, but only the power of the mind. Benjamin Franklin, one of the great men who studied Mesmer, concluded that Mesmer was healing by the power of belief and imagination alone.

God is the only Healer, because all else is belief and imagination. Truth is the healer, and all else is symptomatic removal based on a misplacement of power. When Truth removes illusions, all false beliefs drop away and Divine Harmony is left.

Mesmer was not healing through Divine Mind but through belief, and belief is not true healing. Nothing that vibrates is a true healer, including chakras, beliefs, emotions, energy channels, energy or any form of matter. These relative forms, which are only given power by mind, in and of themselves have no power at all. God is the Only Power, and God is the only Healer.

How to allow the Divine to heal the human being is the theme of the sutras. It is not through just a simple prayer that we find healing occurring. God as the only Healer does not mean that we can simply pray for Him to heal us, and he will. People dismiss God as the only healer and put their faith in mind or matter because they did not get what they asked for from God. Truth is another word for God. People pray that God heals them, but they never ask for Truth. They want their symptoms to go away and for them to still get to believe that they are humans and that matter is real. They never ask for Truth when they are hurting, but for their hurt to be removed and for their illusions to remain the same. True healing is only of God, even if the ignorant mind's prayers go unanswered.

-7:8-

These Truths should never exclude practical forms of hygiene, medical care, proper nutrition, rest and exercise.

As the sutras and their commentary have already stated, we should never deny common sense when it comes to the care of the body and mind. Destructive behaviors come from a deluded mind. When the mind is clear, it takes care of the body the best way it can. Just because God is the healer does not mean that we should neglect the temple of our bodies. The healthier the body is, the easier it is to meditate and contemplate Divine Realities. A person should always live a healthy and balanced lifestyle that results when the mind is in Truth.

Some people will argue that an enlightened being does not need to worry about such things, but this is totally wrong. If a deluded and ignorant person can take care of his body, then how much better can the enlightened being? An enlightened being loves and cares for all of creation. He knows that he is not his body, but he loves and cares for all. Through a healthy body, Divinity manifests much more easily. Therefore, one should take excellent care of the body, relying solely on Truth for guidance and inspiration in doing so.

-7:9-
Most people are not aware of Truth and should be helped on the level that is appropriate for them.

Helping is different from serving. The true healer serves when he heals, because service involves one Child of God assisting another Child of God in knowing the Truth. Helping involves one human being assisting another human being in getting what he wants. Helping is lovely and perfectly fine, but it is not true healing. Through helping, healing can occur; but helping is not directly healing. Because most people are not in a place to heal others or to be truly healed themselves, they should be helped on whatever level they can handle.

Many people are so caught up in the belief that they are their bodies that they cannot grasp healing of more subtle levels. A person who believes that he is his body will not use mind to heal that body. A person who believes that he is mind will not use Divine Mind for healing. However, a person who knows that he is not a person but is Spirit itself will always turn to Divine Mind for healing. Such a person will not neglect the lower levels of reality, but he will honor where the Source of All Power truly originates.

The healer should be wise and compassionate enough to serve on whatever level he is asked to and should not withhold service when another Child of God is in need. An open heart knows this without being told. Love acts spontaneously from moment to moment and is always led by the Divine to act in whatever way the situation deems appropriate. A free being has no rules or restrictions. He simply acts as the moment demands and always knows what true healing is and where it truly comes from.

-7:10-
Healing is not of the body.

Healing is of the mind and not of the body. When the body returns to balance, this may or may not be the result of healing. Symptoms can be removed and physical balance can be restored in many ways, but true healing is only of the mind. When the mind is healed, the body may or may not get better, although it usually does. Healing only occurs on the root level that causes disharmony, and that level is mind. Only Divine Mind is the true healer, and Divine Mind shines its Light of Truth into any mind that will receive it. When this happens, healing occurs. If this does not happen and the body gets better, no real healing has occurred at all.

The Sutras on Healing and Enlightenment

-7:11-
Healing is not done through a rebalancing of energy.

Many so-called healers attempt to rebalance the body's energies in a number of ways. Whether it is through crystals, acupuncture needles, magnets or the use of their hands, these practitioners believe that the power for healing comes through these means rather than through Divine Mind. Quite a few problems with this form of work need to be understood, because this type of practice is so prevalent in the world today.

When power is given to anything but Divine Mind, both the healer and the client become disempowered, because the real Source of their true power has been forgotten. Spiritual healing that does not honor Spirit as the Source of healing is not spiritual healing at all. There is a problem in giving power to objects or energies to rebalance the body's energies because energy is not the root cause of illness, but rather mind is. The human mind causes imbalances in the energy flow of the body, and Divine Mind can rebalance these energy flows when the human mind is brought to Truth again. To simply manipulate energy is not true healing, because this does not include the human mind or the Divine Mind.

The manipulation of energy is perfectly fine but should not be considered true healing. A person can brush his teeth and therefore promote health in his body, but this would never be considered healing. So too a person can balance his own or another's energy, but this is not true healing. If power is given to anything but God and if Mind is not involved, then healing is simply not occurring. Manipulating energy in order to rebalance it, like anything else, can pave the way for true healing.

However, the evolved healer finds absolutely no use for it, because he knows that Mind is the most powerful and in fact the only healing force there is.

When a person's energies are rebalanced through external means, his mind usually becomes much clearer. In that moment of clarity, he can begin to have a glimpse of his True Self; and this can be considered healing in and of itself. In the rebalancing of energy emotions can also be released, and this too can be very healing. The problem is that it is not complete. Healing requires more than emotional release and a glimpse of one's True Nature. If belief systems are not changed and forgiveness does not occur, the person is likely to fall back into his old patterns. A very skilled energy worker can be very close to being a true healer but if he is not relying entirely on Divine Mind, he is not working as the most powerful instrument that he can be.

-7:12-
Healing is not done through chakra balancing.

The same critique of energy balancing holds true for chakra balancing, and the sutras have repeatedly stressed that chakras are not the cause of illness. The human mind causes imbalances in the chakras, which only Divine Mind can truly heal.

-7:13-
Healing is not done through medications, herbs, drugs, needles or homeopathies.

The modalities listed in this sutra include many of the means used in Eastern and Western medicines. Each has their place, but without Divine Mind these are only tools for the relief of symptoms. They can relieve pain, but they

The Sutras on Healing and Enlightenment

do not address the root cause of suffering. The root cause of suffering is ignorance, and true healing is the removal of ignorance with the Light of Truth. If the cause of a person's suffering is not removed, then he cannot be said to be truly healed. The well-evolved healer has clearly seen the shortcomings of traditional and alternative medicines and has come to understand that only Truth can bring about what humanity has always longed for. Again, these other modalities—which are very valuable and do have their place—simply are not true healing.

-7:14-
Healing is not done through massage or bodily manipulations.

Massage and bodily manipulations are not much more than the moving around of symptoms and energy. The body and its energy fields are not the cause of illness. If a person simply uses his hands to move around these imbalanced patterns, then he may relieve discomfort or cause the body's systems to function better, but he has done nothing to remove the root cause of suffering and has not brought in the Light of Truth as the Ultimate Healer. Through a person's loving touch and care for his client, some very profound healing can occur; therefore, massage and other such means can be very powerful. Again, these modalities should simply be seen in their proper place; and any healer working in these areas would do well to take the next step forward into using Divine Mind more and more in his work. The more Truth plays the role of the healer, the better off all parties involved will be.

-7:15-
Healing is not done through crystals or stones.

The Sutras on Healing and Enlightenment

Crystals and stones do have a certain power to them, because nothing in God's creation is lacking power. However, these are subsidiary means to promote change and are not the Source of true transformation. A person who works with crystals and stones has put an enormous amount of energy into these items and has empowered them through the use of his own mind. His beliefs and intentions play a far larger role in rebalancing energy than do the crystals or stones themselves. Intention is the biggest part of this type of healing work. In modalities such as acupuncture, energy work, and crystal healing, it is the practitioner's intentions and beliefs that are far more powerful than what they actually do. The healer who has worked in these types of fields for a sufficient time eventually comes to understand that it is his mind and his client's mind that are promoting change, not actually energy or matter at all.

Many very advanced acupuncturists, massage therapists, or crystal workers have come to realize that physical touch or the use of stones is not necessary at all. The Mind is far more powerful than many healers have come to realize, and through Mind we come to the real Source of all healing. The healer's intentions and beliefs are more powerful than anything he can imagine. When intentions are only for Divine Mind to heal and beliefs are given up for Truth, then the healer becomes a most powerful force.

-7:16-
Without true forgiveness, healing does not occur.

It has been said by many great beings that all illness is a lack of forgiveness. The healer therefore must understand this statement very thoroughly and also must really understand what forgiveness is and the real reason for it. Forgiveness is perhaps the most important part of the healing process, yet in Truth there is nothing to forgive. A person requiring forgiveness is a person caught in illusion. In Truth there is nothing to forgive, because in Truth there is only God. Forgiveness is an illusion used to shatter illusions. When a person needs to forgive, he is in illusion. The belief that he needs to forgive is an illusion itself. Either way, this need is crucial and must happen in the healing process.

Forgiveness is a process. It involves the shift of the mind from its illusions of separation and anger into the Truth of Oneness and Love. When the mind believes itself to be a separate self, then this illusion needs to be forgiven. The mind, which holds itself in any form of a holding pattern, must learn to let go and to allow energy to flow again. Forgiveness removes the blockages to the presence of the Divine within the mind. To make the shift from false beliefs to Truth, the false beliefs must be let go, and this process in its most general sense is called forgiveness.

In the order of manifestation, a false belief that is held in the mind diligently will continue to manifest disharmony. For instance, if a person believes that he was betrayed by his father and is angry at him, then he has a number of false beliefs to forgive. The first is that his father betrayed him. The second is the belief that he can be betrayed. The third is that anger is a useful emotion. The fourth is that his father is a person other than God, and the fifth is that he is a person other than God. If these shifts in Consciousness do not occur, then healing cannot occur. No one is ever betrayed by God, and no one ever got what he truly wanted by being angry and creating separation. When a person forgives his illusions, then Truth can enter into his mind and his thoughts, which now based on Truth will have a very beneficial impact on the order of manifestation as it unfolds into his life.

Forgiveness is a process that must be learned by the healer and then shared with his client. It is a concept that is worthy of an entire book and cannot be thoroughly explained here. The sutras simply make the case that healing cannot occur without forgiveness. Because forgiveness is the means by which Truth can enter the deluded mind, then forgiveness is essential. All illness then is a lack of forgiveness, because false beliefs that are not forgiven continue to manifest disharmony through the order of manifestation.

-7:17-
Without Self-Realization, healing does not occur.

Self-Realization is the ultimate aim of a human incarnation. It is through Self-Realization that true healing occurs. Once a person is able to forgive his illusions, he is able to shift from his world of ignorance into the Truth. Knowing one's Self as the Truth is Self-Realization. Without this, a person cannot be said to be truly healed. Even if a person's body is healthy and he has everything that he could want out of life, if he is still in ignorance about who he really is, then he is not whole. Healing only truly occurs when a person is made whole. Even better said, healing only truly occurs when a person realizes that he already is and always has been whole. There is no division in Truth. Therefore, every Child of God is always perfect, whole and complete. If a

The Sutras on Healing and Enlightenment

being is not aware of this through direct knowledge, then he is not enlightened and, therefore, not healed.

Changes that occur on the physical, emotional or energetic levels of one's being that do not bring about Self-Realization cannot be considered true healing. Self-Realization, a final state, also is a process. If it were simply a final state, then healing would be virtually impossible for a human being. However, each illusion brought to Truth is a healing; and this can occur countless times throughout a human incarnation. The more it occurs, the more enlightened a person will be. The healer's role is to enlighten his client to his True Nature, while transforming false beliefs, promoting forgiveness, relieving suppression, releasing negative emotions and ideally enabling positive shifts to occur in a person's physical reality. This is healing of the highest degree and the only real form of healing there is. Therefore, a true healer's standards should only be of the utmost highest, and he should never compromise Truth in any way.

-7:18-
A human being is never the healer; his skillful means only make room for Truth to enter.

This very important sutra puts the healer into his proper place. The healer is not a doer. He does not function from his ego-mind, thinking that because of him a person is made whole. The true healer knows that a person is already whole and that it is only in his illusion that he believes himself to be other than that. When healing occurs, and a client awakens to the Truth of who he really is, then the healer knows that only Truth could have enlightened his client to Truth. The enlightened healer knows who he really is and knows that he is the Truth. He does not claim to be a separate individual who has done anything. He knows that nothing happens without God, and he never considers himself to be anything but that One Certain Truth.

However, the healer must practice humility always and never claim to be the doer. Every human being, no matter how evolved, still is bound by the use of language. In language we have many words that have to be used in daily conversations, such as I, me, and mine. A person is not necessarily in his ego if he uses these words, but he should never make his client feel that he is the healer. The true healer always credits all healing work to God, because his client still believes that there is God, himself and the healer as three separate individuals. The healer knows that there is only God and that only God is the healer. There is no duality in the true healer's mind. If he says that he is the healer, he would only mean that God is the healer. However, the client is not in a place to hear this and still sees the healer as being separate from God. Therefore, the healer should give all credit to God rather than to his body/mind that the client sees.

The healer will employ certain skillful means. Something must occur from the healer to invoke change. This could be a word, a technique or a therapeutic process, but in the end these means have only paved the way for Truth. If a healer tells his client that he is not sick but is perfect, whole and complete, then the client may simply believe him and have some very powerful shifts in his life. The healer's words were simple but may have been what the client needed to make the shift from ignorance to Truth. The healer's words paved the way for Truth, but the healer should not consider his actions to be the cause of the healing. Words are very powerful, as are certain techniques, but should not be seen as separate means used by a separate person who brought about healing. Truth is all that there is, and there is no duality in Truth.

The healer knows that he himself and his words, actions and modalities are not separate from God in any way. Therefore, the healer and his methods are also God. However, when a healer believes himself to be a separate self and he believes his actions to be his own, he sees himself as a doer apart from God. This type of healer is not a true healer and should always give credit to God for any good that comes out of a session. The healer who is not working as a separate individual also would give credit to God, because he knows that nothing exists but God. He also does this for his client's sake so that the client can begin to honor the Absolute Reality as the Source of all healing and not the separate person whom he sees before him in his illusion.

-7:19-
The belief that healing takes time is a false belief.

Because the word *healing* is often used for lesser means of promoting positive change, then it is often believed that healing takes time. If healing is the removal of a tumor, then it takes time. If healing is the transformation of an emotional pattern, then it takes time. If healing is the reframing of a memory, then it takes time. However, because healing is only a shift from ignorance to Truth, then it takes no time at all. The level where true healing takes place is beyond time and space and therefore not bound by time.

When true healing occurs, the order of manifestation adjusts to this shift. It may take some time for the changes on the more subtle levels to manifest, but true healing can and often does happen instantaneously. A client should therefore be made to know that he is not sick and has always been perfect. The sooner the client stops believing that he is sick, the sooner his symptoms can begin to drop away. The author has worked with many clients who were still having physical symptoms yet were totally convinced that they were perfect in every way. In time, this accurate view of who they were began to manifest harmony in all areas of their life. Healing does not take time, and the healer should never believe that the movement from illusion to Truth is bound by time and space.

The healer working on the deepest levels of mind must understand that there are countless numbers of illusions, that each illusion does not take time to heal, but that healing all the illusions does take time. If a person believes that he is bad but comes to know that he is Pure Goodness, this is not bound by time at all. However, if a person holds thousands of other false beliefs, their transformation will take time as a whole. True healing does not require absolute enlightenment. It is a process, yet each shift from illusion to Truth can happen in an instant.

-7:20-
The belief that it is difficult to heal is a false belief.

Healing is not difficult, contrary to popular opinion. Because healing is often defined improperly, that which is not true healing can be considered difficult; but true healing itself is not hard at all. When a client is willing to change his perceptions and he has suffered enough, it is

The Sutras on Healing and Enlightenment

not hard to get him to let go of his errors and to come back into Truth. When a person has suffered so much from believing that he is unlovable and the healer allows him to see that he is lovable, this does not have to be difficult at all. When the belief has changed, the emotions will change. When the emotions change, suppression can easily change. When all this changes, physical healing can occur. This is not a challenge for the true healer. He should always approach healing with the confidence that it will be simple and easy. He should never believe in his client's illusions in any way.

Healing is easy for the true healer because he knows that his client is already whole. It is not hard for the healer to change his perceptions, because he has learned that Truth is always the answer. Once the healer sees his client as perfect, whole and complete, then healing is easy regardless of the illusions that the client works to perpetuate. Healing is not difficult for the healer, but it can appear very challenging for the client. This does not make healing difficult, but it only means that the client in his illusions will cause himself needless suffering. However, when true healing does occur, Truth was simply allowed to come in. Letting Truth in is not difficult, although a client may put up enormous resistance to it. The important point for the healer to remember is that healing is easy and that the client is already whole. With this attitude the healer does not get stressed, and the client shifts easily because of the healer's confidence.

-7:21-
The belief that symptoms must get worse before they get better is a false belief.

Symptoms may get worse before they get better, but this sutra simply says that the belief that they must get worse first is false. When a client brings attention to his problems, he actually puts more energy into them; and this can cause an exaggeration of symptoms. This is actually good. Any healer will suggest that it is a sign of what is often called a "healing crisis." When this occurs, it shows that the symptoms can change. If the healer can make them worse, he can also make them better.

However, this does not need to be the case; because healing is not difficult and does not have to take time. When healing is instant and easy, symptoms can fall away very rapidly. When false beliefs and negative emotions are transformed, their symptoms do not last long at all. Symptoms usually only get worse before they get better because healing was not able to occur during one session. Healing can be a process. The times between sessions may be difficult for the client; this is inevitable. But the healer should know that when true healing occurs, symptoms can clear themselves during even one session. Time, difficulty and degrees of intensity all exist in the realm of illusion. The true healer does not work on these levels and should never believe that he or his clients are limited by such illusions.

-7:22-

The use of the hands, magnets or energetic transfer is not necessary for true healing.

The use of hands, magnets or energetic transfer is not necessary for true healing, because true healing is of the Mind. When the mind is brought back into Truth, then whatever hands, magnets or energy could do, Mind does even better. There are times, however, when a client feels helpless, powerless and depleted. During those times, a powerful healer's energy can be given to his client to promote healing. This is only necessary in the realm of illusion, because the healer knows that the client can never lose his power. Power can be invested poorly, but it can never be lost. A Divine Child of God is always perfect, whole, complete and never lacking anything. He may believe he lacks, but he never does. He may need to feel that the healer is giving him energy, but he never really needs it. The healer may give or channel energy for the client's sake, but the healer knows that the client is not lacking and therefore only does this for the mind's sake.

The client must come to believe that he can heal. If he feels that the healer is giving him something that he lacks, then he will believe that much more. In the end, it is about belief and not energy. Yet taken a step further, it is not about belief but about Truth. When the client believes he has the necessary energy to heal and then does move back into Truth, he will realize that he was never lacking at any time. The healer must know this always and not think that energy transfer is true healing. Only Divine Mind heals by transforming illusions. Energy work can be very powerful in removing symptoms because the problem area is certainly lacking in energy or is blocked, but to remove this through energy alone is not true healing. If the client is enlightened to his True Nature and his symptoms are gone, then true healing and symptom relief has occurred. The healer can use any modality that he likes as long as the principles of true healing are followed. Symptom relief alone is never complete.

The Sutras on Healing and Enlightenment

-7:23-
True healing can and often does heal the physical body, but not always.

This is another major false belief about healing. The body may not change during the healing process, although it usually does. The body is the result of the mind; if mind changes, the body will change. However, when the body has suffered from tremendous disorganization and entropy and the Soul is ready to move on, then healing can occur but the body may not change. Sometimes it is simply the healer's job to help a person be at peace about leaving his body. Healing the body at this point would be pointless, but healing the mind is crucial.

During other times, an illness in one family member can be exactly what other family members need to work out their own karma or false beliefs. The healer can bring Truth to these situations but does not necessarily have to change the physical body of the person who is sick. Healing can occur for groups of people and, therefore, all factors need to be considered. A mother who births a chronically sick child may end up becoming healed herself because of the child. The healer must know that the Soul is never sick, but that it may choose a body that is sick for the sake of another. Such Souls are very great and may not need healing at all.

It is the healer's job to ascertain what is needed in any given situation. Some clients simply will not see the physical shifts they want to see with their current body. All things are indeed possible unto God, but that does not mean that God always does what we want. The Soul's agenda as it works with Truth is quite a mystery to the human mind. Healing, therefore, must only be

The Sutras on Healing and Enlightenment

considered to be about the Soul's knowing who it truly is. When this happens, it does not matter what the body looks like. If the Soul knows it is eternally free, healing has occurred regardless of physical, emotional or even mental circumstances.

-7:24-
A saint's curing touch is not true healing even if it does partially or fully relieve symptoms, although it certainly can spark true healing.

When a very enlightened being touches another person, symptoms may be removed partially or fully. There are many reasons for this, but the fact is that it does happen. Why it happens is unimportant. The touch could be an energetic transfer, placebo effect or an expectation fulfilled, but it matters not. The important point is that if a client's symptoms go away, that does not mean that he is necessarily healed. Healing must occur from the more subtle levels down to be true healing, and it must begin with mind. Through the interaction with a saint, if a person wakes up to the Truth of who he is, then true healing was certainly sparked by the encounter. The miracles that Christ performed, for instance, did indeed relieve symptoms, but it was only when those around him came to know their own Divinity that they were truly healed. No great healer wants to perform miracles that only remove symptoms, but they may in order to wake those around them to Higher Truths.

In the path of Yoga, there is a term *siddhi*, which is a special power brought about by intense spiritual practice or similar means. However, it is common knowledge among practitioners of Yoga that the use of siddhis can be a big trap in the path of enlightenment. Practitioners are warned not to get caught up in special powers, even if they are used for good, but that they should strive only for full God-Realization. Even fully realized masters will not use their siddhis because they understand what true healing really is and never want their students to get caught up in anything less than complete enlightenment. This is a very important point, because it can save an aspiring healer countless years of wasted time in trying to accumulate healing powers. The greatest of healers only work to enlighten humanity to their True Nature. Through their infinite compassion they may relieve symptoms through their power, but their priorities are clear and their contributions to humanity speak for themselves.

-7:25-
Any modality can spark true healing, even though it is not the direct cause of true healing.

True healing is enlightenment, and no modality can bring about enlightenment. Modalities can cause transformation on many levels, but only Truth enlightens. Transformation brought about on any level can pave the way for true healing, because Truth can be allowed to enter. The healer, therefore, may use many modalities to bring about change in his client; but he knows who the True Healer is and only relies on Truth in the end. The True Healer is God, although certain modalities when used in the Spirit of Truth can certainly assist a person in letting go to open up to God. Modalities can spark healing but they are not the true cause of healing, for the true cause of healing is always God. Doctors can diagnose and treat, but God heals. A person can chew properly, but God digests. A person can clean a wound, but God cures it. And a person can assist another in letting go of illusions, but in the end it is God who is the Truth that makes them whole.

-7:26-
True healing does not stop the body from dying, although it could.

As we have seen before, healing is not of the body but of the mind. The mind may become free, but the body can and eventually will still die. There is no death in Truth, however, because in God everything is eternal; and in the relative world of illusion there is only change. The healer should never be afraid of death for himself or his client, because he knows that there is no death. The more a client can be made aware of this fact, the more truly healed he will be. The client is not his body, and the client never dies. His body merely transforms and also never dies. There is no death in God and only transformation in illusion. True healing has nothing to do with death and only exists as long as there is illusion. The process of healing will exist as long as ignorance exists and has endured long before and will endure long after one physical human incarnation.

True healing can never truly stop the body from dying, although it could delay its demise. The body suffers from entropy when Consciousness withdraws power from it. This is inevitable and will happen eventually. A woman, for instance, who was married for fifty years, whose husband suddenly dies, may begin to also withdraw her Consciousness from the body as she feels she has nothing left to live for. Through the process of healing, if she comes to realize that she still has much to offer in this life, then she will put more energy back into the body; and the body will not suffer from entropy as badly. This woman may heal her beliefs that she is alone, unloved, uncared for, abandoned and betrayed. She may realize that she is one with the whole Universe, is infinitely loved and cared for and is always supported by God. Then she has awakened to the Truth and is healed, and her body most likely will continue to live. However, anyone who has seen a husband die and a wife die not much later understands that when Consciousness decides to go, then it will go. This is perfectly fine, because both beings are free and eternal and can choose whatever paths they like.

There are many other such cases where true healing could prolong the life of the body; but, in the end, true healing is all that matters. The healer should know that true healing is inevitable for any Child of God; therefore, there should never be pressure for healing to occur. It will occur, and in Truth it already has.

-7:27-

A person is not healed simply because the body has ceased to function in what is commonly called death.

Death is not healing, and in fact the belief in death is an illusion itself. A person is not his body, for his essence is Soul. However, the Soul is perfect and is not in need of healing. Healing occurs for the mind and manifests in the vehicles that the mind uses. The mind is a mental body, and the emotions are the astral body. These bodies do continue on after death in Soul. Just because the body

The Sutras on Healing and Enlightenment

dies does not make the mental and astral bodies pure. In an indeterminate time, the mental and astral bodies will begin to form a new etheric body, which will eventually form a new physical body. As long as sanskaric patterns are still held in the mental and emotional bodies, then healing is still necessary and so is a body.

The reincarnation or transmigration theories are very real. The wise healer must understand that the mental and emotional nature of a being does not die when the body dies. The Soul must be made to know that it is free, and only one lifetime is not enough. When the physical body goes through the process called death, profound healing can occur for the mind. But death is not the ultimate healer, for only God is the Ultimate Healer. If during the time of supposed death, the mind wakes up to its True Nature and releases its illusions, then it is healed. But death in and of itself is not the healer. Before a being leaves his body, profound shifts may occur in the psyche toward and into healing, but this can happen at any time and is not dependent on the dying process. Sometimes the dying process fuels the mind to question its own existence and its belief systems, but only a fool waits until that time to do what he can do right now. And truly only a fool waits until his next life to do what he can do right now.

The Sutras on Healing and Enlightenment

Chapter Eight —The Process of Healing

-8:1-
There is no one way to assist a person in healing, yet there are principles a healer should know to make him a more effective healer regardless of his methods.

There are as many ways for a healer to work as there are healers; however, certain principles must be applied if the term healing can be accurately used. What true healing is has been well established throughout the sutras as well as the cause of illness. Regardless of the means that he employs, the healer must understand that only Truth is the Real Healer and that the healer's means are only meant to pave the way for Truth. If the healer follows the guidelines of this chapter, he is certainly on the right path to promoting the greatest good for those who come to him for service.

-8:2-
The most important principle is that the healer knows who he truly is and only sees his client as that One Self—which is pure, free and forever.

A healer is not a true healer if he still lives in ignorance. Knowing that Truth is the only healer, the healer must know this Truth. If the healer believes himself to be anything less than Divine, then he will project his illusions to his client. However, when the healer knows through direct experience that his True Nature is pure, free and forever, then he is able to support his client in this One Certain Truth. In Truth, there is only One Self; although each body, mind and emotions are unique, the

The Sutras on Healing and Enlightenment

Source that sustains and heals them is one. There is only One Truth. When the healer knows this, he knows his client to be nothing short of Divinity Itself. There is no principle more important than this when it comes to true healing.

-8:3-
The healer must not accept the client's illusions as real, including physical symptoms, destructive behaviors, emotional responses or false beliefs.

Not only must the healer know that the client is Perfect Divinity, but he must not see the client's illusions as having any basis in Reality. Only God and His Creations are real. A person's false beliefs, which manifest disharmony, are not real. The beliefs are not real, and their manifestations are not real. A client will argue for the reality of his illusions, but the true healer should never believe in them. Anything that manifests from illusion is illusion, no matter how solid or painful it is. A physical sickness or a violent outburst of emotion is still illusion; and destructive behaviors and their results are also still illusion. The client is convinced that these things are real; but the healer clings fast to the Truth and only knows Love, Goodness and Harmony as real. He understands the order of manifestation and the Infinite Goodness and Intelligence of God and is never deluded by ignorance and error.

-8:4-
The healer must assess his client's ability to heal based on the criteria given earlier.

The Sutras on Healing and Enlightenment

The sutras here refer to the earlier criteria (Chapter Five), which deal largely with the formula for creating and manifesting (Chapter Eleven). This sutra cannot be underestimated. The healer is first asked to know himself as the Self. Then he is asked never to see his client's illusions as real. Now he is asked to assess his client's ability to heal based on the criteria (Chapter Five). We are reminded that the healer is not meant to reject a client because of a lack of criteria, but he is to help nourish these criteria in the spirit of compassion and honesty while trusting in God to handle his client load.

-8:5-
If the client is ready to heal, then the healer should gather a thorough understanding of the client.

This important sutra begins the discussion of doing a thorough intake on the client to assess his complaints and their underlying beliefs and emotions. The healer fills many functions here, as will be explained in sutras to come.

-8:6-
All healing must be rooted in Spirit; both the healer and the client must have a rapport on many levels, especially on the level of Spirit.

The word *rapport* implies a relationship, and good rapport involves trust and commonality. In rapport, two Children of God come together and meet with common interests. It is the healer's role to do what it takes to build rapport through finding where he and his client have mutual interests. The first and perhaps most important

The Sutras on Healing and Enlightenment

place to find rapport is in the fact that both the client and the healer want the client to be free from suffering. The client wants to know peace, and the healer's role is to assist in that process. *Raporter* is an old French word that means "to bring back." Therefore, when the healer is in rapport with his client, he can bring him back to his Divine origins and enable true healing to occur.

All healing must be rooted in Spirit, which is to say that the healer and the client must develop a rapport on the level of Spirit where the client comes to know who he truly is. When there is a true Soul connection between the healer and the client, healing becomes very easy. The more rapport the healer can develop on every level, the more he will be able to connect in Truth. The client should feel comfortable, and the healer should work to connect on the deepest level possible. It is perfectly fine if the client cannot connect spiritually in the beginning, because that is why he is a client. However, the client is a spiritual being whether he knows it or not. Yet as soon as he is led to that place, a profound rapport will develop and exceptional healing can occur.

-8:7-
With rapport established and a good understanding of the client's complaints, the healer should become clear about what the client wants the results of the healing to be.

Once rapport is there and the client has presented his forms of suffering, the healer should become very clear about how the client wants to be when he has completed therapy. The healer is not the one who should decide the outcome, but both the healer and client should mutually agree on this outcome based on the client's level of understanding. The healer knows the Truth and may know far more than his client about what the result of true healing will be. Yet he should never force this on his client. Rapport can easily be lost when a client feels that he is not being heard and when he is being led by the healer's agenda. The healer can suggest possible outcomes. In the end, it is up to the client to share what he wants to get out of therapy. The client may not know what true healing is and what he can expect at its conclusion. But he knows what he wants and that should be honored while never forgetting who he truly is.

What the client really wants is his True Nature, which he already has. He only feels that he is lacking because of his ignorance. Therefore what he wants may not appear to be this at all. However, when he is questioned deeply, he will always come to realize that his highest intentions are always the same as everyone else's. The client wants peace, love, health, happiness, abundance and joy, because these are his Divine birthright. All Children of God want the same thing in the end.

-8:8-

Then the client's underlying beliefs and emotions that cause the physical problem should be brought to Consciousness, along with the negative self-image that goes with this.

The root cause of suffering, as we have seen, is the ignorance of the Self as found within false beliefs. These false beliefs cause negative emotions, yet what we have not examined is the associated mental image. When a client holds negative beliefs and emotions, he also has a self-image that goes with these. The healer is to help uncover these beliefs, emotions and images so that he

The Sutras on Healing and Enlightenment

can work to transform them through the Light of Truth. Perhaps one of the best ways to do this involves feeding back to the client what the healer has heard during his intake process. After the healer has listened very carefully to his client, he can simply ask the client to close his eyes and to get an image of what the healer feeds back. The healer simply tells the client what the client has told the healer, and the client gets a mental image of himself with his problems. Then the healer can ask the client to finish a sentence with a beginning that says, "When I look at myself like this, I just feel so...." This sentence is meant to uncover a client's emotions around this issue, and it should be repeated at least 5-7 times until the healer feels that he has understood all negative emotions surrounding the client's complaints.

Then the healer asks the client to finish this sentence: "When I look at myself like this, I feel like I am...." This sentence uncovers the negative beliefs involved in this issue. This should be repeated at least 5-7 times or until the healer feels that all negative beliefs have been uncovered.

Through this process, it is very easy to uncover the negative self-image, the false beliefs and negative emotions surrounding the client's issues. The healer should be sure to tell the client during this process that he is simply amplifying the problems and that the healer knows that the client is not his problems. It is usually sometime during this process that the client tells the healer that he is much more than these beliefs and emotions. The healer should acknowledge this immediately and explain the need to amplify the problem to solve it. This process brings illusions right into Consciousness where they can be transformed. Therefore, the client should understand this and know that he is not judged because of what comes up.

The Sutras on Healing and Enlightenment

-8:9-

Then the corresponding chakras that relate to the problems should be noted along with their corresponding energetics.

Once the healer gathers the list of negative beliefs and emotions along with the original complaints, he should ascertain which chakras are out of balance. This can be done simply by observing which parts of the body are affected and also through the words that the client uses in his list of beliefs and emotions. For instance, if the client says he feels powerless, the healer might suspect an imbalance in the third chakra. Or if the client says he feels unloved and unlovable, the healer may look to the heart chakra. As the beliefs, emotions and chakras emerge, the healer begins to get a very clear pattern in his mind of what is really happening with the client. At this point if the healer feeds back to the client what he sees in the client's complaints, self-image, negative beliefs, emotions and chakra imbalances, the client will most likely feel very well understood and a deeper level of rapport will have been established.

-8:10-

Once the physical symptoms or behaviors are addressed, along with the underlying beliefs, emotions and chakras, then Truth should be discussed.

-8:11-

The healer must explain to the client the unreality of illusions and assess the client's model of Truth.

Now that the healer has collected his information about the client's illusions, he should discuss the Truth with him.

The Sutras on Healing and Enlightenment

First the healer should let the client know that his symptoms, emotions, beliefs, self-image and imbalances are not of Truth, not eternal and cannot last forever. The healer should first understand his client's model of Truth before he attempts to convey his own. The healer must still maintain rapport and cannot force his own model of Truth on the client. It is important to remember here that the client is not necessarily in Truth yet, so models of Truth are all that can be used at this stage. Truth, in the end, is not debatable; in the beginning, it most certainly is. The healer should be gentle and flexible and should find a model that both can agree on.

The healer should take the time to explain that all suffering is an illusion, that illusions are not real and that which is not real is that which is changing. Whatever is real can never change. It should not be hard for the client to see that the body, feelings, emotions, mind and self-image all have changed, can change and will change. Therefore, they are not eternally real. That which is eternally Real should be discussed, and this Truth should become the basis for all healing work that is to be done. The healer will always be able to dispel his client's false beliefs using their mutually agreed-on model of Truth. In time, however, the Truth Itself will begin to work directly on the client's perceptions, and the healer will find himself less and less important in the process. It is the healer's job to make himself obsolete in his client's life. But until the client has come to have his own relationship with Truth, this will be virtually impossible.

-8:12-
While discussing the Absolute Truth, the client should be made to see the falseness of suffering and be willing to let it go.

The Sutras on Healing and Enlightenment

The beauty of this process is that the client gets to look clearly at his suffering and its cause. The client should understand a workable model of health and healing and also be in agreement with the healer on their mutual model of Truth. The client has been made aware of the unreality of illusions, and now he should be made to see the cause of his suffering and how it only comes from his false beliefs. He should come to know that suffering is due to ignorance and is therefore false. The client should see that his suffering is useless and that he has suffered enough. Once this is clear, the client should be willing to let go of his suffering and, more importantly, the cause of his suffering.

The problem with this is that the client is all too willing to let go of his symptoms but is not willing to let go of the cause of his symptoms. It is easy to have a client say that he wants to get rid of his migraine, but when he is asked to let go of his anger and suppression, then the real work begins. The healer must be sure to have this willingness first before he attempts to proceed further. He should not deceive himself and believe that his client is willing to heal if he is not willing to let go of his false beliefs and negative emotions. Willingness is all that is necessary; without it, very little change can take place. When a client sees the falsity of suffering, has suffered enough and is willing to let it and its roots go, then the healer is ready to move on.

-8:13-

The list of negative beliefs and emotions should be checked against the Light of Truth, and a client should make new lists with words that speak to the Truth of who he is on all levels—physically, emotionally, mentally and spiritually.

The client's negative beliefs and emotions are the cause of his pain. When these are checked now against the Light of Truth, the client will see the uselessness of such patterns. When the client is willing to let these go, each one should be checked individually in relationship to Truth. Therefore, once the healer has established the negative beliefs and emotions held in the subconscious mind and has discussed with his client what the real Truth of his being is, then the healer begins to reframe the negative beliefs and emotions based on the Truth. For instance, if the client has a set of beliefs, such as bad, stupid, not good enough, not worthy, incapable and useless, then the healer would reframe these beliefs by asking the client to reevaluate each belief based on Divine Truth. Each belief is reframed, not with the opposite of the negative belief, but with the Truth. For example, the belief that a person is a bad person should not be reframed so that the person believes that he is a good person. The problem with such a reframe is that the client still believes that he is a person. From the Divine Truth perspective, the client can adopt the Truth into his mind that he is Pure Goodness, which is free from any identification with the body.

Because Truth is the Ultimate Healer, positive beliefs are not to be used. If the person feels stupid, they should be told that they are Divine Intelligence. If they feel not good enough and incapable, they should come to know

The Sutras on Healing and Enlightenment

that they are Pure Goodness and Divine Intelligence who is fully capable and more than good enough. Hearing the Truth is the first and most important step. Healing must include a thorough look into a client's illusions so that he can be freed from them. Making the body feel better through the pacifying of emotions is fine; but for true enlightenment, a client must know who he truly is. The first step in this process is this clear look at illusion and reframing it with Truth. Once the client and healer have the two lists (a list of negative beliefs and emotions and a list of the Truth of these), the healer can begin working to make these shifts on much deeper levels of his client's being. It is not good enough simply to tell someone that he is the Truth. Therapy must be done to transform the negative beliefs and emotions, and the client must be empowered to meditate on this Truth directly.

-8:14-
Then a new positive image of the person should be established in the mind with this image representing his Divinity made manifest in human form.

-8:15-
The client's new image should present himself as he wants to be—free from his suffering and illusions.

A positive self-image is not the Divine Truth of the person but is far better than the old image out of which he was living. As the new model of the client is being formed, the healer is also working to cultivate a new positive self-image based on the person's Divinity made manifest. This new image will have to be based on duality; therefore, it should be positive rather than negative. An image of the Divine made manifest as a human being will always be based on certain qualities; therefore, these qualities should be positive. The reason why the self-image belief systems are made positive is because the person in his essence is beyond belief systems and should not cling to any false identity through them. However, in the world of manifestation, the Soul re-creates itself at every moment through its self-image. This image is of the body and how it will look and act. The image of the person as a body should be healthy and as he would want to be when free from suffering. The thoughts that will accompany this image are not new beliefs but terms that simply describe the client's Divinity as it appears through the order of manifestation.

The new self-image can be as spiritually based as the client wants to go, but it must always relate to his human form so that it can apply to his everyday life. For the client to see himself as nothing but Pure Light is too dissociated from everyday experience. The client should know himself as Pure Light, but must see this Light made manifest. While functioning in the world of manifestation, a positive self-image based on one's Divinity is invaluable. This new self-image is not a false ego, but it is what the person would look like if the order of manifestation were flowing perfectly and without blockage.

The client will be very glad to know who he really is, even if only intellectually, and will be very happy to have a new positive self-image that lives up to his true Divinity. This image is not something that is to be held too firmly, and it should be changed whenever necessary as the client's mind continues to evolve. How the healer establishes this new self-image is entirely up to him;

The Sutras on Healing and Enlightenment

however, it is an exceptionally important part of the healing process. Without it, the client will still be living out of his old self-image, which can be very destructive. A picture is worth a thousand words; and, in the mind, this is exceptionally true. The healer must understand the value of a new self-image and the enlightened Truths that accompany it. When false beliefs are changed to Truth, when negative emotions drop away, and when a positive self-image based on one's Divinity resides clearly in the mind, the person is well on his way to living a self-actualized existence free from suffering. How the healer works to make these shifts will be based on his own training and sanskars. How he works to heal the physical body if necessary will also be unique. In the end, true healing occurs only through Truth, and these past few sutras explain a key part of allowing Truth to begin to enter the client's mind.

-8:16-
This image is then used to dismantle all false images with their corresponding negative beliefs and emotions.

When a positive self-image is established and Truth has been made known to the client, this becomes the basis for all future transformation. Dismantling false images is a process that the healer will do based on his own training and experience. In the end, Truth is the only healer because Truth is what will be left when all false images drop away. The process is actually quite simple and can be understood through example.

A client comes in with severe sinus problems causing a great deal of discomfort. The healer begins to assess the physical complaints, the accompanying self-image and

The Sutras on Healing and Enlightenment

the beliefs and emotions that underlie the symptoms and any corresponding chakras that go along with the overall pattern. He gets a series of lists that look something like this:

Symptoms
Stuffy nose
Congestion
Sinus pressure
Difficulty breathing

Accompanying Beliefs
Not good enough
Incapable
Can't express myself
Out of control
Ugly
Useless
Helpless
Powerless

Accompanying Emotions
Angry
Frustrated
Annoyed
Afraid
Overwhelmed
Sad
Depressed

Chakras
First Chakra—Feeling insecure
Third Chakra—Feeling powerless
Fifth Chakra—Difficulty expressing

The Sutras on Healing and Enlightenment

The accompanying self-image description is not a written list per se but the result of the four lists above. The healer will also have uncovered a lot more information about other symptoms and other beliefs and emotions about other issues. The lists above were gained just from asking about the one major complaint of sinus problems. Once the healer has all the information he needs, he feeds this information back to his client to be sure the client feels that he has thoroughly understood the client's complaints and what is underlying them. The client then can be made aware of the negative self-image that he is playing out as a result of these lists.

It is important for the healer to remember that the beliefs and emotions that come up because of the sinus problems are not the result of the sinus problems but instead are the cause. The chakras that are out of balance are not the cause of the sinus problems but the result of the false beliefs and emotions, which are usually being suppressed.

These lists become the basis for the positive reframes that will follow, which will look something like this:

Symptoms

Stuffy nose—*Clear-headed*
Congestion—*Open sinuses*
Sinus pressure—*Relaxed nasal passages*
Difficulty breathing—*Easy breathing*

Accompanying Beliefs

Not good enough—*More than good enough*
Incapable—*Fully capable*
Can't express myself—*Express freely & easily*
Out of control—*Confident, self-mastery*

The Sutras on Healing and Enlightenment

Ugly—*Beautiful*
Useless—*Important, useful & valuable*
Helpless—*Empowered & powerful*

Accompanying Emotions Angry—*Understanding and forgiving* Frustrated—*At peace* Afraid—*Loving, confident* Overwhelmed—*Clear & centered, self-assured* Sad—*Joyful* Depressed—*Light-hearted*

Chakras

First Chakra—Feeling insecure—
 Feels safe & secure
Third Chakra—Feeling Powerless—
 Feels confident & powerful
Fifth Chakra—Difficulty Expressing—
 Feels expressive & open

The lists above with reframes are examples of how the process might unfold with a real client. The healer should only use words that the client is comfortable with, but words that both the healer and the client mutually agree would be in the client's best interest. Once this second set of lists is established, then the healer knows exactly the client's complaints and underlying causal factors as well as where the client wants to be when the healing work is completed. The healer says to the client, "Okay, you have come in with these problems, and you want to leave with these solutions. Is that correct?" Here the healer is double-checking to see that he understands his client fully and that his client feels heard and understood. By asking that question, the healer is also saying to the client, "Yes, you have come in with these errors as to your True Nature. Wouldn't you like to come back to Truth now?" The client will most likely be very pleased and willing to make the shift from the old illusion to the Divine Truth, and the healer assists in bringing him there.

The healer should always remember that the client is already whole and that illusions do not exist. The healer should be 100% confident that he can lead the client back into this wholeness through the means of Truth and Truth alone. If the healer feels in any way that he cannot help the client to make this shift, then he must discover within himself why this is and release it. If the healer comes to understand that for whatever reason the changes that the client is asking for are beyond his means, he should clearly communicate this to the client and share his expectations about the healing process. The healer is limited by the beliefs he holds about himself in his own mind. The healer should be honest with himself and his client, and let the process unfold organically in Truth. At this stage of the healing process, the healer is aware of what his client wants from him, and it is perfectly fine if he feels he cannot get him there. However, if he feels that he can, he should show the utmost confidence, while still being sincere, and let his client know that he really believes that this shift can occur.

The more evolved a client is, the more the healer can speak about the Absolute Truth that the client is already healed. The client, if he can hear such a statement, will benefit tremendously from it. However, if he cannot yet hear such a statement, then he will benefit enormously by simply hearing that the healer already sees him as whole and that he will know wholeness someday as well.

The Sutras on Healing and Enlightenment

Either way, the healer must always see his client as already healed, and he will use the new words and corresponding self-image to bring his client back into that experience of wholeness for himself.

-8:17-
The new image should access a client's visual, auditory and kinesthetic senses.

Not all clients access information in the same way. Some are more visual, some are more auditory and some are more kinesthetic, which means they access more through feeling than through anything else. Everyone uses all these senses to a degree. Even a blind person sees mental images, and even a deaf person hears thoughts. The Soul and its subtle senses are never impaired; therefore, the client should be made to access his new positive self-image with all his senses. If the healer finds the client more dominant in one sense, then he can cater to that sense; but all senses should be engaged. Therefore, a person should see his new positive image, hear it and feel it. He should see it as a mental image in his mind's eye. He should hear it in the words, sounds and expressions associated with it; and he should feel it in his body's felt sense and emotions. The more a client can tap into the new image, the more powerful it will be in promoting change.

-8:18-
The new image should address his intelligence, ego-sense and mind as a whole.

The new self-image should not be simply on the level of a visual image, but must cater to the client's entire mind. Mind is more than simply thought; it is rational intelligence. Therefore, the new image should be believable and should make sense to the client. Mind also contains the ego-sense, and therefore the new image should not be too far removed from the client's current idea of who he is. If a new self-image is too perfect or too spiritual, then a client's mind may reject it. However, the more evolved a client is spiritually, the further he will be able to go with this. The client should also be made to understand that the new image is his real self made manifest and that it is all right if he cannot fully contain it yet. The healer should push his client just outside of his comfort zone, but not much more. If the client's mind rejects the new image because it seems too good to be true, then progress will be halted.

-8:19-

The new image should address his emotional state and feelings.

Again, we do not want the new self-image to be a flat, two-dimensional model of the client but a fully alive and vibrant reality. The healer should be passionate about the new self-image he is re-creating in his client and should impart that passion to the client as well. The client should feel very good about this image. It should make him excited and happy. He should be able to feel what it feels like to be this "new person" rather than simply see it in his mind. If the client cannot feel it, it is imperative that the healer works to get him into such a state. Words and images are not enough. The client must begin to feel this in his heart. However, until negative beliefs and emotions are truly released, the new image will never go completely in, but it should be felt to some degree while the healing process is beginning. The healer could wait until the negative emotions are released before the new image is felt in the client. But the more it is felt at the beginning, the more faith the client will have that he can be the way he is now beginning to perceive himself.

To make a thought a physical reality, there must be emotion behind it. Creating and manifesting involves not only a visual image and a thought, but also emotive power. Without emotive power, the mental image that exists on the mental plane cannot become manifest on the astral plane, which is the emotional plane. The more the healer understands this and its relationship to the order of manifestation, the more effective he will be. Therefore, a healer who is afraid of his own emotions could never fully help his client to access his own emotions and to become truly free on all levels.

-8:20-

The new image should address the condition of his physical body and his behaviors.

Considering the order of manifestation, we can see why the sutras give so much emphasis to the new image being mental, emotional, and physical. The image should include the client's body and his behaviors. Therefore, the new positive self-image can be more than just a photograph; it can be a movie with actions and responses. If the image is only mental and emotional, it cannot thoroughly come through into the physical plane. The mind should be clear that this is more than just a dream and that it will become an experiential reality on the physical plane for the client and all those with whom he interacts.

The Sutras on Healing and Enlightenment

-8:21-
Suggestions and affirmations should be made that remind the client of who he truly is.

-8:22-
These suggestions and affirmations, along with the new visual images and powerful emotions, should be repeated often in the client's mind.

The new positive self-image should be supported by suggestions and affirmations based on the new words that the client came up with. These words should address the physical symptoms, the emotions, the beliefs, the chakras and the new self-image as a whole. The healer makes suggestions to support the client in qualities that he wants to nourish in himself but feels that he does not already have. A suggestion might be something like, "I am now feeling stronger and more powerful each and every day." Such a suggestion is adding something to the person's experience that he wants to feel more of. Each suggestion needs to be worded in a way that is believable so that the client's conscious mind will not reject it. Suggestions should be incremental, building on each other more and more each day. Suggestions should also have some emotional charge and be short and simple.

Affirmations simply acknowledge something that is already true for the client that he wants reinforced more and more. An affirmation that affirms Divine Truth may be too much for the client to accept right away. An affirmation is meant to reinforce something that is true for the client; it must be something that the client can believe at his present state of evolution. An affirmation of "I am infinite love and all powerful" is true; but the

The Sutras on Healing and Enlightenment

client will most likely reject it. However, an affirmation of "My True Nature is love and power" might go over much better. Affirmations can be much less spiritual, such as "I am a confident and successful person." As long as the client already believes that this is true, this would be a good affirmation because it simply reinforces what he already knows.

Affirmations often do not work for people because they are considered too good to be true and do not get past the client's conscious mind. However, this should never cause the healer to belittle the power of suggestions and affirmations. A person is the result of his thinking; when his thoughts are destructive, so shall be his life. When thoughts are positive, pure and based on Truth, one's life will be a reflection of this. Positive thinking combined with thoughts that only reflect Truth makes for a very functional and successful human being. However, positive thinking alone is not enough where healing is concerned. In fact, in and of itself, it is still illusion. The mind must be made to reflect Truth, and suggestions and affirmations in therapy are very important.

However, the mind only actually reflects Truth when it has been absorbed back into its Source in silence and peace. When the heart is calm and the Consciousness is turned in on itself, the mind ceases to function in its old ways. When this very high state of union is occurring, suggestions, affirmations and positive self-images become obsolete. However, when the heart is still disturbed and the mind is chaotic, the healer must work effectively to promote change. He cannot expect his client to be fully enlightened in one session nor can he expect his client to do the necessary spiritual work to make such a transformation happen on his own. It is the healer's role to transform his client through the power of Truth. Suggestions and affirmations with emotive force behind them based on Truth are an excellent starting point.

-8:23-
It is important to understand that this new positive self-image is not the True Self, but is a healthier construct for the person to live out of.

-8:24-
The new self-image will help to allow for the Light of Truth to come more easily and for illusions to drop away more quickly.

A self-image is by definition not the True Self. The ego—with its thoughts, beliefs and images about who a person is—is a self-concept. A self-concept is only that—a concept—which is never the real thing. A person is not a person at all, but he is the Divine Consciousness made manifest. No image or likeness can ever be made for the Absolute Source of a human being but for a human being who functions through thoughts, beliefs, images and emotions, a healthy self-image is imperative. No one exists peacefully on the physical plane when the more subtle levels of their being are filled with lies, errors, false thoughts and disturbed emotions. The order of manifestation simply will not allow for a harmonious human experience if the mental and emotional bodies are misaligned. For a person who does exist on all levels of being to be complete, his mind and emotions must be aligned to Truth. The new positive self-image then becomes the blueprint for how the subtle bodies will work to form the physical experience. It is not the True

The Sutras on Healing and Enlightenment

Self, but it is a much healthier construct for a person to live out of. The positive self-image is not the Truth, but it can pave the way for Truth. A person who is happy, healthy and free grows much better spiritually than a person who is sick, tired and depressed. Contrary to many religious traditions, suffering is not the answer to freedom. Ascetic rituals and deprivation are not the means to wholeness. A person grows one thousand times better when they feel good about themselves. Therefore, the therapist should work to transform their entire being into a healthy and functional one. Once a client has seen a ray of sunshine, he will want to experience the whole sun. However, when he only knows darkness, then he will simply want to be free of darkness. Yet when he sees Light, he will want more and more Light. To move away from the negative is not the answer for spiritual growth, because this will lead to only lesser degrees of negativity or the opposite illusion, which is to try to be positive. Truth transcends, yet includes, all dualities and is what the client truly seeks. He reaches such heights through Love and not through oppression. Therefore, the healer should work to create this solid base of a healthy self-image through which the client can come to know who he truly is. Therapy may not ever bring Truth, but it certainly can pave the way for Truth to enter.

-8:25-
After a new self-image based on the highest Truth is established, then the underlying events, beliefs and emotions must be dealt with.

This sutra leads the healer into an entirely different realm of healing that now begins to deal with sanskaric patterns in a very real way. The previous stages of the healing process were simply laying the foundation for the real work to come. If a person is told who he is and given images, suggestions and affirmations alone, then healing will be slow and incomplete. Sanskars, which consist of memories, beliefs and emotions, must be released and transformed. Not only must the blockage of energy that the sanskar is creating be released, but also the contents of the sanskar must be transformed for it to be truly let go. This process is again going to be unique to the skills and training of the healer, but it must happen for healing to be complete. The following sutras touch on this very crucial point, but only the practicing healer can really begin to grasp the need for emotional release, belief transformation and memory reframes. This process is only alluded to in the sutras to help lay the foundation for true healing. Yet it is up to each healer to find his own way to facilitate this process.

The sutras are extremely clear that to remove symptoms alone is not true healing. However, now we must see that to simply address a problem and place the solution into the mind is not good enough. We must transform the cause of the problem that resides in sanskaric patterns. Without a complete healing process that does this, energy will remain blocked, emotions will be held on to, negative beliefs will still linger and symptoms will continue to manifest. The healer must get to the root and release and transform it or else healing is not complete. The next sutras shed some light on this complex and important process.

The Sutras on Healing and Enlightenment

-8:26-
Negative emotions must be released so that physical and energetic shifts will occur if necessary.

As we have seen, physical problems that manifest from the more subtle levels always have emotions trapped within. We have seen that emotions also have a cause, which rests in false beliefs; but here we must go into the very important topic of emotional release.

A client's biggest problem lies in the fact that he was never taught how to properly deal with emotions. He has spent his entire life either suppressing or acting out on his emotions; and his emotional body has become a very blocked and chaotic field of energy. In time, his very disturbed astral body affects his etheric template; and the physical body becomes diseased as a result. These emotions then must be transformed; and the astral and etheric bodies must be brought back into harmony.

Because beliefs cause emotions, we might conclude that we should simply change false beliefs and watch the order of manifestation resolve the other bodies; but this seldom works. If a client holds powerful emotional patterns, these must first be released before a change in belief systems can occur. Trying to make a person not feel helpless while he still suppresses tremendous amounts of anger will not work. The person must learn to be comfortable with his feelings and in therapy to release these feelings appropriately, so he can begin to feel less helpless. Healing reverses the order of manifestation of disease and therefore must trace the disease back to its roots.

The healer first addresses the physical problem and then the emotions and beliefs underneath it. To resolve the problem thoroughly, he must unfold the pattern from more dense to less dense. He must get the client to open up his heart and to experience how he feels about his problem and to get those emotions flowing again. When emotions remain suppressed, a client never can fully heal. If there are negative emotions trapped in the system, regardless of physical symptoms, these emotions must be made to move again. The client needs to be authentic in his feelings, and there is not one way that this should unfold. If the client is sad, he must feel fully sad. If he is angry, he must be fully angry. If he is afraid, he must feel fully afraid. This is true for any emotion, for that which is not fully felt is never fully released.

A healer who tries to assist a client without helping the client to open his heart and to be real has not helped his client at all. There are many therapeutic techniques that can help a person be free of symptoms and even emotional imbalances. Yet if a client still shields his heart to life and has not opened up, healing simply has not occurred. A closed heart never knows freedom, even if certain emotions do not come up again for whatever reason.

A healer must not only work to open his client's heart, but emotions that have been held in must be expressed. In the safety of the therapist's office, this can be very effective; but a client should not be encouraged to act out his emotions in his daily life. He should be taught how to deal effectively with emotions on his own and should understand their illusory nature, yet he should be encouraged to free himself of emotional tension in the therapeutic setting. Cathartic emotional release is therefore recommended when necessary.

Cathartic release involves the full and complete expression of emotions that are held trapped in sanskaric

The Sutras on Healing and Enlightenment

patterns. When this occurs, the blockages of energy flow that were contained get released, and deeper healing work can begin. As long as energy is contained in holding patterns, a person will never be truly free. The therapist should encourage authentic emotional release—no matter how intense—as long as it happens in a safe and conducive environment.

Cathartic release alone is not enough because many other steps must happen after the release for healing to be complete. Simply releasing emotion is not enough, and therapies that end at this point have only let the steam out of the cooker, but they have not removed what was burning. A sanskar is more than simply an emotional blockage. To truly transform a sanskar, we must understand it fully. Sanskars contain memories that must be reframed and forgiven and beliefs that must be transformed. Therefore, emotional release is not enough, although the client will feel better.

Because the sutras and their commentary are not a guide for therapy itself, we shall not discuss the process of emotional release. We will stress that emotional release is often extremely necessary, especially in a case where physical symptoms have manifested. There are many ways to release emotions, and it usually must be done. When it is done fully and completely, both client and healer will feel much better off for it. If a client's heart remains closed during a session, energy is not allowed to flow completely, and both the client and the healer will most likely leave drained.

When emotion flows, energy flows. This is a very big part of the key to physical healing. Most physical problems are the result of a blockage of energy, a deficiency in energy or an excess of energy. We must remember, however, that a person can never lose power; he can only

The Sutras on Healing and Enlightenment

invest it poorly. Therefore, when emotions are moved, energy is moved. The healing process will balance out excesses or deficiencies, and blocked energy will flow once again. Through the power of the breath and emotional release, energy can be made to flow smoothly again, and the body will begin to heal itself.

There are many ways to move energy within the body and to get emotions to release, but the more internal the process for the client, the better. What this means is that if the healer uses any method to move the energy, he has not empowered his client to do this himself. This is acceptable and sometimes necessary for external intervention, but the more the change comes from within, the better. Massage, energy work and various types of body work can move energy but always from outside the client. When a client is encouraged to release emotion through his own opening up from within, healing is that much more complete. When a client opens up himself and in his own time, he realizes that he is the one who closed his heart and he was the one who opened it. There are many ways to assist the client in doing this, but the sutras are only here to point out the need for the shift to occur from within the client and with as little assistance from the healer as possible.

-8:27-
The belief that there is a valid reason to be angry must be eliminated.

-8:28-
Anger is love without understanding.

Anger is perhaps one of the most powerful emotive forces within the human system. When it is suppressed, it will wreak havoc on the human body. Anger comes from fear, and fear comes from being hurt in the past. Therefore, anger is simply a young child who has been hurt too much, who is afraid and who is calling out for love. Anger is a call for love. It is love without a thorough understanding of how to get love. Anger never brings us what we want. In the end, we only want peace and love; and anger never brought anyone peace and love. Anger is never justified, although it must move if it has been blocked in the past.

A depressed person has closed down a lot of emotion, and anger is usually one of the biggest of these. It has often been said that depression is anger turned inward, and this is largely true. Other emotions have also been turned inward in depression, but anger is a very important one to deal with because hurt and fear will always go along with it. A person who is angry is also mad at himself, and this will always involve some degree of guilt for something they feel they have done wrong in the past. The guilty punish themselves, and this lowers their self-esteem, which causes more fear and anxiety. The angry person is truly sitting on an enormous amount of blocked energy. Sometimes the anger has gotten to the point where it has escalated to rage and hatred. Such a client will also have frustration, agitation and irritability; but if his anger can be released, tremendous healing can occur.

The healer must not believe in the need for anger but must be perfectly comfortable with it. He cannot be afraid of expressing anger or afraid of his client's anger. Anger is not real—it is a call for love. It is not rooted in Truth, and whatever is not rooted in Truth is an illusion. The healer knows that illusions do not exist and that nothing can ever change Truth and Love. The angry person simply wants freedom and love. The healer can assist this, but only after the client has thoroughly opened his heart and released his anger.

How the release occurs is based on what has been stored in the heart. The important point is that the release is authentic, although it can be amplified. The healer can encourage the client to overact on his emotions to really get them out. Once the emotions are out, the pressure is off, and transformation can really occur. The need for the release of anger cannot be overemphasized, especially if the healer is working to heal the physical body. Once anger is released, the client should be made to see what he really wants, which is love. When he sees this and feels love, he can release his apparent need for anger. Once this occurs, the client will see that anger was simply love without understanding. Anger is love without understanding because once wisdom has been shed on the past events that hurt the person, he will come to understand that people always do the best they can based on their conditioning and given resources. With this, forgiveness can occur.

When the client has released anger, sees no need for it anymore, has understanding and forgiveness, he is truly on the way to healing. Not only will he be free of hurt, fear, anger and guilt, but also his life will improve dramatically. Any physical symptoms that arose from this anger will also drop away rather rapidly. Truly, this aspect of the transformation can be considered a huge step toward healing and wholeness.

The Sutras on Healing and Enlightenment

-8:29-
Understanding, acceptance, commonality, forgiveness and compassion must arise.

At a certain point in the healing process when the client has released whatever emotions he had and has opened his heart, profound healing can begin. True healing only exists if understanding, acceptance, commonality, forgiveness and compassion arise.

Understanding comes from knowing that there is perfection in every aspect of God's creation and that nothing happens by chance. The client must come to understand the reason for his problems, and he must understand that anyone who wronged him in the past was simply doing the best he could do. This is often hard for a client to accept, but once he has really released his emotions, the Light of Truth will bring him understanding very naturally. The healer will not have to work hard to bring the client into a place of true understanding as long as emotions have been sufficiently released.

Acceptance is not a process of simply pretending to be okay with what happened, but truly being at peace with it. If a past event was unresolved in a person's psyche, he must come to accept that the event is in the past and that it was for his greater growth. If he regrets or is resentful over the past, he is not yet free. Acceptance is the process of knowing that everything is in Divine Order and for allowing it to be as it is, was or will be in peace.

Commonality involves bringing a client to a state of mind where unity can begin to appear. When a client feels separate from those in his present or past, he is still in a state of duality. There is no duality in Truth.

The Sutras on Healing and Enlightenment

Therefore, having commonality with other people is a first step toward this unity. The client can feel that he is simply a human being like others and that he too has made mistakes. Even better, he can see himself as a spiritual being, like others, who gets lost and confused in the embodied state. Either way, the client should feel a sense of unity with those involved in his issues and feel that he is neither superior nor inferior to them.

Without forgiveness, healing does not occur. Without forgiveness, anger is never truly resolved. If anger is not resolved, healing is impossible. Forgiveness allows the client to let go of the past holding patterns and to come fully into the present where he can find Truth, for Truth exists only here and now.

Once a client has understanding, acceptance, commonality and forgiveness, he has compassion. This should be explained to him, and he should begin to feel compassion for himself and others. He should have also gained understanding, acceptance, commonality and forgiveness for himself; and then he can have it for others as well. When he does, compassion is there. Compassion is love seeing pain. It is the Soul in its purity witnessing the suffering of its own incarnation and that of others. Compassion does not suffer, and it is not sympathy nor empathy. It is a free state of being that still warmly honors suffering, but does not get caught up with it. Compassion is the state of the true healer, and it should be imparted to the client as a major stage of his healing. When the client has true compassion deep in his heart for himself and others, healing is virtually complete.

The Sutras on Healing and Enlightenment

-8:30-

Past memories must be reframed from the perspective of Truth and present-day spiritual awareness.

With emotional release and the movement into compassion, past memories have already been largely reframed. But it is now the healer's job to be sure that the client has shined the Light of Truth on the past so it can be totally transformed. Because the past does not exist, it can never be changed. Therefore, a client may protest against the need for looking at his past. He will say that it is over and done with, and there is nothing he can do about it. It is over, but it is not done with; and there is a lot he can do about it. The past still exists as a sanskaric imprint in the client's heart. To the degree that he is not at peace with it, to that degree he will suffer because of it.

Reframing the past first involves the release of blocked emotion if necessary. If anger, fear or sadness is still strong, the pattern is still held too firmly to reframe it well. Once the emotional charge is off a memory, the Truth can be brought in to see what really happened. Memories are not exact historical information, but rather the result of a younger and less evolved part of us that interpreted a situation based on our capacities for understanding at the time of the event. A child does not see an event the way an adult does, and an unenlightened being does not see an event the way a God-realized being does. There is no truth in memory, but only interpretation. It is the healer's job to transform the way a memory was perceived into a perspective of the highest Truth. Again, this can happen in as many ways as there are healers, but it must happen if a person is to be free of his past.

-8:31-
False beliefs must be transformed to Truth.

Now we finally come to perhaps the most important point of healing, because we are now ready to be here. False beliefs are the root of all suffering, but to change them often requires many steps before they can be transformed properly. Beliefs lie buried in the subconscious repository of sanskars, which rest suppressed far away from the conscious mind and infused with powerful emotional charges. They are well guarded in most people and cannot be changed thoroughly without many other steps happening first. A closed heart will never change belief systems well. A suppressed emotional body will never allow for the mental body to be truly accessed. An unforgiving mind will never be willing to change its perceptions of who it is, and someone who is holding onto anger is way too convinced of who he is to ever want to be free of it. All of these issues must be resolved for beliefs to be truly transformed in the most powerful ways possible.

Suggestions and affirmations have to work their way through so many layers that only intense repetition will ever even make a dent. Most suggestions and affirmations are rejected because of the suppressed sanskars that are held so deeply within. If sanskars are not released of their emotional charge, their beliefs never really go away. Enough repetition will gradually erode them, but this could take years. Once emotional release occurs, the heart is opened, and the other steps have been followed, beliefs change very easily.

We will remember that false beliefs cause the entire order of manifestation within a human system to become out of balance. The mental level is the root cause of

The Sutras on Healing and Enlightenment

illness, but mind alone does not cause illness, because mind itself is inherently Divine. The individual mind, which is full of false beliefs that manifest into the astral, etheric and causal bodies, causes illness and imbalance. Unfortunately, these beliefs are deep and are not changed easily until the heart is truly freed; but once this happens, beliefs drop away very easily.

Because false beliefs were the cause of the entire problem, Truth is the solution. Now we can see why Truth is the ultimate and only real healer. The entire order of manifestation was disturbed by error, and only Truth can resolve this. The healer who is one with Truth has no problem in being the perfect channel for Truth to flow to his client. This can happen in an infinite number of ways because there is no limit to God, but it must happen in the end. Truth must replace illusions, or the client is simply not healed and enlightened. When false beliefs are removed and Truth is what is left, then the client can be said to be truly free.

-8:32-
The new self-image should replace the old self-image; the healer must be sure that the client knows who he truly is aside from this more beneficent new model.

At this point of the healing process, the healer can revert to his original work with the client and bring in the new self-image that was cultivated earlier in their time together. The healer showers the client's mind with the words they mutually agreed on to discuss the Absolute Truth. The healer should also paint the picture in the client's mind of the new self-image with emotions and suggestions. Whatever method is used, the client should be brought all the way back into the Source of his own being and allowed to know himself as Pure Consciousness. He will also hear about the Truth of who he really is while seeing an image made manifest into human form. The client must know who he truly is, and he should also be made to see the value of his new re-creation of himself.

The client at this stage should be enlightened through direct experience as to who he really is. Of course, this requires that the healer has a very good sense of this for himself as well. Once this happens, the client will realize that he cannot create himself, because he already is who he is and that can never be changed. However, he does have the power to consciously re-create himself as he would like to be. The client has previously re-created a world for himself of suffering and pain, and no one did this to him but himself. Now he is empowered to use the Divine Power of his mind to begin to see himself and declare himself as Perfect Divinity made manifest. This is truly a profound step in the healing process where the client knows his own Divinity and re-creates it in his own life.

-8:33-

Visualizations and suggestions for symptomatic relief should be given if necessary.

This stage in the healing process is the place to address any physical symptoms that need to be healed. The false beliefs and negative emotions have now been transformed. Energy shifts have occurred. The heart has been opened. Forgiveness has been established, and compassion has arisen. The client is now truly ready to let go of his physical problems. The order of manifestation will no longer support these physical problems if true healing has occurred, and the client can begin to use his mind to heal the body even more quickly.

For this to truly happen, the healer should be aware of the causal idea of the part of the body that the client is working to heal. The healer must understand that things are thoughts and that God, on the causal plane, holds the perfect thought for every thing. For instance, if the large intestine needs healing, the healer should go right to the source of the pure idea of a large intestine. This is not as mystical as it may appear. The perfect idea of a thing is not hard to come by. The causal idea of a large intestine is simply a perfect large intestine in perfect health. The large intestine on the causal plane does not exist as diseased or imbalanced in any way. God simply did not create ideas that were not useful. The perfect ideas of God are perfectly functional and useful realities that only operate in harmony with all other perfect ideas. The healer simply needs to tap into that image and impart it to the client's mind.

Again, we can see how Truth is the only real healer. The Truth of a person's being would only allow for a perfect manifestation of a large intestine anyway, but now at the end of the healing process, this perfect idea is directly introduced to the client's mind. This is not positive visualization, because the perfect ideas of God are not positive or negative; rather, these ideas are Truth made manifest, which is Pure Goodness and Harmony. The client therefore should hold only this idea in his mind while thinking of his intestines, and the healer should help by guiding his mind through visualization and suggestion.

The Sutras on Healing and Enlightenment

From the beginning, the true healer never saw his client as sick and now the client must begin to see himself as perfectly whole as well. The client is not under the illusion of healing now, but he is healed—as he always has been. His mind, heart and body are now one with God and the perfect ideas of God. God only knows Himself and His perfect creations. God does not know illusion; therefore, God never could see any of His Children as lacking anything essential. He knows that they are perfect as they were created. The true healer knows this as well, and now ideally his client does also.

-8:34-
Chakras that were out of balance can be visualized with their corresponding locations and colors.

-8:35-
A chakra's emotional energetics can be placed into suggestions to balance a specific chakra or chakras.

Just as the vehicles of the human system have been brought back into balance, so too should the chakra system be brought back into balance. Just like the physical body will most likely heal on its own, when Truth has been re-established, visualizations and suggestions help to speed up the process. The same is true with the chakra system. It will realign itself in Truth, but the healer can help to speed up the process.

The healer was aware of chakras that were out of balance because of his thorough intake. Now he can ask his client to visualize the chakras and their colors. This will bring the Light of Consciousness to each chakra that needed assistance. This awareness itself will bring the necessary balance now that the emotions are released. Each chakra's energetic qualities can also be stressed, allowing even more reinforcement. For example, the healer can give suggestions that the client is pure power to help balance the third chakra that held a belief of powerlessness.

-8:36-
Through these steps, if negative beliefs are transformed, emotions are released, forgiveness occurs and suggestions and visualizations for symptomatic relief are given, then success will be easy.

-8:37-
True healing only occurs when a person is enlightened to the Absolute Truth of his being.

-8:38-
False beliefs and self-images must be replaced with healthier ones, but in the end only Self-Realization can be considered true healing.

These sutras simply summarize the process of healing: when healing is done completely, success is very easy. As long as a person is enlightened to his True Nature, healing can be said to have occurred regardless of any other beneficial changes that may have taken place. Healing is a process that usually takes time. A client in Truth is always whole, but this may take time to manifest as their false beliefs are dropping away. However, as long as the Self comes to know itself in the end, nothing else really matters. The human being is always limited and can never be truly free. All of his bodily vehicles are limitations,

The Sutras on Healing and Enlightenment

but the True Self is pure, free and forever. There are no limits to the real Truth of a human being; and the body, mind and emotions do not become enlightened. What becomes enlightened is enlightenment itself. The body, mind and emotions—which are changing and will eventually fade—are not the real aim of true healing. True healing is enlightenment, and this happens only for the Self itself. When Self-Realization occurs, freedom is the result regardless of the condition of the body, mind or emotions.

The body will eventually die, but the Self is forever. The emotions and mind will always change, but the Self never changes. Therefore, healing must be based on only the highest realization of Self where no suffering exists. In the Absolute Truth of a human being, there is only eternal freedom. If this is not the aim of healing, healing is a process that will eventually result in suffering again. Healing cannot be of the body, mind or emotions, which are all in the field of duality, and duality is always changing. True healing, therefore, is not even of the mind because the mind comes and goes. True healing is enlightenment, which in the end has nothing to do with body, mind or emotions. When the healer can bring his client to this place, his work can truly be considered great and valuable beyond all other works that he could do.

Chapter Nine—The Breath

-9:1-
Here we begin an explanation of the breath-within-the-breath.

The breath plays a vital and often missed role in the process of healing. Every client who comes to the healer is breathing, but often their vital energy is blocked due to an improper use of the breath. Although the breath is vital for sustaining the life of the body, an even more subtle essence flows with the breath that is important to address in healing. The breath-within-the-breath is the real link between Spirit and matter. It is through the inflow and outflow of breath that the body stays alive; without this breath, the body would obviously cease to function. However, this simple process is often taken for granted. The breath can be exceptionally powerful as a catalyst for promoting profound healing on all levels.

-9:2-
The word breath here is synonymous with the body's life force energy.

The breath-within-the-breath is what is known as life force energy, called Qi in Chinese, Ki in Japanese, and Pran in Sanskrit. This energy has been acknowledged since human beings have sought to understand the human body and its process of health and disease. The basic premise concerning life force energy is that when it is not flowing properly disease manifests. However, as we have seen in the sutras repeatedly, energy blockages are not the true cause of disease and removing them is not true healing. The flow of vital life force energy must be restored, but this alone is not enough. Without the process of enlightenment itself, the release and revitalized flow of energy will not be complete in the true healing process.

Breath, life force energy and mind co-existing within the mind-body system go hand-in-hand. When the breath is very slow and calm, the mind is also slow and calm. When the breath is fast and chaotic, the mind is also fast and chaotic. The important factor in healing is to understand that when the breath is stopped, so too is the energy of the heart-mind. The most efficient way to suppress emotions and negative thoughts is simply to tense the body and to stop breathing for a moment. When a person consciously or unconsciously suppresses emotions, he often tenses the body and stops the breath. The vital life force as e-motion (energy in motion) is blocked, and a sanskaric imprint is created within the psyche.

Sanskars, which are intimately linked with the breath, can be removed through the breath. Sanskars themselves block the life force energy from flowing. When this energy is increased with a conscious increase in the rate and depth of breathing, these blockages can be brought to the surface, resolved and removed.

-9:3-
This life force energy is the breath-within-the-breath.

The breath itself can be considered to consist of various gases as found within the atmosphere that help to nourish and sustain the human body. It can also be seen as being composed of other gases that are by-products of the breathing process itself. However, the breath-within-the-breath is an essence more subtle than oxygen or carbon dioxide. The breath-within-the-breath is not only to be considered as energy, but also as the flow of conscious energy within the human system. When the body stops breathing, and what is commonly called death occurs, the breath stops; but, even more importantly, the breath-within-the-breath no longer associates with the body. This is important because, as we have seen, if Consciousness is pulled away from an area, then blood and energy are also pulled away from that area. When a body is "dead," the breath-within-the-breath is no longer flowing and has gone on with the more subtle bodies of the Soul itself.

When the Consciousness of Soul no longer attends to the physical body, that body will not last very long. The conscious energy, or life force, of the Spirit itself is what animates and motivates the more subtle bodies. If this is suppressed or blocked in an attempt to avoid life experience, the process of dis-ease and separation begin. This flow must be unblocked so that the meridians of the body flow properly to promote balance and nourishment of all organ systems, and the blocked sanskars are released to awaken the client from the illusions held within them.

-9:4-

Unless this energy flows freely and in balance, illness will manifest.

As we are discussing, life force energy is so much more than just the breath or even simply the breath-within-the-breath as the body's vital pran or Qi. This energy is intimately linked with the psyche and its feelings, emotions, thoughts, memories and belief systems. When energy gets blocked, energy and blood is restricted to vital organs and cells and the system's beliefs, emotions and memories get knotted up. By increasing the amount of breath energy within the system, blockages can be brought to the surface and thereby released and healed.

-9:5-
The biggest cause of the blockage of breath energy is emotional suppression and denial.

In the natural order, life force energy flows freely and easily. Emotions are fully felt and mind is never rigid. Harmony is meant to exist within all manifest beings. When the ignorant mind puts up walls between itself and what it experiences, then disharmony arises. Where there is resistance, there will be suffering. As the process of healing occurs with the intention to eliminate suffering, these blockages and denials of Self must be removed. When a person closes his heart and resists any life process, whether internal or external, he initiates within his system causes of illness and disharmony. Healing involves bringing the being back into a state of unity with the benevolent harmony of things. Therefore, to the extent that a person is still suppressing his emotions by stopping the breath or breathing improperly, to that extent there will be suffering in his life.

-9:6-
To stop emotion or thought, one can stop the breath; yet this blocks life force energy.

A simple experiment can be done to see how easy it is to show the relationship between mind and breath.

Simply ask a group of people to stop thinking. Then wait a moment and ask by a show of hands how many people were holding their breath. The majority of people in the room will most likely raise their hands, because all have this natural ability to control the mind by controlling the breath. In Yogic pranayam exercises, the life force energy is consciously regulated to help to calm the waves of the mind. Most people do this unconsciously and destructively when they stop the flow of breath energy through suppression. Again we are reminded that breath energy must always flow. In the midst of any emotion, memory or feeling, a person must be encouraged to relax and to keep breathing.

-9:7-
Blocked energy must be made to flow freely again.

-9:8-
Within blocked breath energy are mental impressions that house memories, beliefs and emotions.

-9:9-
These must be released and brought to Consciousness.

Methods for removing blocked breath energy and releasing trapped patterns include Rebirthing, Holotropic Breathing and Integrative Breathing, which activate the life force within the breath. These similar processes encourage a long period of time where the person breathes slightly rapidly, deeply and rhythmically, increasing the amount of life force energy in the system.

During this process, a person's symptoms can be brought to the surface and healed. Usually physical

The Sutras on Healing and Enlightenment

symptoms get amplified first, followed by feelings, then emotions, then beliefs and then memories. The process of Breath Work simply reverses the order of manifestation of disease from the most gross to the most subtle. This is not always but is usually the case where the blockages unfold as if from the outside in. Once the layers have been exposed and a person is fully in the midst of his issues, the healer can use the processes discussed in previous sutras to resolve the imbalances that have surfaced.

Using the breath greatly facilitates physical healing and also powerfully removes and restores the proper flow of the life force. As the physical symptoms are surfacing and the energy is being intensified by the breath, the underlying beliefs and emotions that caused the problem are brought to the surface with their underlying memories attached. Through proper facilitation, not only are the underlying patterns transformed, but also a client can be easily led into a state of profound awareness of who they are as Pure Spirit. Through the intense emotional releases of Breath Work, combined with good solid therapeutic technique, a client can make great strides in knowing himself as that immortal and unchanging Self of Love and Light.

-9:10-

This is done exceptionally well by the healer assisting the client through Breath Work.

Assisting a client through a Breath Work session requires training and skill. A client is in a very intense situation and only someone who is thoroughly trained and confident enough to deal with the material that comes up should engage in the process. It is not difficult to hold the space for a client to engage in Breath Work, but it is at the point of catharsis and healing that the healer must be able to finish the job successfully.

When the process is done well, the client is often freed of many physical, mental and emotional symptoms. His negative beliefs have been transformed, and past memories have been "cleaned up." In the end, the client should be united with his True Self in a process of true healing. If the client's symptoms are all relieved and he comes to know himself as the Divine Self through proper facilitation, the healer has indeed done his job very well.

-9:11-

The breath will reverse the order of the manifestation of disease.

-9:12-

The breath will expose suppressed mental impressions, which the healer can transform with his client.

As we have seen in the sutras repeatedly, nothing exists on the physical plane without existing in some form on the more subtle planes first. As the link between the planes where Spirit manifests into matter, we can see how the breath is active on all levels of the order of manifestation. When the breath is intensified, the order of manifestation unfolds within the client's psyche. It is as if the intensified breath goes into the problem and shows the client's mind the underlying roots of the problem. When the client feels the associated feelings, re-experiences memories and shares these with the healer, he and the healer work through these together.

-9:13-

When this is accomplished and true healing occurs, the client must be taught never to block this energy again.

After the healing process is complete, healer and client must have a post-talk where they review the session and the client can understand what he just went through. The order of manifestation of disease will now make sense to him from his own direct experience. He must come to understand the destructive nature of emotional suppression and the problems that come from closing the heart. He should be made aware that the false beliefs he held about himself were clearly erroneous and that he is so much more than he imagined himself to be. The client should be led into the real world, where there is only the benevolence of God and where he can feel safe and secure to live with an open heart and a free-flowing breath energy.

Chapter Ten—Long Distance Healing and Taking on Karma

-10:1-
Healing can occur regardless of whether the client is physically present or not.

It has been known by humankind for ages that one person can heal another whether he is physically present or not. The well-evolved healer who truly understands the process of healing can enter into his own meditative state, tap into his client and work out his client's karma in his own body. Great Gurus and Saints have been known to do this for their students and disciples frequently, yet in their humility they never advertise the ability. Not to mention that one person—no matter how great— can only deal with transforming so much of the world's illusion.

The following sutras will explore the fascinating concept of helping another person to heal without even being physically present with him. It has been proven time and time again that prayer does heal the sick, but it has never adequately been proven how. The belief that God offers his grace to those who ask is sweet, but it is also very naïve. God is Infinite Love and Grace and has never withheld his Love and Healing Power from anyone. The Truth is there—everywhere—and the healer and client only need to tap into that power to let it work for them. Our discussion of creating and manifesting gives a formula for dissecting prayer and seeing why it really works.

It is no longer debatable that prayer works, but we will begin to explore the mechanics of prayer and come to

The Sutras on Healing and Enlightenment

understand the profound ability of the healer to work out his client's karma in his own body. Of course, there are reasons not to do this work (which the sutras will explain); and no one should enter into it lightly. Most people are not healed enough themselves to even begin to consider healing another person's issues in their own bodies. The well-evolved healer, however, has come to a place where he is healed enough in himself to understand how healing truly works. His confidence in the unreality of disease makes it very easy for him to consider being of service in this way. The information in this chapter will be for most simply an interesting topic that may empower them to heal themselves. At mankind's current state of evolution, it is not recommended that the teachings in this chapter be practiced by those who are not totally confident in their abilities to promote healing and enlightenment for others within their own bodily system.

The topic of taking on karma is one of the reasons why a saint might get sick. Technically speaking, a saint is a free being whose mind is no longer bound in the duality of illusion. He is totally attuned to Truth. Therefore psychosomatic illness could not possibly manifest in his body. Yet one of the reasons (and not the only one) is that he is working out other people's issues within his own system. Not all saints do this; for many, it is simply not their purpose. Yet those who do have truly given of themselves selflessly. The statement that Christ died for our sins refers to the fact that he was working out an enormous amount of humanity's karma in his own body. The notion that Christ, the Truth, can die is absurd; but his body was a vehicle for the liberation of mankind. For a totally free being to give himself so fully for humanity's salvation is perhaps one of the most profound examples of this work.

The Sutras on Healing and Enlightenment

-10:2-
The healer and the client are not two separate realities and are not limited by time and space.

In order to understand the theory behind healing another person "long-distance" we must acknowledge the inherent Oneness of the Whole. In Truth, there is only one Reality without a second: God is not two. There is not the Infinite Consciousness of God and then some other reality called the physical universe. Because in Truth there is nothing but God. the healer knows that he and his client are one and the same Reality. He knows that, in Truth, time and space cannot possibly separate them, because time and space only exist in the relative field of mind. The client does not have to know this, but the healer must. The healer must be established in the field of Unity Consciousness to be able to be one with his client. In this Oneness, there is no separation; and there is only One Mind because in Divine Mind there is only Oneness. Any aspect of the Whole can affect change on any other aspect of the Whole.

The human being is a hologram of the Whole, which means that all of the entire creation is contained within him. Nothing exists in the Whole that does not exist within the part. However, taken even deeper, we can see that the Consciousness of the healer is the Consciousness of the client and that they are the same Reality. For the healer then, all suffering is his suffering. The compassion that exists within the healer is not sympathy for another's pain but an overwhelming Love for the whole of creation as his very own Self. For the true healer, nothing exists but God—which is indeed his very own Self. Therefore, as long as there is still suffering, the healer will be of service.

The Sutras on Healing and Enlightenment

-10:3-
True healing, which is the transformation of illusions into Truth, happens only on the mental level.

As we have seen throughout the sutras, healing is synonymous with enlightenment; and enlightenment is the transformation that occurs within the human being where a shift is made from illusion to Truth. In Truth, the Self is perfect and does not need healing. The problems, where suffering exists, are only in the human mind. Only the mind gets sick, and therefore all healing is mental healing. The more subtle bodies that the mind uses have no power of their own; these are vehicles for the Soul to experience through while using the vehicle of mind as well. When the mind falls into illusion, all the bodies it uses will suffer accordingly. This point has been made very clearly throughout the sutras and need not be elaborated here. The major point to be understood then is that the healer can work to heal his client long-distance, because the healing is not happening on a physical level, but on the mind level. If we then understand that healing is not on the body level, we can see that all long-distance healing and any true healing is only happening on the mental plane. The healer must know this to be able to fully tap into the root cause of his client's problems.

-10:4-
The healer is again reminded not to acknowledge illness or error as real.

When the healer begins his process of working on his client long-distance, he first goes into a deep meditative state where he accesses the Truth of his being. He moves into the state of Pure Consciousness, where the illusions of body and mind have fallen away and where only Self-Alone exists. Here, the healer knows himself as the Divine Truth—the Source of all healing, love, goodness, power and grace. The healer might not declare to the masses that he knows himself as the Divine Itself, but nothing can change this Truth. The healer moves into this Space and takes as long as he needs to center himself in this Truth.

In this Space, he only knows Truth. He cannot possibly see error, illusion, illness, birth, sickness, old age or death as real. He knows that the Self is unborn and undying. He knows that the Self never ages or gets sick. He knows the Truth and therefore cannot possibly believe in the reality of illusions. Illusions have no reality; therefore, in this Space he can safely work out his client's illusions within his own system. Any person not deeply established in this highest Space of Truth is simply not qualified for the work of healing another person's karma within their own system. The healer must know the Absolute Truth of the Universe, or he is not ready to tackle another person's illusions.

-10:5-

The healer is to visualize his client and to see him only as perfect, whole and complete.

While in the Space of deep meditation, the healer allows the image of his client—as he currently is—to come into his awareness. The image is the client with any of his problems. Now the careful reader will have noticed that a previous sutra says that the healer should visualize the client as perfect, whole and complete; yet here we are told that the healer should see the client as he is currently manifesting in his illusion. The reason for this is because this work is not for the novice. The sutras do not mention going too deeply into someone else's illusions but would rather have the inexperienced healer focus only on the goal rather than the problem. This way is safer for him, and he will not take on the client's karma nearly as much.

The true healer has come to deeply understand that illusions must first be brought to Consciousness to be truly released. Just visualizing a person as being perfect, whole and complete is the practice of a less evolved mind that still sees people as being their forms. A person is Pure Consciousness in the healer's eyes. Therefore he does not need to visualize his client as perfect, whole and complete because he already knows that they cannot be anything else. Therefore, the first step the healer takes in the field of Pure Consciousness is to allow the client's illusions to manifest in his mind. It is from here that he will begin his work. When the work is done, both healer and client will both know that they truly are perfect, whole and complete. The healer's work is far more complex than simply a positive visualization. However, this sutra has purposely been kept vague so that only the sincere reader and dedicated healer will be instructed that he must be willing to open up to the client's illusions and not simply his perfectly visualized form.

Opening up to the information coming to him in meditation, the healer simply is to trust his first impressions and not analyze them. When he taps into the client's energy, the healer is opening himself up to impressions that the client himself may not be aware of. The healer should only do this work if he has permission from his client or if he feels that he is totally in harmony with Divine Goodness in doing so. Therefore, with his client's willingness and his mind fully open to receiving, he can begin to tap into the real root of his client's issues—beliefs, emotions, chakra imbalances, negative self-images and physical symptoms. It is with this information that he begins to work, not simply on trying to visualize a positive self-image for his client.

-10:6-
He should deny the client's false beliefs and affirm only the Truth.

Again, the process of healing from a distance is more complex than the sutras go into. Before the healer can begin to deny false beliefs, he has to first know what these beliefs are. He must also open up to all other imbalances that are occurring within the client on all levels of his being. This can be considered a psychic exercise, or it can also come from information that the healer already knows about his client. Impressions will come into the healer's Consciousness from many data points. The information can come from many sources, from those that are truly clairvoyant to those that are very common and practical. For instance, the healer may pick up on the thoughts of the client and discover his belief systems, or he may simply know them from having worked with his client in person. It does not matter where the information comes from, because the healer will simply acknowledge any error and affirm only the Truth.

The healer is basically to work with his client in his Consciousness the way he would in person. This does not need to be explained in depth here. The major point

The Sutras on Healing and Enlightenment

is that in the end, the healer will have transformed all the client's illusions in his own meditations. In short, he does this by acknowledging his client's false beliefs, denying their reality and affirming only the Truth. However, the more levels he can work on (e.g., the causal, mental, astral, etheric, physical, energetic and chakric levels), the more effective he will be.

-10:7-
The healer must believe that it is possible to heal a client in this way.

The next sutras are a brief version of the Creating and Manifesting Formula. These will be elaborated on more in the next chapter. For now, we can see that if the healer does not believe or have faith in the process, he will seriously limit his ability to do this work. The more experience he has in this type of healing, the more his faith and belief in the process will grow. The stronger his faith and belief, the more powerful his healings can be.

-10:8-
The healer must want to do this.

This sutra goes without saying: the healer must want to do this work because in Creating and Manifesting, the desire aspect of the work is much more than meets the eye. The healer must not only want to heal his client, but he must acknowledge that he wants his client healed. God has given all His Children the free will to re-create themselves as they wish. He will never go against this. If a Child of God is willing to heal and the healer is willing to assist in the healing, it must be acknowledged that both want the healing to occur because God will not go against His Child's will. Desire is very important.

-10:9-
The healer must be willing to accept this power and any responsibility that goes with it.

Acceptance is also a key component of Creating and Manifesting. Simply stated, anything that a Child of God re-creates he must be willing to accept. There is a responsibility in having creative-healing power, and anyone who chooses to wield it must be willing to accept the outcome. Because the outcome in healing is only for the greatest good, this will never be a problem for the healer, who simply must acknowledge that he is willing to accept his role, the power that goes with it and the responsibility of using such power.

-10:10-
The healer must expect that his efforts will yield the results he imagines.

What we expect tends to be realized. The healer should affirm that he expects that this healing will occur. The healer simply should know that he must completely expect that his efforts will produce the results he is working for. These results are only a shift from illusion to Truth within his client. The healer knows that all healing is mental. He can expect that this healing will occur, because all Children of God will eventually be enlightened in the end. The healer knows who the client already is and easily expects the healing to occur, because in his mind it already has.

The Sutras on Healing and Enlightenment

-10:11-
The healer must surrender the outcome with non-attachment.

The Ultimate Healer is the Truth, not some vague idea of a healer as separate from Truth. Thus, any part of the healer that feels he is the doer must surrender the outcome of his actions with non-attachment. When ego-mind becomes part of the healing process, then surrendering the outcome is the only option for the healer. However, when the healer knows himself as the Self, he knows that he is not the doer and that healing is simply what is happening.

-10:12-
It is possible for the healer to read the mind of the client during a long-distance healing session and to become aware of the negative beliefs that are causing the problem.

-10:13-
The healer can then work out those beliefs within his own mind.

-10.14-
Karma is belief in action.

It is impossible to understand thoroughly the concept of karma without understanding belief systems, and a healer can never fully take on karma unless he is proficient in resolving false beliefs. The word *karma* is often misunderstood. Literally, the word means "action," yet there is no action by itself. All karmic-based action is motivated by mind, but all action is not karmic. For the average human being, there is still the false belief in a separate self who is a doer. This masquerading Self actually believes it is in charge of its own life and its actions are based on the false notion that it is the one actually doing. God alone is the doer. Therefore, karma only applies to the false Self and its false beliefs—the individual who feels that he is the doer. Karma then is false belief in action.

Karma is a dualistic theory that ties into the belief in individual responsibility, yet this is only a theory based on illusion that never really helps to free a person from his suffering. Karma—and its partner theory, reincarnation—are very simple, linear and limited models of what is really happening in creation. Karma and reincarnation are very valid theories in the world of duality, but in Truth they are far from what is really going on. The Self is never born and never dies. It never acts, nor is it acted on. The Self is pure, free and forever and has never incarnated into a body in the first place. Therefore, when the healer works on the client's karma, he simply is aware that he is working in the realm of the client's illusions and transforming them into Truth.

Because this occurs within his own awareness, he cannot believe in his client's karma, or false beliefs made manifest; in the healer's awareness, there is only Truth. While the healer is in this Space of Truth, he can open up to the client's energy and tap into the client's karma or negative belief systems and how these are manifesting. The more open he is and the more skilled he is, the easier it will be to tap into a client's energy system and to "read his mind" so to speak. Mind-reading is a simple term and not really what is implied in the sutras. The healer will not know every thought that his client is thinking, but will intuit the beliefs that underlie the symptoms of his client. For instance, if the client is suffering from endometriosis (a severe irritation of the uterine lining), then the healer will bring the client into his awareness with this condition in mind. He will then open up to what is underlying his client's symptoms and receive the answers. While meditating on this client, the healer might find underneath her endometriosis a belief that she is dirty, ugly, shameful, disgusting, bad, sinful and stupid. He then can begin to work on transforming these beliefs within his own system.

The well-evolved healer knows that his client is never truly sick, but when he focuses his attention, the client's problems may begin to somehow appear in his own body. He will feel the symptoms, because he has held the beliefs in his mind that cause them. If he then heals the false beliefs within himself, the symptoms will drop away within his own body relatively quickly. This will absolutely help his client in her healing. Because there is only One Mind, when false beliefs are removed from that Mind, Truth simply manifests very easily.

Taking on a person's karma is complex, because the healer in a sense becomes his client. He takes his Consciousness and owns the person's beliefs, emotions, chakric imbalances, energy blockages and even physical symptoms while engaging in the healing process in this way. However, because the healer is not blocked and is working from the inside out, he does not need to go through all the more dense levels of manifestation for healing to occur. He can simply go right to the mental level and heal false beliefs from there. In this way, the symptoms will fall away within his own body.

Karma is sanskar. A person's sanskars are their mental impressions from past events with their corresponding beliefs and emotions. These patterns cause an ignorant person's behaviors and what they attract into their lives. Sanskars house the false beliefs that motivate action and manifest disease. Therefore, sanskars are the karma that the healer can take on within his own system.

For the enlightened being, however, there is no notion of being the doer any more. He realizes that he is not a separate self who is motivated by karma. He knows that he is the Source and is beyond action and inaction. He is the Knower, the Witness or the Supreme Self who watches the dance of creation unfold, never for once believing that he is doing any of it or that it is separate from himself. He knows that karma is an illusion and that he actually frees his client from the dream of being a separate individual when he takes on his karma. Because all true healing is enlightenment, the healer is actually enlightening clients to the Truth of their being through this process—the only real aim of any human incarnation. A human being exists to know himself as God. The healer must support this during any type of healing work, or it is not true healing.

-10:15-

If the beliefs are very strong, then the healer may experience the client's symptoms within his own body.

When the healer taps into the energy fields and belief systems of his client, he is setting himself up to feel whatever the client is feeling and even to experiencing similar symptoms. A client's strong beliefs will take longer to transform. Belief systems seldom come one by one, arriving in packets intimately woven together. If the client believed that he was not good enough and was getting a nervous stomach because of it, the healer would resolve this belief in his own mind for the client, and it would be rather simple. However, healing rarely works this way.

A client presents himself as a walking maze of illusions, and the list housing these errors is usually quite long. The person with the stomach problems does not simply believe that he is not good enough. He also feels unworthy, useless, not important, incapable, valueless, small, weak and powerless. We can then see that the patterns are usually much thicker and more complicated than we would like; and the work is therefore that much more complex. It could take a healer many days to unravel a client's patterns within his own system. During that time, the symptoms of the client may begin to appear in the healer's body. The more quickly he can work them out, the better.

-10:16-
If the healer is well evolved and does not believe in the client's false thoughts, emotions and symptoms, then the healing can be quite rapid.

-10:17-
If the healer does hold similar beliefs, then the healing will take longer only because now the healer must heal himself as well.

The real problem with this type of healing—taking on karma—is that the healer himself is usually holding the same beliefs as the client. These beliefs may not be as strong in the healer and may not cause physical symptoms; nevertheless, he houses these beliefs just the same. In these cases, the healer has to work out his own karma and his client's at the same time. The healer and the client are the same being, and false beliefs healed for one are healed for the other. When the healer and client come together, truly a relationship is developed, and it only takes one person to change a relationship.

The healer may still hold beliefs in sickness and may actually be afraid of manifesting the same sickness that the client has. The healer must then work out his belief in the illness and his fear about getting it. During this time, he may certainly feel the client's symptoms in his own body. Unless he can work out the false beliefs that manifest the symptoms, these could truly become his own, and he would not have helped his client very much at all.

If the healer is well evolved and does not hold karma similar to his client's, it will not be difficult at all for him to embrace, deny and transform his client's false beliefs and symptoms. There is a real beauty, however, in the fact that the healer is healed in the process if he does hold similar beliefs as his client. The healer is usually the more conscious force. In his humility, he understands that a relationship is never an accident and that his clients are for his own growth as well. He is grateful for the opportunity to have a mirror placed before him where he can see his own issues amplified in the client. If he is bold enough to work out his client's issues in his own mind, he will see that he has tremendously benefited from this process. In healing his client, he has also come to heal himself.

The Sutras on Healing and Enlightenment

-10:18-
A healer should never attempt to take on another person's karma without the total confidence that he can resolve it quickly and easily.

If the healer does not feel confident in being able to work out a certain issue in his own system, he should never begin. If a client's karma lingers in the healer's system for weeks or even months, it can debilitate the healer, and he will not be able to assist other clients. A healer should be very cautious about this process and should never take on more than he can handle. If he does not feel exceptionally confident in his abilities, he should wait until he does and continue working directly with his client in person.

-10:19-
It is an unparalled act of selflessness and compassion to even consider this.

-10:20-
A healer must find his own limit as to how much he is willing to work this way with his clients.

To be willing to suffer to free another person from their suffering is a great act that takes an enormous amount of selflessness and compassion. The unity within the healer's heart and mind causes him to want to see all beings free at whatever the cost. But he must only work in harmony with the Divine Will, and he must understand his own limits. A healer may still be young in his body and need his full health and energy for his own daily life, and this is perfectly fine. He should respect this and honor himself as the highest priority. However, if he knows that it is possible and safe for him to help a client in this way, he can easily do this work without care or concern.

He also must find his own limits to how much of this work he will do. He knows that people do, for the most part, need to work out their own karma on their own. To simply take away someone's pain would not help that person to grow from the pain. Karma is not a punishment system. Karma is a communication system that shows a person his own denials of who he truly is. The system is perfect as everything in the Universe is perfect. Therefore, the healer must understand his place here and never deny someone the opportunity to live his or her life fully. Often it is perfectly in harmony for the healer and client to work together on many levels to assist the client in becoming free. The healer should simply listen to his inner guidance and respond accordingly.

-10:21-
Because of this ability for an evolved Soul to take on another being's karma, a healer who does not believe in illness may have sickness within his own body.

-10:22-
Healing and enlightenment are synonymous terms, yet a fully liberated being can appear to have a sick body. He knows that he is not the body and can work out another's karma in his body.

-10:23-
As long as any Soul still believes in sickness, then it will still exist.

Why a saint could get sick is a very important issue. If a saint is someone who no longer lives in illusion, why would his body ever get sick? Without an answer to this important question, we cannot ever fully have faith in the teachings of the sutras. The sutras make it clear that sickness originates in the mind and that all illness is psychosomatic because the body itself—as the result of the mind—is psychosomatic. Therefore, why would a fully enlightened being get sick if he is totally free?

Among many answers to this question, a fully enlightened being may find his body physically sick because he is simply working out the karma of his students or clients on his own body. The manifested illness results not from his own karma but from the karma of those whom he loves and wishes to serve.

Another major reason why a great saint would get sick is that he is simply not as evolved as we would all like to think. As we examine closely the lives of saints, we see that many experienced tremendous personal growth during their lifetimes. Very few beings are born totally free. Those who are almost free usually have very sensitive and finely tuned nervous systems that have to handle an enormous amount of energy and transformative power. Many saints come into this life with their own karma to work out and with bodies exceptionally suited for rapid evolution. Their bodies often became easily out of balance as a result.

We can also see that when a certain saint incarnates during a certain period of time in human history, his physical body is part of a mass consciousness that is creating a consensus reality where illness is simply part of the game. For instance, large epidemics that can kill hundreds of thousands of people can be seen as part of a group consciousness of false beliefs. The saint may not hold the beliefs of the masses, but the group energy still may have a profound effect on his body. As long as there is even one being who still believes in sickness, then sickness will still exist. In the world of duality, there will always be up and down, hot and cold, healthy and sick. The human body, no matter to whom it belongs, is still a part of this dualistic world where sickness is always going to exist. Remember that the world of duality itself is a consensus reality, and Souls who still believe that it is real give it an enormous amount of power. The more people wake up to the Truth of their own being, the less sickness there will be. Because most of humanity is still asleep, then the saint—no matter how great—still has a body that interacts with that field and can become sick because of it.

We must always remember that true healing is not of the body and that it does not matter if the body is sick or not. The True Self is never sick, and true healing is to know one's Self as this Self. The evolved being knows that he is not his body and can willingly take on another person's karma and work it out in his own body, and he can simply know that he is totally free regardless of the condition of his body and regardless of the cause of his illness.

Despite the outward appearance of the manifest world, people are not as separate as we might think. A physical body is part of one unified field that is multidimensional and holographic. The Whole is contained within the part, but the Whole is infinite beyond belief. As long as there is sickness in the Whole, then there can be sickness in the body of a great being who is beyond ideas of "myself and my own" and knows that the world's suffering is his suffering. He does not claim that his body is his or that any illness in that body is his. He is the Whole and works

The Sutras on Healing and Enlightenment

and lives for the Whole. He knows that freedom does not lie in making the physical body perfectly healthy. Because he clearly understands what healing and enlightenment are actually all about, he sees physical healing in its proper place and understands that freedom is infinitely more than simply having a healthy body.

-10:24-
The more evolved the healer, the more influence he shall have over creation, whether he is present or working long-distance.

Regardless of the condition of his body, the evolved healer is a very free being who has tapped into the Source of all power. He no longer buys into the beliefs of the masses. Because he is so deeply aligned with Truth, he has a profound influence on the world around him. He knows that time and space are not absolute concepts, that healing can occur regardless of the distance between two beings and that the process is not much different from when he is with a client physically. He knows that he can certainly work out another's karma in his own body. The client's false beliefs all must get resolved in the end, and the healer most certainly can help that process within his own system. The more evolved the healer is, the more power he will have to do such work even if his own body is not perfectly healthy. All healing is mental healing. Therefore, the well-evolved healer can continue to heal those in need no matter what the state of his physical body.

Chapter Eleven—Creating and Manifesting

-11.1-
Anything that exists physically was created on more subtle levels and then manifested in form.

The healer can use a very powerful system termed Creating and Manifesting to help bring about changes in his client. In truth, anyone can use the process for any purpose once he understands the basic premises. In the context of healing it becomes the foundation for consciously and voluntarily bringing something into manifestation that was not there before or for balancing what is there that needs adjustment. The process is simple, and anyone who has come this far in the sutras should easily grasp the essence of the formula.

Nothing can exist physically that has not already been created on the more subtle levels of reality. The order of manifestation is the basis for what is formed in the physical world. The Creating and Manifesting process uses the concept to bring about good for those who would receive it. This is prayer dissected down to its essence. It explains why some things manifest in our lives and other things do not. It takes out the concept of petitioning a personal god and allows for a non-dualistic universe where Truth is All That Is. By utilizing this formula with wisdom and intuition, the healer can make very profound changes in his life and in the lives of others, because he knows that things are simply thoughts and only exist because the thoughts already existed on the more subtle levels.

-11.2-

An evolved being who is in touch with his Source can easily use a simple formula to create and manifest on any level of creation.

In truth, anyone can use this formula. The more evolved a being is, the more powerfully he can use this, because it works best when it happens from Source. When a human being is in touch with his Source, he taps into the Field of Pure Potentiality. From this field, all things—that ever were, are or will be—appear; and nothing exists that did not come from this Space. The true healer knows that he is this Space and that this Space is the Source of All That Is. The enlightened healer is deeply empowered by this Knowledge and can be said to co-create from it.

It is important to understand that every Child of God uses this process in everything that he does, whether he knows it or not. The semi-conscious human being is not aware of his true power and believes that he is the victim of chance, thinking that he is simply a body-mind. However, he is God whether he knows it or not; and his power is still from Source because it cannot come from anywhere else. He is still one with the field of Pure Potential even though he may not know it. He is also still governed by universal law despite his ignorance. The way things manifest for him is the same way things manifest for the enlightened healer, although he simply does not know this.

Whether we are conscious of it or not, we are manifesting the world we see. There is no other power than the power that we are as Pure Consciousness. The healer is simply aware of this fact, understands universal law and knows how the order of manifestation works to bring about a time-space reality. The Creating and Manifesting process simply empowers the healer and eventually his client to use this formula for manifesting good into the world.

-11:3-
This process can be applied to healing or anything else that one would wish to manifest.

Anything can be plugged into the formula for Creating and Manifesting. However, this present work is about healing, so this shall be our focus. To deeply understand this process, we must look at the words *creating* and *manifesting* to better understand this formula. The word *creating* implies the ability to conjure up an idea on the causal plane and then to manifest it physically. However, God already created everything that was created. The causal plane has already been created, and all pure ideas already exist there in their perfection. The healer should understand this and not try to create his own realities out of thin air. Although he is not the creator of all causal forms, he understands that as an apparently separate individual he can tap into and allow all causal forms to manifest physically. For instance, God has already created the perfect idea of a kidney. If the healer is working to heal a client's kidney, he does not need to create a new organ to replace the malfunctioning organ. He simply can tap into the pure causal idea of a kidney that has already been created. He will then work to help that pure idea manifest physically in the client's body as a healthy and useful kidney. The kidney already exists causally and it even exists physically, but the healer can work to manifest the pure idea into form, which will bring about health and harmony.

It is important to know that God has already created all pure ideas that are useful and valuable. Ideas, which simply float in the causal plane waiting to be tapped into and manifested, do not need to be created again. The human being is not the doer; and he does not need to create ideas of health, prosperity, harmony, happiness, peace and love. God has already done that. The healer only needs to tap into these ideas and open up the appropriate channel to help manifest them in his life and in the life of his clients. Manifesting then is actually the more relevant term here, because the healer is not really creating anything at all. He simply uses this formula to manifest the Goodness of God, which is not flowing perfectly in his client's life.

-11:4-
This process should only be used for the greatest good.

In a book like this, Sutra 4 should go without saying, but the point will be stressed simply because anyone using this process should know that the law of cause and effect is always operational. Anything plugged into this formula that is not for the greatest good can and will only do harm to the healer and the client as well. The perfect causal ideas of God are only Pure Goodness. There is no evil in God, and therefore there simply is no evil. Any maliciousness exists only in the illusion of the individual mind, which is an illusion itself. If this mind attempts to manifest something out of harmony with the Love and Goodness of God, then it can only cause suffering for all those involved.

The Sutras on Healing and Enlightenment

-11:5-
It should only be used to heal someone who is willing to heal and who has asked for help.

-11:6-
In the case of those who cannot ask for help, it is up to the healer to listen to his inner guidance and to act only from the highest intentions and intuitions.

-11:7-
This process works for healing whether the client is physically present or located at a distance from the healer.

-11:8-
If both the healer and the client do this process together, it is even more powerful.

Healing can never be inflicted on anyone, and the person who is to be healed, whether he is present or not, must be willing to heal. The Divine will never go against His Children's will and therefore neither can the healer. It is important then that the client asks for help, and then the healer can feel free to work directly with him or long-distance using the Creating and Manifesting Formula. If the client is unable to ask for help (such as in the case of coma), the healer is to trust his intuition and only act from the highest good. If the client is willing, the power of an evolved healer can be an immeasurable blessing in the client's life. When the client is also empowered with this formula, the power is greatly amplified. The more people using this formula for a specific aim, the more powerful it will be.

The Sutras on Healing and Enlightenment

-11:9-

Although the more people involved the better, the healer must be aware of unevolved or disharmonious minds that could sabotage the process.

The more creative power behind the manifesting process, the better. However, the healer who thoroughly understands the process should be sure that all those involved are in harmony with it. Even people with good intentions may not fit the formula well. Their lack of belief, desire, acceptance, expectation or willingness to let go could sabotage the process. The Creating and Manifesting Formula is the basis for how things come into being. If it does not appear to work, the healer must evaluate whether someone's mind, including his own, has possibly gone against what was trying to be manifested.

-11:10-

First, one must become clear on what is to be created and manifested.

The first step, clarity of intent, is the most important part of the formula. To use this process, the healer must know what he is using it for. Although this may sound simple, when another person's healing is involved, it is not always simple. The initial intake with the client should have established his chief complaints and how he would like his life to be different after these problems are gone. Healer and client should have mutually agreed on the desired outcome, which is then put into the formula. The intention can be general or specific. Both the healer and the client can visualize one area of his life or his entire life improving, but the more specific the manifestation is, the sooner the client can see the process begin to work. However, if the person or persons using this process are not clear about what they truly want, then the order of manifestation will not know how to respond. Clarity of intent is therefore the first and most important part of the process. The Chinese have a saying, "If you do not know where you are going, how will you get there?"

-11:11-
Then he should only act with intentions set for the highest good for all involved.

The healer first sets his intention clearly in his mind or verbally out loud and then simply affirms that this process is being used for the greatest good of all those involved. The clearer the healer is about his own personal values and life principles, the more easily he can know whether what he is about to do is consistent with his highest morality. The healer will know in his heart whether or not what he is working to manifest is in harmony with Divine Goodness. If it is, he can rest assured that no harm could come from his actions. He should affirm this in his mind or out loud by also saying, "Only goodness can come out of my efforts here."

-11:12-
Next, he should be aware of and work in accordance with universal laws.

Certain laws govern all aspects of the manifest universe. The more familiar the healer is with these laws, the more he can manifest in harmony with the laws and the more powerful he will be in this process. For instance, the simple law of karma says that every action has an equal and opposite reaction so you shall reap what you sow. Almost everyone knows this, but the healer simply makes sure that he lives up to what he knows. This is wisdom.

During the Creating and Manifesting Process, the healer simply listens to his heart and checks in to be sure that he feels that nothing he is doing violates or acts out of harmony with universal laws. He can affirm this in his mind or out loud by saying something like, "Knowing that we are in harmony with universal law, then we know that we can safely go ahead with this manifestation."

-11:13-
He is then to go into deep meditation and access his Source, the place of Pure Potentiality, Pure Consciousness and creativity.

Once the healer has clarity of intent, knows that he is acting from the highest good and is in harmony with universal law, he can begin to access a deep meditative state for himself and anyone else involved. How long this takes is up to the healer, but the more time spent the better. Typically, at least five minutes should be spent accessing the Space of Pure Consciousness. This Space is the Source of the entire manifest universe, and the healer and those involved should be led into that place of Pure Potentiality beyond time and space. From here, the true work of manifesting can begin.

-11:14-
Here the image of the desired result is to be held in the mind.

-11:15-
The visual image should be seen as if it already exists with all those involved.

Once the healer and anyone else involved are firmly established in a deep meditative state, then the mental image of the desired result is to be brought forth in the mind. This image should be as real as possible and seen as if it were already so. Those visualizing should see the desired result in its completed state and not as progressive or evolving. There should be joy in the picture, and the people involved should be in the picture as well.

During visualization work, we should be reminded that God has already created everything that has been created. Therefore, any image that is held in the mind should be one that is tapped into from the causal plane. The ideas on the causal plane are perfect and Divine. There is nothing lacking in them in any way. For instance, if a person is working to manifest health in the physical heart, he should tap into the Divine Idea of the heart and use only that as his template. The healer does not have to create a new idea for a heart, as God has already taken care of that. The healer simply needs to hold in his mind the perfect idea of heart and use the Creating and Manifesting Formula to allow the client's heart to begin to match the pure idea, which already exists. Therefore, the first step is to hold the image of the person whose heart is being healed in his mind with the perfect idea of heart as well, seeing the person perfectly whole, healthy and complete.

Of course, we are reminded that visualizing symptom improvement is not true healing. Therefore, we will also want to be sure to add to our visualizations the real Truth of a person's being and affirm his Divinity, not only his bodily healing.

-11:16-
Intense positive emotion should be added.

As the positive image is being held in the mind, intense emotion should be added to it. This involves getting excited about the outcome and feeling joyful and happy about it. An image alone contains very little power, but an image with emotion is truly charged. The healer should do or say anything to increase emotional energy in himself and anyone else involved.

-11:17-
Thoughts affirming the outcome should be added.

Once the positive image is firmly in place and emotion is added, then the healer should affirm the outcome in words. He should state what the desired result is as if it were already so. However, if he feels the need to be incremental in his approach, he can use suggestions that this manifestation is occurring more and more each day. In the ignorant mind, Divine Realities do not appear to exist but the illusory realities of the world do. A sick mind sees sickness and may need to be slowly paced back into Truth; therefore, this mind can be told that health is coming more and more each day and that the positive image held in the mind is manifesting over time. In this case, the healer may want to state a certain time frame about when this will be fully manifest. Such a statement could be phrased, "On or before such and such a date, Bob's heart is perfectly healthy." This statement says that the outcome could happen before this date, which is important, so that instantaneous healing can still occur.

-11:18-
The healer then affirms his belief that this will work.

Now the first major aspect of Creating and Manifesting is complete. Clarity of intent was established, and we became clear that a perfectly healthy heart was the desired outcome. We also affirmed that this manifestation was for the highest good and was in harmony with universal law. We held in the mind the image of the person already healed and empowered this image with emotions and thoughts. Now the healer simply repeats three times in his mind or out loud, "I totally believe this is possible."

Anyone else involved should repeat this phrase in his mind while the healer repeats it out loud if he is working with a group. This important statement helps to cancel out thoughts that might sabotage the creation. For instance, someone in the group might be saying in his mind, "I really do not believe that a heart can be healed using the mind alone." The problem with this thought is that it is false, but it is still powerful nonetheless. By repeating three times, "I totally believe this is possible," the negative and false thoughts can be transformed. The more a person believes, the better. Therefore, the healer should work to convince his client or the group he is working with that this process really does work. This is best done by telling success stories about cases in the past where it has worked before. This leads us into the first major aspect of why prayer works, often associated with the term *faith*.

We now look at prayer in relationship to healing. When a person prays to God, he obviously has some belief that Deity, whatever that may be to him, can heal the person for whom he is praying. A lack of faith will only hinder the power of prayer. A person goes into prayer with an idea of having health restored for the person involved. He is seeing the positive outcome in his mind. He is often very emotional and repeats over and over the desired result that he wants in thought. This mental energy in visual form, emotional form and thought form is very powerful. The power of faith, or belief, makes it even stronger. This is how prayer works. It is not that a god is petitioned until he has been bothered enough to get annoyed at the incessant begging, wave his wand and cure the ailing.

God is Infinite Love and Goodness, and His Grace is Eternal and Omnipresent. There is not a single thought, word, emotion or mental image that is separate from this Field of Pure Potentiality. Prayer is a scientific process that can be repeated over and over again, getting verifiable results if it is understood. Certain laws within the universe can never be changed. When we act in harmony with these laws and understand that God created all that was created, we can easily manifest His pure ideas into physical form or restore imbalance to those manifested forms. Prayer works, and this sutra simply honors its major component, which is belief.

-11:19-
He then affirms that he wants this to happen.

After belief has been affirmed, the healer still must go on to ensure that other key components of the process are in place. He must now affirm that he wants this manifestation to happen. The healer and anyone else involved must repeat three times, "I really want this to happen." Again, we can acknowledge that the Divine will never go against its Children's wills, and if a Child of God does not want something to manifest, then Divine Power will not be behind it. This does not mean that a Child of God will never experience what he does not want to. It simply says that God will never go against his will.

In our example of healing the physical heart, if the person who we are trying to heal does not want to be healed, then he will sabotage this manifestation. We have seen that if he did not believe he could be healed, he would sabotage himself. We can also see that if he does not want to be healed, he can also sabotage himself. He therefore repeats three times in his mind, "I really want this to happen." This helps to cancel out any secondary gain or negative pay-off that gets something out of having a problem.

-11:20-

He then affirms that he is willing to accept the outcome.

Next, the healer and anyone involved is to repeat three times, "I am fully willing to accept this and all of the responsibility that it brings." The point here is that manifestation requires responsibility. A person can manifest a new job but not wish to get up and go to work every day. He sabotages his own creation if he is not willing to fully accept it in his life. He may end up manifesting it, but he will end up sabotaging it sometime down the line. Most of the time, if a person is not willing to accept the outcome of the manifestation while using this process, it simply will not happen.

The Sutras on Healing and Enlightenment

-11:21-
He then affirms that he expects this to manifest.

The next step in the process is to repeat three times the phrase, "And I totally expect and know that this will manifest." This statement is very powerful because it removes any doubt in the mind. What we expect tends to be realized. If we truly know that something will manifest, our thoughts are well aligned to allow it into physical form. The important thing to remember is that what is being manifested already exists. The true healer is only bringing forth already created causal ideas and has full faith that these ideas are available to be manifested into form. He simply needs to affirm that he expects that this will happen and that he knows it already exists. Things are nothing more than thoughts. The healer knows through tremendous personal experience that this process works and that whatever is plugged into it is bound to manifest.

-11:22-
He affirms his commitment to the process of doing what must be done to achieve the result.

The process is largely complete at this point. The last two steps simply ensure that what is being manifested really gets to come into being and that those involved can let go of their attachment to the outcome. This sutra begins that process by affirming three times, "I am totally committed to making this a reality, and I will do what I need to do to succeed." The reason for this is that no one prays for something unless he truly wants it. If someone truly wants something, he works to make it a reality. Therefore, this step is important for two reasons. One is that the person commits to doing the Creating and Manifesting Process until he gets his desired results and does not give up after only one or two times. The second reason for this step is that the person must act on this desire and do what he needs to do in his life to make it a reality. A person cannot pray for a healthy heart and then never exercise or eat a healthy diet. He must do what he needs to do to succeed. If he is not willing to, the healer should assist him in being willing to. If that is not possible, then the healer should not work with him.

-11:23-
He then surrenders the outcome to God through non-attachment.

This last step is perhaps the most important step in the whole process. The entire process of manifestation is given up to the Universe to let the Universe handle the details. When the final result is held in the mind and not the intermediate steps, the Universe finds a way to manifest what has been put into the formula. Therefore, the healer and those involved simply need to let go and let God. They should imagine that the image simply floats away into the universe as they affirm three times, "We now let go and let God, and let the Universe take care of the details. With non-attachment and surrender, we trust that this will become our reality."

If those involved truly let go of attachment and are not in desperation and worry but stay in trust and faith, then what they are asking for will manifest much easier. Worry is inverted imagination, and it is powerful as a creative force. When we worry, we visualize what we want not happening or happening as the case may be; and we do it with fear, actually using the entire Creating and Manifesting process against us. The more we can surrender and trust in the Goodness of God, the faster we will see what we want in our lives.

-11:24-
The process is repeated until the desired result manifests.

The Creating and Manifesting process should be repeated at least twice a day and more if desired. It should not be done too often, however, because this puts unnecessary stress on this very powerful process. Twice a day is usually more than enough. Sometimes once is all it takes; it depends on the scope and magnitude of the manifestation and how much energy has already been put into it. For instance, a building that is 95% complete and only needs some more positive energy to get it finished may only need a few Creating and Manifesting sessions. However, a major construction project that is a recent idea in a builder's mind may need hundreds of these sessions along with an enormous amount of physical work. The building comes about through this process, whether it is done consciously or not; but the more this process is used, the faster and easier the results will be.

-11:25-
The healer understands that present knowledge supercedes prior commitment.

This important statement ties in with the idea that some things we try to manifest may not manifest. Some of these things, we might find, were not for our ultimate

The Sutras on Healing and Enlightenment

good. The knowledge that we have in the present moment may supercede and be more informed or wiser than the knowledge we held in the past. Prior commitments are from an earlier time in a person's evolution through time and space. What is known now may not have been known then. Therefore, present knowledge supercedes prior commitment.

There should be no pressure or attachment to whether a certain idea put into the Creating and Manifesting process appears or not. One may find that he simply no longer wants to put energy into the creation or that this creation really is not for his greatest good. A person often makes a decision and later realizes that this decision no longer serves him. Every human being has the right to change his mind. There is nothing wrong with putting countless hours into manifesting something only to decide or realize later that this manifestation would no longer serve him.

Given free will to re-create himself at every moment, a Child of God is constantly doing so. He has the free will to manifest anything he wants to put energy into. If he finds that his re-creation is causing him suffering or is not serving him anymore, he simply can change his mind. There should never be guilt about letting go of a past commitment, because anything that no longer serves should simply be let go, and the person should move on.

-11:26-
The client is also to use this process in conjunction with his other methods of transformation.

The healer and client doing this process once together for the client's healing will not be enough. The client must be empowered to use this process on his own, and any creative way the healer can get the client to do this can only help. The client must be empowered to heal himself and use the Creating and Manifesting process in conjunction with anything else he is doing.

-11:27-
The highest use of this process involves the healer being totally in harmony with the Will of God and not acting selfishly or with ulterior motives.

How much energy should a person put into trying to get what he wants out of life with a Creating and Manifesting process? There is no doubt that the human mind is a creative force. Yet how this force is used is important in order to live a life that is free from suffering and joyfully fulfilled. Getting what one wants can be an immense curse and is not the real source of a person's happiness or salvation. In fact, many wisdom traditions acknowledge desire to be the cause of man's suffering. Desire is rooted in the belief in a separate self—a self who thinks that he exists apart from everything else and needs to get what he wants to be happy. This is never the real answer and can only lead to more and more misery. The answer to true happiness does not lie in fulfilling desires but in being free from the false self that has these desires.

When the false self is dissolved, then only God remains. The Will of God then is not different from the will of His Child. A Child of God who is totally one with His Source only follows His joy. God is joy, and being in harmony with God is joyful. God is only goodness and abundance, and there is no suffering or lack in God.

Being in harmony with the Pure Love of the Universe is the best way to assure that what we wish to manifest can come into being. However, we must remember that the world itself is changing and will always be a realm of polar opposites or dualistic. Our freedom never comes from making the world the way we want it to be. Unless we want the world to be a changing field that never remains the same, then we will suffer.

There is no certainty in the world of duality. Creating and Manifesting must be in harmony with this. If the healer acts only from the highest good, is free of the illusion of being a separate self, and trusts completely without ulterior motives and without attachment, then wherever he directs his energy can only yield beneficial results. With non-attachment and surrender, the healer can joyfully send positive energy and intentions to his client who is in need of healing without having to ever worry about being out of harmony with the Divine Will. When true healing is understood for what it is, it can never be disharmonious to offer it to another.

The Sutras on Healing and Enlightenment

Chapter Twelve—Empowering the Client

-12.1-
Clients must be empowered to discover the True Self on their own outside of therapy.

The healer can never live every moment with his client. If the client is not empowered to engage his own process of healing, he really is not healing at all. Life is the greatest healer, and the healer certainly has come to know that God is Life. God is the only true teacher and healer. If the client is not brought in touch with this Reality through the therapeutic process, he has been done a great disservice. If the client does not come to know that he can heal himself through Truth outside of the therapeutic setting, he has not gained much of anything from his time with the healer.

The healer must work to become obsolete in the client's life and should never attempt to prolong therapy for any reason. The client should be made into a healer—if not a healer of others, at least a healer of himself. He should leave knowing as much about healing as the healer knows and should be empowered every step of the way to be an active participant in the healing process.

Most of the time the client should work harder than the healer for his healing to occur. The healer is only there to assist in the process of wholeness and should never feel that he is being paid to fix his client as if he were broken. Because the true healer sees nothing wrong with his client, it is up to the client to say what is wrong and be willing to do something about it.

True healing is not analysis. The healer never tries to find something wrong but only affirms wholeness. The client must come in with a complaint if the healer can begin any therapeutic processes. If the healer tries to find something wrong with his client, he will; but it is only up to the client to present his illusions. Once the healer knows the client's complaints, he can suggest ways of healing them. The healer does not need to have all the answers. He simply tells his client what he thinks would work best for the healing to occur. Then the client can choose what feels best for him. Healing must be a mutual process where two minds come together in Oneness. The client should feel comfortable with the healer's modalities and ideally chooses which modality will be used.

The beauty of empowering the client is that it puts the majority of the responsibility on the client. The client presents a problem, chooses what modality to use to heal himself, and then must use this modality and any others available for his use outside of the therapeutic setting. This takes a good deal of the responsibility off the healer and gives it to God and the client as God. The healer knows that the client is God and only treats him as such.

-12:2-
They should be taught to meditate very early on in the therapeutic process.

This chapter on empowering the client discusses what the client can do outside the therapy setting to heal himself. Meditation is perhaps the most important tool a client can use to get closer to Truth. There are many paths to God and many ways to meditate. The healer should always help his client learn the basics of meditation and be sure his client is meditating daily. A beginning meditator should be taught to sit in meditation at least five minutes every morning and evening. He should be told the benefits of meditation and learn to do it easily and naturally. He should not force himself or consider it a discipline, but rather a peaceful exercise toward his own personal empowerment.

-12:3-
They must learn to keep the heart open.

The client should be taught why and how to keep his heart open. If the client stays closed to life in any way, he fails to grow to his fullest potential and is therefore not open to true healing. The true healer understands the immense value of an open heart and must come from that Space with his client. He then should give the client any technique or teaching that can help empower him to stay open and allow his heart to be purified. If the healer is unsure about this, he should review the sutras that elaborate on this theme, perhaps the most important part of empowering the client. Along with meditation, there is nothing more valuable in the process of attuning to Truth.

-12:4-
They should understand not to suppress or act out on their emotions.

-12:5-
They must learn what to do with their emotions—not to block, suppress, deny or act out.

A client should come to know the healing value of neither suppressing nor acting out his emotions. Through meditation and living with an open heart, the client can easily allow emotions to transform themselves without being suppressed or expressed. This most important process helps to burn away sanskaric debris and to leave the heart and mind in a state of clarity and Truth.

-12:6-
They should be taught how to breathe properly and to relax.

As we have seen, the breath is a vital part of healing. When the breath flows normally and naturally, the body remains healthy and energy does not get blocked. One of the best ways to suppress emotions is simply to hold the breath. The client should be taught proper diaphragmatic breathing and also how to breathe in meditation and how to breathe into emotions. When the breath is natural and flowing smoothly throughout the entire body, the client will continue to unfold into the full expression of his Divinity.

The breath also helps the client to relax when he is breathing properly, important both for stress relief and for purifying sanskars. If a client tenses and holds his breath during intense emotion, then he blocks this energy in his body. He should be taught to relax and breathe into emotions and to witness his emotions from the place of Higher Consciousness (also known as Witness Consciousness). Only through meditation, an open heart, proper breathing and relaxation can the process truly work to its fullest.

-12:7-
They should be taught when the voice of ego is communicating to them or when it is the voice of Truth and how to tell the difference.

As the client is coming to know Truth, he must be taught the process of discernment that discriminates the real from the unreal. The real is God—the voice of joy, delight, comfort, peace and love. The real does not cause suffering and is eternal and forever unchanging. The voice of ego, however, always causes suffering in the end and causes tension, worry, discomfort, heaviness and grief. The client learning to observe his body, mind and emotions from the place of Higher Truth must also learn what is eternal and unchanging from what is temporary and fleeting. He must also come to hear the voice of God within him and discern it from the voice of illusion and error.

The process is actually very simple. When a thought is attuned to God, it will bring joy and comfort on all levels. When a thought is attuned to ego, it will bring misery and discomfort somewhere within the bodily systems. The client should be taught to trust the communications of God and to choose only Truth in his thoughts, words and actions.

The client can also learn to discern the real from the unreal in meditation, where he chooses to focus on that which is unchanging rather than that which is changing. In meditation, the attention is constantly brought back to the Consciousness, which is real, and is not placed on the object of Consciousness, which is always changing and therefore considered unreal. These two processes of learning to listen to God and discerning the real from the unreal will greatly empower the client in knowing who he truly is and in living his life in peace and health.

The Sutras on Healing and Enlightenment

-12:8-

They should be taught how to witness their body, mind and emotions from the seat of Witness Consciousness.

The seat of Witness Consciousness is the real essence of daily meditation. Anyone not rooted in this seat is totally identified with his body, mind and emotions and has no idea who he really is. His Consciousness has identified with the object of Consciousness, and he cannot discern himself to be the Eternal Reality as apart from what he observes and will suffer from whatever discomfort the body feels. He no longer knows himself as the Eternal Self, but believes that he is the changing vehicles that he uses to experience the world. However, because the world is a dualistic field of pleasure and pain, the ignorant Soul will always try to hold on to what is pleasurable and push away what is painful. He lives in constant fear of death because he now believes that he is something that can die.

Witness Consciousness transcends this mode of suffering by helping the practitioner to be able to observe without being the body, mind and emotions. This is not detached, and it is not a true separation. It is simply becoming established in the unchanging yet non-dual Truth of one's being. It is only through constant meditation that this can happen. Without meditation, the person who tries to practice it will not have a well-established place to pull into in the midst of the storm. During difficult times, the Consciousness of a well-seasoned meditator can automatically pull back into the seat of observership and know that he is untouched by what he observes.

-12:9-
They should be taught how to meditate on the Knower.

The Knower is another word for Consciousness. It is awareness and always remains pure, free and forever. To know this Self, one simply places his attention on the formless field of Consciousness over and over again, especially during periods of silent sitting. The more attention placed on the Self, the more one becomes identified with it. In healing this is crucial, because true healing is the enlightenment of the human being as to who he truly is. Without knowledge of the Self, healing simply is not occurring. Meditation is the most effective way to cultivate this awareness, and therefore all clients should be taught this very early on in their healing work.

-12:10-
A client should understand that illness is a call for Love and that Consciousness is Love.

-12:11-
A client should be encouraged not to withdraw from or deny pain, but to bring the presence of the Knower directly into the core of the pain.

-12:12-
The Knower is Love, and Love is the most healing force there is.

The sutras make it very clear that illness is a false belief, and a false belief is a lack of Truth. A lack of Truth is a lack of Love, and therefore all illness is a call for the organizing and healing power of Love. Consciousness is Love. Usually during times of trauma, the awareness of the individual tries to pull away from any pain. When this happens, life force energy is robbed from the part of the body that actually needs it most. To reverse this process, the meditator is taught to place his attention directly on the Knower and then bring that Pure Awareness right into the core of the problem area. This process is very scary for some, but its healing effects are worth every ounce of fear that arises.

During times of pain there are many options available for the Soul, but the best one of all is to go directly into the core of the pain and to see what is really there. In the order of manifestation, physical pain also must exist on the etheric level, the astral level and the mental level for the Consciousness to even perceive it. Therefore, awareness placed on pain must go through the other more subtle vehicles first to become fully intimate with the sensation itself in the physical body. When this happens, the meditator's Consciousness is no longer separated from the pain by emotions and mind. He becomes the pain and realizes what is truly there. What he discovers is a call for Love, and in Truth he discovers Love.

The core of any manifested phenomena is Consciousness itself. Consciousness placed on any object of Consciousness long enough begins to perceive the true essence of the object of Consciousness, which is Consciousness itself. There is nothing but Consciousness in this universe; and, therefore, there is nothing but Love. When there is separation, the part that feels separate will call out for Love, even if it must call out with pain. When Consciousness goes directly into that pain, profound healing can occur; because Love is the most healing force in the entire universe. The client should understand this and learn how to be intimate with his pain and not try to avoid it.

By bringing attention to suffering, we stop creating a duality between the subject and the object—between Consciousness and that which it observes. There is no duality in Truth. With compassion, understanding, insight and acceptance, the Consciousness simply embraces its despair. No more resistance occurs, and Love is brought to that which was calling for it. All discomfort can be handled this way. When it is, miracles happen. Every client should be instructed in this process when he is mature enough to stop resisting his human experience and to embrace it fully.

-12:13-

When Consciousness finds the core of a problem, then the problem is seen to be non-existent.

This sutra touches on a deeper truth that is found in the concept of embracing despair. In Buddhist Philosophy, we find the word *shunya*, which is often translated as "void" or "empty." However, the Universe is not empty or void because it is the Whole, which includes all manifest phenomena and Pure Consciousness as one Reality. A deeper understanding of the word *shunya* is that all manifest phenomena are simply empty of a separate self. Because the Universe is non-dual, there cannot be pain and also Consciousness, or a physical problem and then something else called Truth. There is only Truth, and in Truth there is no birth, old age, sickness or death. There is no pain in Truth, and there are no problems in Truth.

The Sutras on Healing and Enlightenment

When Consciousness finds the core of a problem, the problem is seen to be non-existent. This does not mean that it is not really there. It is a relative and changing existence that is empty of its own separate identity. Consciousness becomes One with the area calling for attention. When this happens, there is no longer a problem. Pain in the body, when fully embraced, is seen to be empty. This does not remove pain per se, but it removes the one who feels separate from the pain. In Oneness there is no pain, because there is no one to be feeling the pain. Pain as a separate self is illusion, but pain in its essence is only Consciousness. As long as Consciousness feels separate from what it observes, it will always suffer because it has a belief in two-ness. In Truth there is only One, and that One is nothing but Love.

This concept cannot be intellectually understood: it must be experienced directly. The healer or the client who practices this will discover the Truth of it for themselves. This is the only way these sutras will make sense.

We must clarify the difference between being the Knower or the Witness Self and becoming one with the object of Consciousness in which there is no separation. Witness Consciousness is actually a false dualism that is a necessary stage in spiritual growth. The beginning practitioner is still totally identified with his body, mind and emotions, so he is asked to observe these and to discover his True Nature as the Knower. However, the more he meditates, the more he will come to know that Knower is all there is. In this realization, he will understand that he is not a separate observer from forms; he will know that Knower alone is. In this, we see how Consciousness, touching the core of pain finds only itself. Any apparent paradox being the observer and

The Sutras on Healing and Enlightenment

becoming one with what is observed is only reconciled in the non-dual state of enlightened Consciousness. Even though the philosophy behind this concept is deep, the client should be empowered to become established in the observing Witness and also to embrace his despair fully by moving into its core.

-12:14-
Many times illness arises because the person has withdrawn his Consciousness from a certain region of his body due to fear, shame or judgment.

-12:15-
The remedy is a state of maturity that is willing to be fully intimate with What Is and to embrace What Is totally and completely.

-12:16-
In the core of any manifested phenomena resides the Self.

-12:17-
The client must learn how to take his Consciousness and place it on the Consciousness within a problem.

-12:18-
It is then that the client will discover his wholeness, and he will see that there is only one Self and not two separate realities.

As commentary has largely explained these concepts, we can move on knowing that these truths must be practiced in order to be fully grasped.

The Sutras on Healing and Enlightenment

-12:19-
They should learn how to forgive and to practice forgiveness.

The process for forgiveness is rather simple, and a client should fully understand and practice it. First, he must learn the need for forgiveness and see that the only person who really suffers from his anger and judgments is himself. The client should understand that his suffering is largely due to his failure to forgive and that he simply needs to learn how to let go and let the Truth come into his mind. He should understand that forgiveness must come from the heart and not the head and that it cannot be faked. If the heart still harbors anger, the client should not be told to deny his anger and try to forgive.

Forgiveness never occurs by simply thinking about it and saying it in the mind or out loud. The heart will not change because of this. In therapy, forgiveness is often best done through emotional release and then a forgiveness formula; but in a client's life, he simply has to do two things and surrender the rest to God. First, he must understand why he would want to forgive and have the willingness to do so. Once he comes to the place where he is willing to let go, he should simply ask the Divine for help in forgiving. God is the healer, and the client alone cannot heal his own heart. He must simply affirm that he has suffered enough, that he is willing to forgive and then simply ask God to be healed so he can forgive. He should not suppress his anger, but should honor its presence and acknowledge that he is ready to let it go.

The problem with many people is that they forgive when they are still angry. They are never expected to heal their own anger and therefore are never expected to be able to forgive on their own. They should give their anger to God and ask for Truth to come into their mind when the heart has been cleared out. This is the only real formula that can work for the client because he needs to understand that he is not the doer. He follows this simple process and leaves the rest to God. God may bring a healer to assist, or it may happen in an infinite number of other ways. However, when a Child of God is willing to be free and asks, then he can rest assured that the Divine is always there to help. The healer may have certain ways of helping his client in therapy to forgive. However, in the client's life, he should simply be empowered with the instruction to be honest with his feelings, to admit that he is ready to let go and that he has suffered enough, and to simply ask that he be able to forgive.

-12:20-

They should be taught how to feel, identify and communicate their problems clearly.

A client is taught not to act out or suppress his emotions. Therefore, in daily life when he does need to communicate with others, he should be able to do so consciously and clearly. He should also be able to present to the healer how he feels and to be able to share this without ambiguity or confusion. Meditation helps the client to be present to his feelings through Witness Consciousness. The client should be taught to practice sharing his feelings with the therapist and with other supportive people in a conscious way, acknowledging responsibility for his own feelings without projecting blame or guilt.

The Sutras on Healing and Enlightenment

The client must first be able to feel. This requires an open heart and a mind that will never suppress again. He should also be able to identify the problem, which means that he can describe his physical sensations, emotional responses and thoughts that go along with this. He should then be able to express clearly how he feels on all levels of his being without suppressing his feelings and without acting out on them. Conscious communication is not acting out, it is a very healthy way to ask for help and to bring Oneness to situations where duality exists. Revelation breeds intimacy, and the more a client can share of his heart, the better.

-12:21-

The healer should recommend appropriate books and give homework.

A client should always be empowered with useful and relevant information; and the healer should frequently give homework for the client to do. If the client is not willing to do homework, then his willingness and desire to heal should be questioned. The client must work harder than the therapist, and the client should be empowered to help educate the therapist on his problem and the solutions he has found for it. The client, rather than the healer, is the one who should be learning how to heal himself. The healer simply assists in the client's process of healing. He is not expected to have all the answers, and he is not the one who should be researching the client's problems. The healer can do this, but the client must—or he is not a suitable client ready to be empowered to heal himself. The healer can help to nourish these qualities in his client, always assessing his client's willingness to heal himself; and this is a great way to find that out.

The Sutras on Healing and Enlightenment

-12:22-
Lifestyle changes should be suggested when necessary.

Even though the healer is working to change the client from the inside out, the client must work to change himself from the outside in. He must make changes necessary to promote a healthy lifestyle and healthy relationships. The healer should gently suggest certain changes. At the same time, the healer understands that until beliefs and emotions that fuel behaviors are changed, then the client will not change much on his own. It is important for a client to be empowered with skills that nurture his body, mind and emotions in this world. It is not necessarily the mental healer's job to discuss lifestyle changes, but sometimes the client simply needs the authority of the healer to tell him what to do, and then he will do it. The healer should never underestimate his power of suggestion when working with a client and how easy it is to get someone to do something that is good for him when the suggestion is given in just the right way and at just the right time.

-12:23-
A client should be empowered with the creating and manifesting process and taught to visualize properly.

The client should be using the Creating and Manifesting process in conjunction with his other therapeutic processes, both on his own and in therapy. The client should be taught the process, and the healer should be sure that he knows how to do each step. If a client claims that they cannot visualize well, the healer can help them in that area. Other times, the client

The Sutras on Healing and Enlightenment

may need to understand the use of phrasing suggestions properly or which emotions are appropriate to use when manifesting. The healer should be sure they are doing this process correctly and that they are doing it at least twice a day with their meditations for manifesting their own healing. When this process is combined with the other components observed in this chapter, then the healer will become obsolete in his client's life, and the client will in time become his own healer.

Chapter Thirteen—The Knower

-13:1-

Without knowledge of one's True Self, healing is meaningless and can never be considered true healing.

The sutras began with a clear understanding of what the Self is and now they close where they began—with a reminder of man's highest Divinity and the importance of establishing this within the client for true healing. The process of healing unfolded over these pages, and in a healing session this process unfolds in a client and in the healer as well. When the work is complete, both healer and client should be rooted deep within the Knowledge of who they truly are. Regardless of the physical, mental or emotional changes that have occurred, if both the healer and the healed are established in Truth, then the process was successful. This is the ultimate aim of healing; however, it is a process, and any steps in the process are part of the path of true healing, regardless of the factor of time.

-13:2-

Meditation is the process that brings the practitioner to an awareness of his Unchanging Formless Divinity.

There are many ways to meditate; however, all paths do indeed lead to the same place in the end. The process of healing as synonymous with the process of enlightenment must involve some form of meditation where the attention of the practitioner is placed on the Unchanging Formless Divinity of his own Consciousness. All paths eventually lead back to the essence of the human being. Regardless of what this is called, it is there for all to experience. Meditation is simply placing one's attention on this Space of Pure Awareness and learning to identify with this Space rather than on the body itself. The process of discernment is crucial here, for the meditator learns where his Consciousness should be placed. When this discernment is clear, he will joyfully want to spend time diving deep into the inner recesses of his own Soul. All clients who are serious about the path of healing should be taught to meditate on the Self as early as possible in their healing work.

-13:3-
Effort is required by the practitioner of meditation to become established in the Truth of the Knower.

Success in meditation comes in time, because the more attention that the practitioner places on the Self, the deeper he will move into it. The Self is the Truth; and it is also called the Knower because it is Pure Consciousness and is aware of All That Is. As the Knower, it is also the Source of All That Is—the true essence of man and the Universe. With persistent practice, the meditator begins to reside more and more in this "Higher Self" rather than in his lower self of body, mind and emotions. This takes effort because the mind is far more prone to focus on the object of Consciousness than on the Consciousness itself. A client should be taught that the Knower is the Source of All That Is and that meditation is about placing one's attention on this Source. In true meditation, awareness is placed on the subject rather than the object. This takes time and effort to develop simply because most people are usually focused on the object of Consciousness, and this old habit must slowly wear away.

-13:4-
The Knower—which transcends the body, mind, emotions and the entire chakra system—is pure, free and forever.

The more one meditates, the more he becomes firmly established in the realization of who he really is. He comes to know himself as the Immortal Knower who is pure, free and forever. Nothing can ever touch his True Self, and here he rests in peace beyond the body, mind and emotions. The chakra system acted as a ladder for Consciousness to ascend and descend. But in the end when meditation is well established, even the chakra system is transcended. The Self is more subtle than even the most subtle, as it is the Source of all vibration. When the client discovers this place within, he is certainly rooted on the path of true healing.

-13:5-
The Knower is found in the Space above and between the two physical eyes.

The actual Knower itself is everywhere; however, in meditation the practitioner is encouraged to place his attention in the Space above and between his two physical eyes. Here he will experience a Space of blue/black Consciousness. Without force or control, he should bring his awareness here constantly while sitting still with eyes closed. The mind should not be stopped through the power of the will. Only the attention needs to be placed on the Space of the Self. In time, the mind will quiet down on its own and will not be noticed as an obstacle to meditation. It is fine to use mantra, counting or breathing during the sitting period; however, the attention should always be placed back on its Source. In time, the Space of the Self will become more clearly known as the essence of one's being and all the qualities of the Self will be known as one's very own.

-13:6-
Through meditation the mind is stilled of the fluctuations of Consciousness until Self alone remains.

As a client is instructed in meditation, he should be told that he is not supposed to try to stop his thoughts. Thoughts continually move, as is their nature. Part of the reason that a client is a client in the first place is because he tried to stop his mind and emotions in the past thinking that this would bring him peace. Such an action never brings peace and only causes more separation in the psyche. The attention should simply be taken off the mind and placed on the Soul. When this happens, the mind is robbed of all the power it was given, and it naturally becomes quiet on its own. The mind is a very useful God-given tool, but when all the attention is placed on it and it is relied on so heavily, it becomes out of control. Simply by placing one's awareness on the inner Space, which never moves, the mind will be stilled of the fluctuations of Consciousness, and the Self will be all that remains.

-13:7-
Then the practitioner realizes his True Nature as the Source of the entire universe.

The Sutras on Healing and Enlightenment

Self-Realization always leads to the same place, and true healing and enlightenment also lead to this very same place. When a client undergoes the process of healing and learns to meditate on the nature of his True Self, he discovers the great secret that mystics have proclaimed quietly for thousands of years—namely, that "Thou Art That!" The practitioner comes to know that his Source is the very Source of All That Is and that he in fact is this Source. In this realization, he comes to rest in the Peace of the Self and never becomes bound again.

-13:8-

Here, there are no forms, no sensations, no mental impressions, no desires and no individual sense of a separate self.

For Consciousness fully established in the Soul, there is no longer any sense of form, sensation, mental impression, desire or sense of individuality. For the realized one, Self-Alone is, as being One without a second. This is the absolute state of meditation where subject and object completely dissolve and only Oneness remains. Such a state does not affirm or deny the world; it only acknowledges that Self is all that there is. In the Self there is freedom from all manifest existence, because there is no longer any sense of individuality. When a being is here, he is healed, he is enlightened, and he is free. In Truth, he is beyond even those limited concepts. The state of meditation, when complete, is a state of true liberation where one rests in the exquisite Peace of the Self.

-13:9-
Here, the practitioner is beyond dualistic experience and knows himself to be Absolute Bliss Consciousness, One without a second.

In the state of complete realization, the practitioner has realized his true and essential Self and now knows Himself to be the Non-Dual Oneness of Absolute Bliss Consciousness. The sutras end here with the state of the Master, the state where the process of healing and enlightenment is complete and the need for the drama of life is no more. At this point, the Master becomes a Light for all others, as he no longer exists for himself as a separate self. He is One without a second and is a beacon for all who seek truth, peace and liberation.

Chapter Fourteen—The True Spiritual Path

-14:1-
In the truest sense of spirituality, the health of the body has very little to do with enlightenment.

This important chapter in the sutras clarifies what true spirituality really is—not from a specific tradition or path but in universal terms that put healing and enlightenment into proper perspective. Some may conclude that the health of the body is a sign of spiritual enlightenment because the sutras declare that illness manifests from false beliefs. The body, however, does not define the Truth of the Soul. The body resides in the realm of duality where pleasure and pain, health and sickness, and apparent birth and death will always exist. The condition of the body therefore has very little to do with the enlightened awareness within the Soul of a human being.

The physical body can get sick because of the mind, but this does not mean that all illness is because of the false beliefs of the one who is ill. Tremendous guilt can arise from believing that all illness is the result of false thinking. All illness is psychosomatic because the body is psychosomatic, but this does not mean that all illness is the result of ignorance. The body is psychosomatic because it is nothing but mind-stuff. The body is a thing, and things are thoughts. However, not all things decay or get out of balance because of false thoughts. Entropy begins when Consciousness is withdrawn from any given system. In a human being this may be due to ignorance, but it may not. The body simply may not serve the Consciousness any more, and it therefore simply begins withdrawing its life force from it. There are also other reasons why the body can get sick that are not based on a person's individual mental patterns.

True spirituality is about the Self knowing itself within a human being. The Soul comes to know the Soul in a human being regardless of his physical condition. It is exceptionally helpful in the process of enlightenment for the body to be healthy so that the mind can attend the Soul rather than a painful body; but after true enlightenment the condition of the body is irrelevant. We must therefore as healers understand the nature of the physical body and its manifestations. More importantly, we must understand what true spirituality is so that we do not place ourselves or our clients into guilt and end up believing that all sickness is self-created.

Bodies do get sick, but the Soul never does. Bodies do age, but the Soul never does. Bodies transform back into their constituent parts in the event called death, but the Soul has no parts and never dies. Spirituality is therefore about living in the awareness of Spirit and not about the changing and fleeting physical body. True spirituality is about knowing one's immortal and eternal nature and not about making the physical body more than it is. True spirituality is about Eternal Truth, not about temporary illusions.

The evolved healer can certainly help to relieve suffering and promote healing on all levels. He must always keep in mind that healing and enlightenment are synonymous terms that have nothing to do with the physical body. The body is a reflection of the mind, and the body and mind are not two separate realities. All levels of the order of manifestation are part of the relative field, but the Soul is absolute and the real essence of spirituality. The relative field changes and is only a mirage. Although its condition reflects the illusions of the mind, it itself is illusion and should not be given very much power. Therefore, the Truth of spirituality, which is Spirit alone, must always be held in the mind of the healer.

-14:2-
The health of the body is not a valid indicator for the spiritual evolution of the Soul.

Biographies of the great saints of the world's great wisdom traditions reveal that many of these very evolved beings do get sick and eventually die. The spiritual evolution of the Soul in knowing itself is the real indicator of spiritual growth. The healer should not forget that the body can become sick through mind, but this is not always the case. In the end, the condition of the body does not matter at all. When one knows himself as Soul, his body can be rotting away, but he remains free. However, if a person is manifesting illness due to false beliefs, negative emotions and suppression, most likely this person does not have the complete knowledge of who he truly is. In this case, the health of the body is a reflection of a disturbed mind. If true spiritual growth is complete, the body can get sick, age and die; and the Knower of the changing form still remains forever free.

-14:3-
True Spirituality is based on the degree to which a human being is aware of who he truly is.

The health of the body is not an indicator of true spiritual growth. The degree to which a person is aware of his True Nature is the only indicator for how evolved on the spiritual path he is, and this is very difficult to measure. Many people are perfectly healthy with very beautiful bodies, but they have not an ounce of Knowledge as to who they truly are. A being who knows his True Nature knows that he is eternally free and one with the Whole. In him there is no separation to speak of, because he has gone beyond the dualistic mind of most humanity. Only in this enlightenment is true spirituality real. However, because healing and enlightenment are synonymous terms, healing in the mind can help a person go beyond dualism regardless of whether his body heals or not.

-14:4-
Only the Self is an end in Itself.

"Only the Self is an end in Itself" refers to the fact that no effort made by a human being that does not promote his eternal and immortal nature is ever going to bring lasting peace and joy. Any means that ends in a temporary result cannot be considered true spirituality. It is perfectly wonderful for human beings to make efforts that improve the quality of their lives and the world around them; however, these aims are always subject to change and are not ends in themselves. Only the Self is an end in itself, because the Self never changes. It is the only worthwhile investment that a human being can make, because it is the greatest treasure that there is. The knowledge of the Self is all anyone really wants, even though they will claim to want many other things. It all comes down to the fact that there is only one reason for a human being to exist— to know the Self. A life without the awareness of Truth is a life not fully lived, a life void of true spirituality and real meaning.

The Sutras on Healing and Enlightenment

A human being can engage in many thoughts, words and actions. Thoughts, words and actions that lead himself and others to the Self are beneficial. These thoughts, words and actions lead away from the Self will only result in suffering. Only the Self is an end in Itself; therefore, it is the only real spirituality that a man can engage in. Religion and spiritual paths are very diverse in their approaches to knowing Truth, and this is fine. These paths are all valid as long as they provide true healing and enlightenment of Self in the end.

-14:5-
Enlightenment is not dependent on the condition of the body, the emotions, the belief systems or the chakras.

Any existence in the relative field is changing and constantly seeking balance. True Spirituality transcends this world of balance and change because the Consciousness ends up placed on Consciousness itself, which never changes. Therefore the state of a realized being's awareness is not within the realm of time and space, although he fully interacts with time and space and often very masterfully. His bodily vehicles often do remain healthy and in balance, and his beliefs and emotions are often very pure. His systems do tend to remain quite balanced, because he is not making a mess out of them through poor uses of his mind, yet his enlightenment is not based on how balanced his lower vehicles are. The enlightened mind is free. It is not bound to any conditions or dependent on them. The body, emotions, beliefs and chakras are all tools of the Self, but they do not ever change the Self in their quest for balance. When enlightenment arises, then the manifest

The Sutras on Healing and Enlightenment

world of vibration is seen as being quite insignificant, just as when the sun rises a candle is not very bright.

-14:6-
The knowledge of one's True Nature transcends all manifest reality.

The essence of Truth is unmanifest eternal existence, even though it can appear to manifest into form. Knowledge is Self. The Eternal Truth is Self-Alone, and the Knowledge of the Self is Self Itself. Therefore, the knowledge of one's True Nature is said to transcend the manifest world because if one knows who he truly is, his Consciousness rests in the Source of All That Is. This is true spirituality, as it is not dependent on the manifest world. True spirituality involves knowing the Self as the Source of all manifest existence and therefore has nothing to do with the body, mind, emotions or their condition.

-14:7-
The health and harmony of the lower levels can help one to attain the goal of Self-Realization; therefore, healing is beneficial for this reason.

A person engaging the spiritual path to attain Self-Realization can be given many recommendations to structure his life to promote awakening. If his body is sick and his life is not in harmony, then he will not find it easy to meditate and to place his awareness on his Source. He will constantly find his mind pulled to the lower levels of reality in an attempt to find peace and comfort there. True peace is never found in the lower levels of reality; however, without some sense of ease and comfort, the

The Sutras on Healing and Enlightenment

mind will never get to soar to its Source. The spiritual seeker is therefore advised to make his body, mind and life situation as simple, healthy, balanced, strong and functional as possible through whatever means it takes. By taking good care of the lower levels of reality, the seeker will find it much easier to come to know the Source of these levels.

-14:8-
The lower levels do not ever change the Self and the Knower of the Self, which is the Self.

The Self and the Knower of the Self are one and the same. The Consciousness of the Divine Source and the Knower of that Source are exactly the same essence. Within the Self is the power of the Self to know the Self and also within the Self is the power to know the objects that it perceives. Even the objects the Self perceives are not separate from the Self in any way; in fact, these objects are also nothing but Self. Everything that the Self perceives can be considered as a lower level of reality. When Self is split into subject and object through the use of language, then the Self is the subject and what it perceives is the object. The Self in this case is called the Higher Self, and the object of Consciousness is called the lower self, or a lower level of reality.

These lower levels can never change the Self in any way. The Self is said to be transcendent to the lower levels, but not in the way that the sky is transcendent to the ocean and is therefore never touched by it. The more appropriate analogy is of the ocean and icebergs. The ocean is Pure Consciousness, and the icebergs are the forms of this Consciousness. Nothing that happens

The Sutras on Healing and Enlightenment

to the icebergs can actually affect the ocean. The ocean remains the same regardless of the dramas existing in the ice. Within the human system, whether the object of Consciousness is physical, etheric, mental, emotional or causal, nothing can touch the Knower of these realities. The Knower transcends time and space, while still being intimately one with time and space. True spirituality, therefore, is to place one's attention on this unchanging Space of Pure Consciousness so that the being becomes firmly rooted in that Eternal Truth. When this happens, healing occurs regardless of the lower levels of reality.

-14:9-
The true spiritual path is about one's ability to discern that which is changing from that which is not.

Even though the Self remains forever the same and is never touched by the objects of Consciousness, the human being must begin to discern who he is as opposed to what he is not. Many people exist under the illusion that they are the objects of their own Consciousness. This is a case of mistaken identity where the Knower believes itself to be the body and mind that it knows. The body and mind are not the pure and eternal forever-unchanging Self but are objects of Consciousness. The spiritual aspirant is then to begin the process of discerning the difference between what is changing and what is not.

This process begins with a sincere questioning rooted in the simple question, "Who am I?" When the mind is ready to release all of its beliefs about who it thinks it is and is willing to practice the process of discernment, in its humility it can come to know itself as the Self. As long as it is attached to an identification with an object of

The Sutras on Healing and Enlightenment

Consciousness, it will never know its True Self as Source. All that needs to happen is for the aspirant to ask, "Who am I?" in a methodical manner moving through various bodies and planes of reality.

The questioning begins with, "Am I the physical body or anything on the physical plane?" The answer is always "No," but the question must be asked regularly to detach from the countless numbers of associations with the body. The healer can ask his client, "Are you this sick body?" The moment the client truly realizes that the answer is "No," in that moment he is healed. The body may not change at all in the moment of awakening; but, according to the definition for healing and enlightenment, we can truly say that healing has occurred.

The process must continue through all planes of reality and their associated bodies with the aspirant asking: "Am I this feeling?" "Am I this emotion?" "Am I this thought?" The questioning and denying must continue until the Consciousness resides within itself and knows itself as the questionless state. In the mind there are always questions, but in the Self there are none. The mind must discern its way all the way back to the place where it no longer needs to ask "Who am I?" because it now rests in the place where "I Am I." Self-Alone does not need to affirm or deny its existence, for Self-Alone cannot be changed and is eternally existent.

There is nothing except this Self. In the process of discernment the aspirant must know that the Self is not any limited perception of the senses or the mind but that the Self is the Whole. When the mind is still discerning separate parts in relationship to the Knower, it must be made clear that "separate parts" are not the Self. While these parts are technically the Self—made of the same substance as the Self—parts should never be considered as the absolute, eternal and unchanging Self. To call an object of Consciousness "the Self" is to create dualities where there are none. The process of discernment is a technique, not an end in itself, because it too is dualistic. Only if the vision of "Self-Alone" remains can it be said that true and absolute healing has occurred.

-14:10-
It is the ability to discern the real from the unreal and to know who one truly is in Truth.

That which is eternal, absolute and forever unchanging can be considered real; however, that which is temporary, fleeting and changing must be considered unreal in the process of discernment. The objects of Consciousness are said to be unreal, but this does not mean that they do not exist. To deny their existence is only to affirm their existence. These are interdependent realities with no eternal or separate existence of their own that should not be considered unreal in the sense that they do not exist, These exist in a relative and dependent way where their nature is not that of the eternal and immortal Self. This is important because Consciousness, if attached to these changing objects, suffers due to its resistance to that change.

The relative field, always in a perpetual state of flux, never stays the way it is for long. Nothing that vibrates is eternal, and all objects of Consciousness are in a state of vibration. Anything that vibrates is discerned as an object and therefore as unreal; however, we are again reminded that unreal does not mean nonexistent. Anything with a relative and temporary existence is made up of nothing

The Sutras on Healing and Enlightenment

but mind-stuff. Therefore, in the realm of healing, we come to know that only the Self is the True Power and that nothing has its own power apart from the Self. Nothing exists on the relative plane without the energy of the Self fueling it, and nothing in relative existence can last when the Self withdraws energy from it. In the case of healing where the lower vibratory bodies are concerned, the client must begin the process of discernment so that whatever is eternal and forever free can know itself as Itself apart from the disharmonious relative reality.

Once the Self can know itself and observe the problem area with love and compassion, then Consciousness can be placed back on the problem area, and the power of the Self will then be a Healing Power. When the Self within a person is unaware of itself and is identified with the object of Consciousness of the body and its problems, then the state of agitation that occurs in the mind only makes matters worse. However, when the Self is conscious of itself and with dignity, compassion and intimacy embraces the area that needs attention, then the Healing Power of the Self becomes immediately active.

Wherever Consciousness is placed, energy follows. In the human system, wherever energy goes, blood follows. If Consciousness is withdrawn, then energy is withdrawn. If energy is withdrawn, then blood is withdrawn. In a state of misidentification with an object of Consciousness where the mind and heart are confused with false beliefs and emotions, the dis-eased areas are not improved when Consciousness is placed on them. In such a case, the Consciousness brings with its presence all of the lies and stresses of false beliefs and negative emotions and only makes matters worse. However, purifying the heart and mind through the process of discernment and then placing the Consciousness on a disturbed area will bring healing.

When Consciousness, which is filled with sanskaric patterns, is misidentified and unconsciously placed on the object of Consciousness, the energy patterns in this area will be disharmonious. Over time, blood flow will become disharmonious and limited, and cells and organs will not receive proper nourishment. However, if Consciousness has been purified by a true spiritual path and placed consciously on a problem area, that area will be fed with life-giving, healing energy and blood. The process of discernment is therefore not simply about the enlightenment of Consciousness into itself, but it also is about healing in the sense that whatever this enlightened Consciousness touches will be turned to gold.

-14:11-
When the Knower of the Self is fully established in his True Nature, then healing and enlightenment are completed, and there is no more healing and enlightenment left.

There comes a point in one's evolution where there is simply no more evolution, because the Consciousness has been so firmly placed within the Self that the being knows that for him there is simply no more change. Evolution requires change, but the Self is not changing. The body, mind and emotions will always be subject to change and will therefore always be subject to evolution. However, the Self remains forever the same. Healing and enlightenment, processes of evolution, appear to occur within the realm of time and space in their observable manifestations, making it appear that within the realms of healing and enlightenment there is evolution. In

The Sutras on Healing and Enlightenment

Truth, healing and enlightenment take no time at all, but their manifestations may. However, the fully liberated being has come to know that he is not, and never has been, in the realm of evolving, healing and enlightening within time and space. He knows that he is not a process and also that he is not the result of manifestation.

The fully liberated Soul knows himself to be the Self and knows that he never can change in any way. He is not in need of healing, and enlightenment is no longer an issue. He no longer dwells in the realm of enlightened or not-enlightened. He is self-effulgent and knows himself as the Self. There is no gain or loss, no birth or death, and no ignorance or non-ignorance; and thus there is no healing or enlightenment for the fully liberated being.

Made in the USA
Middletown, DE
22 December 2016